Nineteenth-Century Major Lives and Letters

Series Editor

Marilyn Gaull
Boston University
Editorial Institute
Boston, Massachusetts, USA

This series presents original biographical, critical, and scholarly studies of literary works and public figures in Great Britain, North America, and continental Europe during the nineteenth century. The volumes in *Nineteenth-Century Major Lives and Letters* evoke the energies, achievements, contributions, cultural traditions, and individuals who reflected and generated them during the Romantic and Victorian periods. The topics: critical, textual, and historical scholarship, literary and book history, biography, cultural and comparative studies, critical theory, art, architecture, science, politics, religion, music, language, philosophy, aesthetics, law, publication, translation, domestic and public life, popular culture, and anything that influenced, impinges upon, expresses, or contributes to an understanding of the authors, works, and events of the nineteenth century. The authors consist of political figures, artists, scientists, and cultural icons including William Blake, Thomas Hardy, Charles Darwin, William Wordsworth, William Butler Yeats, Samuel Taylor Coleridge, and their contemporaries.

The series editor is Marilyn Gaull, PhD (Indiana University), FEA. She has taught at William and Mary, Temple University, New York University, and is Research Professor at the Editorial Institute at Boston University. She is the founder and editor of *The Wordsworth Circle* and the author of *English Romanticism: The Human Context*, and editions, essays, and reviews in journals. She lectures internationally on British Romanticism, folklore, and narrative theory, intellectual history, publishing procedures, and history of science.

More information about this series at
http://www.springer.com/series/15032

J.C.C. Mays

Coleridge's Ancient Mariner

palgrave
macmillan

J.C.C. Mays
Department of English
University College Dublin
Dublin, Ireland

Nineteenth-Century Major Lives and Letters
ISBN 978-1-349-95866-5   ISBN 978-1-349-94907-6   (eBook)
DOI 10.1057/978-1-349-94907-6

© The Editor(s) (if applicable) and The Author(s) 2016
Softcover re-print of the Hardcover 1st edition 2016
This work is subject to copyright. All rights are solely and exclusively licensed by the Publisher, whether the whole or part of the material is concerned, specifically the rights of translation, reprinting, reuse of illustrations, recitation, broadcasting, reproduction on microfilms or in any other physical way, and transmission or information storage and retrieval, electronic adaptation, computer software, or by similar or dissimilar methodology now known or hereafter developed.
The use of general descriptive names, registered names, trademarks, service marks, etc. in this publication does not imply, even in the absence of a specific statement, that such names are exempt from the relevant protective laws and regulations and therefore free for general use.
The publisher, the authors and the editors are safe to assume that the advice and information in this book are believed to be true and accurate at the date of publication. Neither the publisher nor the authors or the editors give a warranty, express or implied, with respect to the material contained herein or for any errors or omissions that may have been made.

Cover image: "An Exact Prospect of the Town and Harbour of Ilfracombe" by John Walters. Courtesy of the Ilfracombe Museum.

Printed on acid-free paper

This Palgrave Macmillan imprint is published by Springer Nature
The registered company is Nature America Inc. New York

Ad Manes

R. C. Carthew
Inez Conibear
J. F. W. Conibear

Preface

That ships, when they are a little shattered, must...refit themselfs the best they can.

Samuel Pepys[*]

I became involved with studying Coleridge by accident. He seemed at the time to offer wider scope to read and think than most of the authors on an old-fashioned English Literature course. My dissertation was concerned with what you could call his prose interests; I had very little interest in his poetry; indeed, most of my literary interests were in writers who did not appear on any English syllabuses at that time, because they were either recent or American. I found more in Samuel Beckett than Samuel Coleridge.

I returned to Coleridge at a later stage to edit his poems, and anyone who has found themselves involved in such an enterprise will confirm that the process of editing a text is very different from thinking about it in a literary way. Of course, matters of value are involved but one is largely comparing and sorting, and making choices in a medial position between the writer and his readers. The version of poems they expect to find has to be put on the scales against the one an editor might prefer. Every poem has to be treated alike although you might hardly think this fitting. And there are house rules affecting the edition in hand with which you must reach a decent compromise. In short, it is a job that is best done without

---

[*] *Diary* 4 July 1666; ed. Latham and Matthews 7:194.

departing too far from certain conventions and expectations, which have their good reasons, and as far as I thought seriously about poetry at all, meanwhile, it involved off-road writers whom I read for my own pleasure and instruction. It was only when I had done with editing projects that I began to think seriously—for myself—about Coleridge. This is the third book to come out of that process, following one about Coleridge's poetry in general and one about his father.

Coleridge's Experimental Poetics was an attempt to challenge the notion—surprisingly prevalent and persistent—that Coleridge is to be understood as a failure who wrote three great mystery poems (the other two being "Christabel" and "Kubla Khan") and then retreated into impenetrable prose. My argument was that his career as a poet hangs together and that the poems he wrote later in life are continuous with, if not in some ways more impressive than, the poems he wrote earlier on. I have given occasional lectures, some of them published, on particular poems that I hope elaborate the same point, but I embarked on the present extended commentary on his best-known poem for other reasons.

First, it is a special case, being the first of a famous trio: the poem in which he discovered the need to extend and perfect the manner that subsequently served him so well. Second, it is a poem so wrapped about in commentary that it deserves more space than I was able to give it when it was part of a larger argument. I cite previous commentary here not to give the poem another lick of paint but to burn it off and start afresh from the bare wood. Third, following Wordsworth—the poem's first critical reader—the "Ancient Mariner" is at the core of Coleridge's two-hundred-year reputation as it developed phase by phase. By setting the insights—and the blindness—of successive generations of readers against a reading of this central text, one becomes particularly conscious of prejudices one might have inherited, as well as more humble in the views one wants to hold.

Many questions arise. For example:

- How central is the killing of the albatross to the story, and how serious is the moral at the end? How can a poem written in such simple language contain a complicated meaning?
- Why did Wordsworth, who began the poem with Coleridge, turn on it savagely when it was republished? Did Coleridge take notice of what Wordsworth thought when he revised his poem?

- Does the "Mariner" stand separately from Coleridge's criticism and other poems? For example, he wrote another ballad towards the end of his life, "Alice du Clós," where a near-innocent victim is slain by a hastily thrown lance (not arrow). Or how to read the retrospective comments in *Biographia Literaria*?
- Why was a poem that was so very popular for the first sixty years of its life not included in Palgrave's famous anthology, *The Golden Treasury of English Songs and Lyrics*, only to become one of the best-known poems in English during the next forty years, translated into many languages?

I add that I deliberately introduced poets of the present day (or at least my day) who helped me understand what Coleridge was trying to do. It is important that he quickly gave up the idea of becoming a professional poet after he met Wordsworth and realised that this was not an admission of failure. Seen objectively, it was the platform of his future success: the realisation enabled him to do things in poetry that he could not have done otherwise, and I compare him to J.H. Prynne, who appears to have made a similar decision after his first volume. He, too, was viewed with suspicion for withdrawing from the race but slowly found "fit audience, though few," and now, fifty years on, is finding a larger public on his own terms. Separately, one casualty of the divide between Coleridge's criticism and his poetry that emerged with twentieth-century criticism, to the detriment of the same, was the hitching of his poetry to the standard biographical fiction of failure.

When the poetry is read alongside his thinking in prose—about ideas of the numinous, in particular—it can be very helpful to compare it with the work of contemporary poets like Susan Howe. I wrote about Coleridge in relation to poets and theorists of poetry like Charles Olson and Robert Duncan in my earlier book, which is not to say that he is not of his own time: he is, of course, and I say a lot about Wordsworth, along with Hazlitt and Hunt, in particular. Byron has been canvassed as the Romantic poet closest to the spirit of the early twenty-first century, and if that is true in a particular sense, Coleridge is equally so in a more generous way as an experimental poet.

The cover illustration reproduces an "an exact prospect" of Ilfracombe harbour which I suggest in Chap. 1 is the only possible actual place that can have been in Coleridge's mind when he wrote the poem. Note the lighthouse atop Lantern Hill at the centre, Holy Trinity Church on Parish

Hill to the left, and a pilot's boat attached to the ocean-going vessel to the right. The original watercolour by local artist John Walters in 1805 is in the care of Ilfracombe Museum and reproduced by kind permission. I am especially grateful to Sara Hodson, the Manager, who went out of her way to provide a copy at very short notice.

It only remains to thank others who helped me along the way. I become ever more aware of those dolmens round my childhood, and this book is dedicated to their memory. Otherwise and as always, I thank my wife, Marianne, my uncompromising first reader. I am also most grateful to three Coleridgean friends who advanced my education: Peter Cheyne, Graham Davidson, and Gerald Janzen. Finally, like so many authors who have tried to bring the understanding of Romantic period writing up to date, I sincerely acknowledge the help of Marilyn Gaull, the series editor, along with the team at Palgrave Macmillan in New York, from the moment this book went into production.

J.C.C. Mays
Dublin, Ireland
December 2015

Abbreviations and References

The following abbreviations are employed in references to and quotations from Coleridge's writings. They are identical with those employed in the Bollingen Collected Coleridge.

Lyrical Ballads is included in the list and referred to in the notes as *LB*. References are to the first editions unless otherwise specified, for example, *LB 1800* and *LB 1802*.
Bolded numbers following a poem title or alone in parentheses within the text refer to poem numbers in the chronological arrangement of *Poetical Works* below.

AR S. T. Coleridge. *Aids to Reflection*. Ed. John Beer. Princeton, NJ: Princeton UP, 1993—Collected Coleridge IX.

BL S. T. Coleridge. *Biographia Literaria*. Ed. James Engell and Walter Jackson Bate. 2 vols. London: Routledge and Kegan Paul; Princeton, NJ: Princeton UP, 1983—Collected Coleridge VII.

C&S S. T. Coleridge. *On the Constitution of the Church and State*. Ed. John Colmer (London: Routledge and Kegan Paul; Princeton, NJ: Princeton UP, 1976—Collected Coleridge X.

CL *Collected Letters of Samuel Taylor Coleridge*. Ed. Earl Leslie Griggs. 6 vols. Oxford: Clarendon Press, 1956–71. References are to page numbers, not letter numbers.

CM S. T. Coleridge. *Marginalia*. Ed. George Whalley and H. J. Jackson. 6 vols. London: Routledge and Kegan Paul; Princeton, NJ: Princeton UP, 1980–2001—Collected Coleridge XII.

CN *The Notebooks of Samuel Taylor Coleridge*. Ed. Kathleen Coburn, Merton Christensen, and Anthony John Harding. 5 double-vols. London: Routledge

and Kegan Paul; New York and Princeton, NJ: Bollingen Foundation and Princeton UP, 1957–2002. References are to item numbers, not page numbers.
EOT S. T. Coleridge. *Essays on His Times in The Morning Post and The Courier*. Ed. David V. Erdman. 3 vols. London: Routledge and Kegan Paul; Princeton, NJ: Princeton UP, 1978—Collected Coleridge III.
Friend S. T. Coleridge. *The Friend*. Ed. Barbara Rooke. 2 vols. London: Routledge and Kegan Paul; Princeton, NJ: Princeton UP, 1969—Collected Coleridge IV.
LB [S. T. Coleridge and William Wordsworth]. *Lyrical Ballads with a Few Other Poems*. 2nd issue. London: printed for J and A. Arch, 1798.
LB [followed by date] William Wordsworth. *Lyrical Ballads with Other Poems in Two Volumes*. 2nd ed. London: T. N. Longman and O. Rees, 1800; *Lyrical Ballads with Pastoral and Other Poems in Two Volumes*. 3rd ed. London: T. N. Longman and O. Rees, 1802; *Lyrical Ballads with Pastoral and Other Poems in Two Volumes*. 4th ed. London: Longman, Hurst, Rees and Orme, 1805.
Lects 1795 S. T. Coleridge. *Lectures 1795: On Politics and Religion*. Ed. Lewis Patton and Peter Mann. London: Routledge and Kegan Paul; Princeton, NJ: Princeton UP, 1971—Collected Coleridge I.
Lects 1808–1819 S. T. Coleridge. *Lectures 1808–1819: On Literature*. Ed. Reginald A. Foakes. 2 vols. London: Routledge and Kegan Paul; Princeton, NJ: Princeton UP, 1987—Collected Coleridge V.
Lects 1818–1819 S. T. Coleridge. *Lectures 1818–1819: On the History of Philosophy*. Ed. J. R. de J. Jackson. double-vol. London: Routledge and Kegan Paul; Princeton, NJ: Princeton UP, 2000—Collected Coleridge VIII.
Logic S. T. Coleridge. *Logic*. Ed. J.R.de J. Jackson (London: Routledge and Kegan Paul; Princeton, NJ: Princeton UP, 1981—Collected Coleridge XIII.
LS S. T. Coleridge. *Lay Sermons* [being *The Statesman's Manual* and *A Lay Sermon*]. Ed. R. J. White. London: Routledge and Kegan Paul; Princeton, NJ: Princeton UP, 1972—Collected Coleridge VI.
OM S. T. Coleridge. *Opus Maximum*. Ed. Thomas McFarland with Nicholas Halmi. Princeton, NJ: Princeton UP, 2002—Collected Coleridge XV.
PW S. T. Coleridge. *Poetical Works*. Ed. J. C. C. Mays. 3 double-vols. Princeton, NJ: Princeton UP, 2001—Collected Coleridge XVI. While poems alone are referenced by a poem-number, note that quotations are referenced by volume plus page.
SW&F S. T. Coleridge. *Shorter Works and Fragments*. Ed. H. J. Jackson and J. R. de J. Jackson. double-vol. London: Routledge and Kegan Paul; Princeton, NJ: Princeton UP, 1995)—Collected Coleridge XI.
TT S. T. Coleridge. *Table Talk*. Ed. Carl Woodring. 2 vols. London: Routledge and Kegan Paul; Princeton: Princeton, NJ: Princeton UP, 1990—Collected Coleridge XIV.
W S. T. Coleridge. *The Watchman*. Ed. Lewis Patton. London: Routledge and Kegan Paul; Princeton: Princeton, NJ: Princeton UP, 1970—Collected Coleridge II.

Contents

1 Taking Bearings, Setting a Course   1

2 What Does the Poem Do?   25

3 As a Poem of the Imagination   47

4 Wordsworth as Collaborator and Contributor   71

5 The Shadow Cast by Wordsworth   93

6 Revision, Gloss, Choice   117

7 A Reputation by Default   139

8 Today and To Do   163

Appendix A The Rime of the Ancyent Marinere   185

Appendix B Reading "Alice du Clós", and for the Birds   207

Bibliography   233

Index   253

CHAPTER 1

Taking Bearings, Setting a Course

> The providence that's in a watchful state
> Knows almost every grain of Pluto's gold,
> Finds bottom in th' uncomprehensive deep,
> Keeps place with thought, and (almost like the gods)
> Do thoughts unveil in their dumb cradles.
>
> William Shakespeare[1]

1.1 What, When, and Why

Owen Barfield wrote a particularly trenchant, characteristically insightful review-essay on *The Friend*, edited by Barbara Rooke, when only one volume of the Bollingen edition had appeared. One of the several points he made concerns the way Coleridge hoped his writing would be read and why it is often misread:

> Much of what has been written about the mind of Coleridge in the last forty years is of a very high quality. One recalls, for example, Humphry House's Clark Lectures (1953). But there is one feature that is common to nearly all of it; and that is its excessive absorption in the two related "problems" of chronology and plagiarism. Did Coleridge change his opinions much in the course of his life—or not? Did he only borrow from everything he read, or did he sometimes think for himself? It began with De Quincey and it was still going on last year in Thomas McFarland's packed and learned

Coleridge and the Pantheist Tradition. The "when" and the "why" seem to take precedence of the "what" so powerfully that one sometimes feels rather uneasy—like a man listening in to a sophisticated argument about different wines and rival vintage years and suddenly afflicted by a qualm of doubt as to whether the disputants had ever actually *tasted* any of them. (76)

Of course, the proportion of "when" and "why" did not grow less as the Bollingen edition advanced. It was applied to throw light on the substance of what Coleridge had to say, with startling results; Barfield would surely have approved the volumes prepared by George Whalley and Carl Woodring, no less than many others. Still, the point he makes is important and it distinguishes the value of his own commentaries. He restates it again in terms borrowed from Coleridge himself:

> We must have discovered the truth ourselves by other means, before, out of the mass of traditions, assertions, and fables, we can discriminate what really was Coleridgean and that it *was* Coleridgean. (cf. *Lects 1818–1819* 1:170)

Such is the ideal. Unusual difficulties nevertheless remain when the task is faced. First, Coleridge often wrote to discover or improve his grasp on what he sought to say—not just to communicate what he had already determined in his mind—and, second, times have changed. Not only must the fog between then and now be dispersed: there are also differences between the same thing seen at different times. The words in the "Ancient Mariner" are simple, the overall story can be appreciated by a child, and all this can come adrift, leaving one lost among the changes of position, shifts of mood, and the way apparently random things happen in the poem. The ingredients are recognisable, but what is being done with them? The logic of a more recent "difficult" poem like T.S. Eliot's "The Waste Land" can seem easier to follow: at least, if specific details are annotated. By contrast, a serious reader of the "Ancient Mariner" can be brought up short by the recollection that Coleridge began the poem light-heartedly as a mock Gothick parody. The words are the same, but what is the entity we are reading? Are we looking at a picture of a duck or a rabbit?[2]

I recall one group of students who found a way to situate themselves when they imagined marking up the poem for a film-shoot (this was a class in Los Angeles, with Hollywood nearby). They fastened on the rapidly changing shifts of scene in the opening stanzas, how the tempo settled and mounting expectations replaced it; how the action was interpreted all the time by changing focal lengths and points of view; and how situations built up only to crest or crumble and go into reverse. The narrative progresses in this way throughout. The hold on cause-and-effect loosens further as episodes follow each other; events happen with neither reason nor justice. Beauty, horror, hope, and incomprehension are sustained by the momentum of a voyage out and back, although that too contains unexplained gaps. The narrative returns to its starting place; but home safe and sound are not the right words because the mixture of emotions at the close is particularly, and most subtly, the most uncomfortable of all. The Mariner is haunted by ineradicable memories and remains in a forever unsettled, somehow compromised position. In what way has he come through, and how can one really say his story is finished?

Working over the poem with greater care, at this stage of the reading process, risks dulling initial impressions that are all important. One might notice, for example, that traces of Part VII appear to be anticipated in Part V (lines 341–61). What to make of this? Is it a deliberate foreshadowing or the trace of a change of plan? The purpose of a poem is—as Coleridge repeatedly emphasised—to give pleasure and in this case it is better to begin with the thought already suggested, that Coleridge's first casual intentions were overtaken in the course of writing. If the basic story of voyage out and back became less of a parody as it progressed, the pattern of what he discovered may provide the next step in describing the puzzling rationale of the poem. The neutral word *describing* is important here: an over-anxious wish to understand can destroy the half-grasped mystery of what is there. Coleridge came across deeper themes in the course of composition that troubled him. His attempt to comprehend them better led him to revise and expand the very first (lost or, as likely, never written down) version in 300 or 320 lines (*PW* 1:365 gives refs), and to continue to make further changes, large and small, following the first published version. Only when this incomplete dimension of the poem is acknowledged—the mystery in the poem confronted—should analysis cross from facing the "what" to begin to discuss the relation of the same to the "why and when." The transition derives from the same necessity Coleridge faced in Chap. 14 of *Biographia Literaria* when he argued that it is not enough to understand how a *poem* works by reading carefully and slowly. To understand how the same may or may not be *poetry* involves one differently in an argument about intention, which—I emphasise—does not involve the personality of the author. The poem itself is, in Shakespeare's words at the head of this chapter, a "dumb cradle." The "gold" contained in its "depths" waits on the assistance of "watchful providence" that has "kept place with thought." The life of the material poem is infused by an activity almost like that of the gods. So much can be said simply now, and before I elaborate, it will be helpful to set out what each chapter contains.

Several kinds of reader are likely to look into this book. One might look for thoughts on, or help with, a specific aspect of "The Rime of the Ancient Mariner"; another might possess an interest in Coleridge's writing as a whole and how the poem fits into it; yet another might have no more interest in Coleridge and his poem than in many other poets and poems. The ambition must be to cater to an interest in all three categories equally.

1.2   Peculiar Distractions

Anyone writing seriously about Coleridge's best-known poem faces peculiar distractions. Coleridge's personality has been part of the story since his years at school, where he was a star pupil. A formulaic understanding of his career was reached by 1816 by a curious coincidence of judgements between friends and enemies (Wordsworth and Hazlitt), and this has remained essentially unchanged down to the present time. It turns on the argument that the trio of poems of which the "Mariner" is one (the others being "Christabel" **176** and "Kubla Khan" **178**) marks the climax of his early years of promise and the beginning of his years of decline. It matters less whether the biographers are hostile or sympathetic—for example, E.K. Chambers or Richard Holmes—than whether they possess a firm grasp of what was going on in Coleridge's mind. Without that, whatever they write of the earlier years, and however enthusiastically, is likely to be distorted. Coleridge's later writing is now available in printed editions, and there is nothing to prevent the two phases from being brought into relation with each other.

The importance of the task is perhaps not generally understood. Equally important is the uncommon relation between Coleridge as the subject of biography and Coleridge as the poet. I wrote about this in *Experimental Poetics*, and the topic will recur in the chapters that follow. It applies to the "Ancient Mariner" very obviously, in that the story is pure invention: outside Coleridge's time and place on earth. The storyteller enters it by accident, his telling is driven by a particular theme, and in the course of its development, Coleridge clearly discovered that the processes of his own invention drew on feelings he did not know he had. In this way, undercurrents that threatened to usurp it complicated the advancement of the story. In the following chapters, I do my best to describe this process. It is made easier by knowing how the conflicts in his mind—emotional and intellectual together—subsequently advanced towards reconciliation and dynamic coherence; although there is always a danger that the backward explanatory projection will clarify too much the confused seedbed of a life-long project. For the moment, enough to say that although Coleridge is an experimental, not overtly experiential poet, the experiment was rooted in and nourished by experience. It is unimportant to worry about whether he began to take opium or wrote "Kubla Khan" before, during, or after the "Mariner" was substantially complete; or when he decided that what he was writing was too long or too good to publish in the *Monthly Review*, as was initially intended; or whether his preoccupation with the poem interfered with his obligations as a husband and father.

Take another example of what one could call interference deriving from the particular circumstances of the poem. Those who turn off Route A39 to visit the Coleridge Cottage at Nether Stowey, refurbished and extended by the National Trust, often continue afterwards to Watchet because it has been claimed as the port from which the Mariner departed and returned, and where there is now a prominent statue showing him with an albatross hanging from his neck. The modern visitor to Watchet will try hard to find the snug, sheltered village sketched by J.M.W. Turner in 1811 and engraved by George Cooke in 1818, and since reproduced many times down to the present (e.g. *PW* 1:369), but a further problem remains. Although the village has long possessed a church on a little rise, St. Decuman's, it lacked the lighthouse twice-over mentioned in the poem: there was no lighthouse at Watchet until 1862, and they were rare constructions indeed along this stretch of coast in 1797–1798. The assiduous biographer, then, must suppose that Coleridge walked to the western end of the Exmoor tourist trail, where the only lighthouse of the time was to be found, prominently situated, at Ilfracombe. This, converted from a chapel dedicated to St. Nicholas at the time of Henry VIII, still stands high above the harbour, with the parish church on a lesser rise behind in the town: the top cover of the present book shows the prominence of these two features at the time the poem was written. It seems to me quite likely that Coleridge's attention was drawn to the Ilfracombe lighthouse—as it had been to the chapel at Culbone and Ash Farm nearby (and also perhaps Lord King's strange Kubla-like construction above Porlock Weir)—by Richard Warner whom he met at Bath.[3] Thirty years afterwards, Coleridge associated Ilfracombe with his favourite walk towards Lynton from Porlock (*TT* 1:205). There is no other reason for him to know and remember the name of Ilfracombe—which Warner makes clear was worth visiting mainly for its lighthouse—although the town came into the news when it was blockaded by four French warships in February 1797 (as Coleridge possibly remembered in the spring of 1798, when he wrote "Fears in Solitude" **175**).

Thus, Ilfracombe has as good a claim as Watchet to be the little port Coleridge had in mind, if not a better one. However, the church in the poem is described as a "kirk," which is appropriate in a poem masquerading as a Border Ballad, but the ports on the Scottish Borders could not have sent ships to the Antarctic or Pacific Oceans any more than any small port other than Ilfracombe on the coast between Bristol and Bideford: note the ocean-going vessel attached to the pilot's boat on the cover scene. In short, while a biographer like Holmes could make a very good case for Ilfracombe while treading further in Coleridge's footsteps, and while a tourist might like to drive onwards so far because the lighthouse is indeed picturesque and the museum contains further watercolours by John Walters, the hunt to connect the poem to real-life locations and events is a pleasure utterly separate from the pleasure the poem itself offers. This book is concerned with the latter alone: with the make-up of Coleridge's poem, its ideas, its complicated interrelation with poems written by Wordsworth, its different versions, the ways it has been read differently during its 200-year history, and its relation to poems of a similar kind in the present day. The lighthouse and the church stand together as emblems of physical warning and spiritual rescue, creating an image of departure and return.

1.3   Almost Like a Subplot

The present chapter stands as introductory to a connected sequence in which Chap. 2 addresses the primary question head-on: how to confront the "Mariner" for what it is, or appears to be; and Chap. 3 enlarges the focus by considering what was in Coleridge's mind when he wrote it, that is, replaces the emphasis on technique with an examination of its content. Chapter 4 turns to the specific poetical context—the beginning of the poem in a joint venture with Wordsworth—and develops (in Chap. 5) into a consideration of Wordsworth's response to the result. This was the first criticism the poem received and it remains the most searching. It proceeded by way of a different poetical treatment of the same themes and motifs, as well as by critical redefinitions, by the end of which Coleridge came to modify the text of the "Mariner" several times. It was therefore appropriate to pause and consider the differences between the major versions and Chapter 6 forms a "landing-place" in the argument (*Friend* 1:148–49), a place to settle this matter of importance before moving on. Chapter 7 returns to the story of the many further reactions to Coleridge's poem across the nineteenth and twentieth centuries, before the concluding chapter addresses the situation of reading in the present. There are things to be learned from each of the several ways of reading, even if only to clear their shadows from the page.

Some additional considerations affect the way the poem was written and responded to, and determine the way it is seen now. They press to be taken into account because they enrich the story, even while they threaten to derail it. They are interconnected, and bear a relation to the main part of what I have to say, almost like a semi-independent subplot. A sample will explain what I mean.

To begin with, a distinctive and most surprising thing about the "Ancient Mariner" is its continuous appeal to a notably diverse spread of readers. Children and professors have fallen asleep over it; sonatas have been based upon it, and also graphic novels; it has held its place as one of the most popular poems in the English language for over 200 years while others have come and gone, or risen and fallen in fashion. The groups of readers involved are for the large part separate in a way that is matched only by Shakespeare, whose audiences laugh and cry at different things; those who once thought *The Merchant of Venice* was comedy being replaced by audiences who find it food for solemn thought. The text of the "Mariner" has likewise enjoyed a mixed reception on many levels simultaneously at all stages of its career. Wordsworth was evidently made anxious by it, while Macaulay forever treasured it as a simple childhood thrill. A hundred years later, one artist (Mervyn Peake) found it mirrored the horrors of war, while another (Duncan Grant) took it as an invitation to escape from the same. Such diverse responses certainly pose a vexatious question for Reception Theory, not least because the poem is not presented as a riddle.

An effort to pursue this consideration by exploring the Coleridgean context goes round in a circle likewise. The poem was written at a moment of change in its author's circumstances. It reflects ideas and attitudes with which he was becoming dissatisfied and the beginnings of the alternatives which replaced them. That said, his unresolved state of mind continued for almost two decades before it reached a determination. It has been natural to turn to the interim retrospective account given in the *Biographia*—his most extended critical statement, whose argument centres on this poem he began with Wordsworth—but this seemingly promising context turns out to be infirm ground. Coleridge's argument in the *Biographia* is couched in terms Wordsworth employed in the Preface and Supplementary Essay to his *Poems* (1815), and forms an answer to a discussion of Imagination and Fancy of a kind that had become increasingly outpaced by Coleridge's philosophical thinking. The mismatch prompted his argument to deflect onto an over-reliance on Schelling, the result being a confused account of where his own position had arrived. The consequence has been a similarly muddled and unresolved discussion in the middle decades of the twentieth century that attempted to match Coleridge's compromised theory with Wordsworth's practice as poet. It might have been more successful if an attempt had been made to match the confused *Biographia* theory with Coleridge's own poems; or Wordsworth's theory with those poems of his that directly answer the "Ancient Mariner," "Kubla Khan," and "Christabel" (as I describe in Chap. 5).

As it happens, the Bollingen project has at last made all of Coleridge's later prose writing available in a well-edited form, and the aberrant nature of the *Biographia* formulation of Imagination is clearer: as a faculty, it stands between Reason and the Higher Understanding, as Fancy does between the Lower Understanding and Sense. Coleridge's 1817 distinction between Primary and Secondary Imagination is likewise clarified by his subsequent thoughts on the Trinity. The position reached in the course of the 1820s contains elements that had been there from the beginning: call them Unitarian and Neoplatonist, or whatever polar equivalent is preferred. It encompasses logical and theological difficulties, but it was the most satisfactory clarification of Coleridge's mental, moral, and emotional processes that he managed to achieve. For this reason, if no other, we are now better placed to work back from Coleridge's final position to estimate its status as a concept he shared with Wordsworth at the beginning of the long period of uncertainty. The period was one of extensive reading and hard thought, as well as personal anguish, and these factors need to be borne in mind to comprehend his relative silence while Wordsworth was simultaneously establishing himself as a major poet. While the latter was increasing in confidence, and at the same time using poems by Coleridge to help define his position, Coleridge had other things on his mind to which Wordsworth was largely blind.

The relative situation of the two poet-friends is the foundation of a great irony. Wordsworth's response to the "Ancient Mariner"—from the 1800 edition of the *Lyrical Ballads*, through his own poems and in critical prose, and ending in 1819 with *Peter Bell*—was never satisfactory, even to himself. He bypassed the fundamental questions raised by the "Mariner" (for instance, concerning the nature of innocence), misunderstood them by translating them into his own terms (for instance, the supernatural into superstition), and could only attempt to bury his failure to understand in humour and common sense. Nothing he wrote or is recorded as saying engages directly with the central issues at the heart of the poem, and it is unsurprising that Coleridge appears to have ignored his friend's response. He might have pruned the old spellings of the 1798 "Mariner" at Wordsworth's urging, or allowed Wordsworth (unsystematically) to prune them; and he might have made other changes of a similar kind at Wordsworth's suggestion then and later. It has also been assumed that Coleridge added the gloss to the "Mariner" in 1817 in order to underline the moral reading Wordsworth obviously preferred, but I suggest in Chap. 6 that this is not necessarily the case. For one, the addition of the gloss makes the verse impossible to read at the same time, and this indeed may be the point Coleridge is making. For another, his new epigraph introduces a tale that the majority of readers had already come to understand as primarily to do with crime, penance, and restitution in a way that reinforces its supernatural dimension, before tying the tongue of any reader attempting to read prose and gloss together. This is not Derridean *bon esprit*: the literally unreadable version makes the poem even sadder and wiser than the first one. As a final response to Wordsworth, it caps the lengthy dialogue more conclusively than the *Biographia*.

However, the loose-fitting gloss was accepted as a confirmation—not an unsettling—of a too-easily-made assumption, and the long-term consequence of Wordsworth's fundamental incomprehension thereby makes an even greater irony. It came about as follows: The success Coleridge wished on Wordsworth created the way poetry was read in his time and this of course included Coleridge's poetry. Consequently, by the time of the laureate's death in 1850, the "moral" interpretation of Coleridge's poem was firmly entrenched. The "Lost Generation" at the end of the century found ways to rescue something of what this proto-Victorian interpretation failed to take into account, but the earlier view prevailed to dominate the critical consensus throughout the following hundred years. Indeed it was cemented into place by biographers, who repeated with little change except selective detail the old canard that Coleridge wrote only a couple of poems worth reading and his later life was a regrettable failure. In literary criticism, Coleridge's Imagination was used to explicate Wordsworth's verse while Wordsworth's understanding of the "Mariner" usurped Coleridge's own. The topic of Imagination was fought over for decades, and the symbolic importance of the Albatross likewise, until Wordsworth and with him the whole "Romantic Ideology" was dethroned by Deconstructionist and Materialist theorists in the 1970s and 1980s. Coleridge suffered differently again in the inevitable collateral damage.

Two further strands of this situation in which the fortunes of Coleridge's poem were steered by factors beyond his control deserve mention. First, the question of the Reading Public to which I will return in Chap. 8.

Coleridge was glad to assign Wordsworth the honour of becoming the poet of his age, not least because it left him free to do otherwise: to devote his main energies to his philosophical researches and at the same time to write poems to please only himself or likeminded others. By escaping the demands of readers on whom he was reliant for a living, he joins others, in the twentieth century in particular, who did the same. I emphasise that neither he nor they sought to write for a coterie, nor were they averse to making a profit from their labours. They held to the idea that whatever they did would be less distorted by pressures to match expectations that were not integral to what they themselves chose to undertake. Thus Ezra Pound wrote in Canto XXXVI, a poem dependent on Cavalcanti's meditation on *amor* as an emanation of *nous*, "Donna mi prega," and therefore in close sympathy with many of Coleridge's poems that make use of similar sources:

> Wherefore I speak to the present knowers
> Having no hope that low-hearted
>   Can bring sight to such reason. (177)[4]

Coleridge was tempted by the same notion of Gnostic "knowers," an esoteric audience who would understand what the majority would refuse or misapply. Anne-Lise François has a nice epithet—"nonemphatic" (xvi)—for this kind of revelation without insistence and rhetorical underscoring. And if Coleridge did not withhold his meaning as adamantly as Pound ("I have no will to try proof-bringing"), he certainly exercised reserve in many matters that concerned him deeply. I mentioned in the Preface that there are comparisons to be drawn between Coleridge and a contemporary poet with a reputation for elusive meaning, J.H. Prynne. Neither is difficult if approached on their own terms; that is, if you are prepared to attend. Their shared assumption is that truth does not come cheaply, is not to be compromised by making it more comprehensible, although a lot of readers' firmly held assumptions must be loosened if they are going to see the point. Take, for instance, the truism voiced by W.B. Yeats with reference to (again) Pound that the successful poet must get "all the wine into the bowl" (xxvi). This is patently untrue of the "Ancient Mariner." Indeed, the way Coleridge does not get everything into the poem is both its theme and the reason that it is so haunting. One might say that, if any poet working on the same principles as Coleridge did manage to say all he had to say, he would need to write no more. Beckett was famously explicit about the matter: "Try again. Fail again. Fail better."[5] The "Ancient Mariner" asks to be read like an opening of the field in Robert Duncan's sense and, like all Coleridge's poems, "not to reach a conclusion but to keep our exposure to what we do not know."[6]

The second strand of the situation beyond Coleridge's control is as follows. I centre my discussion throughout on the earliest version of the "Mariner," published in *Lyrical Ballads* 1798, referring sparingly to other versions for reasons of comparison and postponing the topic of revision until Chap. 6. There are good reasons for doing this. The 1798 version preserves the element of parody (distancing) involved in the initial joint project that most of its first readers (including Wordsworth) appear to have lost touch with fairly quickly, while the hankering for the last-revised copy from Coleridge's hand is in the end a sentimental fetish. I can think of only two editions of Coleridge's poems that printed the 1798 version alone, as *the* poem, in the past 200-plus years of its history.[7] This is surely a good reason, by itself, for a rethink. The first version has as much claim to be the default as the last; indeed it might be held to emblematise the project of the larger argument (main plot?) of the present book, the recovery of the poem Coleridge wrote from the misunderstandings under which it has laboured.

A nice irony lies here in discriminating between editions. Editors easily become excited at the prospect of multiple versions they have to work with. They can argue that, if one word or punctuation change constitutes a new version, there are forty and upwards versions of the "Ancient Mariner." Add on digital technology and reading becomes redefined as a giddy process of fast toggling. With this in mind, it is a chastening thought that the non-authorial versions of Coleridge's text have circulated far more widely and have been far more instrumental in keeping the "Mariner" alive than the "transmissional" texts from which "authoritative" texts are constructed. From the 1820s onwards there has been a confused, multitudinous mass of unauthorised editions of the poem that mix up the versions or dump the gloss, and then supply a photograph of an American Coleridge-*faux* as frontispiece, or make the poem into a picture book for five-year-olds or for rich investors: all this to cater for the diverse group of readers that has always, uniquely, been there, hungry for the poem if not always respectful of its author's concerns.

1.4 And Further

Appendix B comprises a previously published essay of mine on Coleridge's late poem, "Alice du Clós" (**655**). It earns a place here because it completes an argument that arose out of the spectre-ship episode of the "Mariner" Part III and prompted the poems Coleridge wrote afterwards: "Christabel," "The Ballad of the Dark Ladiè" (**182**), and "Love" (**253**), among others. The narratives of these poems develop and clarify themes that are murkily entangled in the "Mariner." And the issue on which they turn—an innate sense of compromise and separation; a troubling speck of doubt and frailty; its causes and implications, psychological, philosophical, and theological—haunted Coleridge's thinking and writing throughout his life. The "Alice" poem is his final statement on the matter, omitting the supernatural dimension and focussing instead on psychological and moral issues. One might say that the bequest of the nightmare figure Life-in-Death in the "Mariner" is understood in "Alice" as fatal hesitancy, incompleteness of Will: a diagnosis that underpinned the Trinitarian resolution in Coleridge's late theological writing. The abbreviated references to many philosophical matters in Chap. 3 and elsewhere below take this larger context for granted.

The manner in which "Alice du Clós" is structured, along with other stylistic features, also makes for an illuminating comparison. The end of "Alice," although foredoomed, is sudden and dramatic. The poem works as an intricately integrated whole—every detail connecting a situation from which there is no exit—very different from the "Mariner" where everything apart from the protagonist's physical return is suspended in uncertainty. The same contrast is communicated in smaller stylistic features. "Alice" contains only a few regular ballad stanzas: for the most part they are extended and elaborated in ways much more various than in the

"Mariner" or even "Christabel"; they also come together in more tightly organised fashion. Allusions to parallel situations in mythology and other books manipulate the reading of words on the page in a way from which the "Mariner" is free, despite all that John Livingston Lowes wrote about its sources. The later poem is a deliberately constructed reprise and its plot snaps shut with the finality of a prison door.[8] The aspects of technique that are shared with the earlier poem are employed more self-consciously and with determination. The shared human narrative appears abrupt in the clearly focused perspective, as indeed it must.

My essay was written to speak up for a poem that has been much underrated but completes a journey Coleridge began thirty years before. The end is likewise sad and wise, but finally more clearly understood—a frank acknowledgement of unsolved mystery—and the comparison points up the richer options, even the sometimes lack of control, cradled by the earlier sea-story. The condensed structure of "Alice," its compacted style, prompts the thought that the looser, earlier, longer "Mariner" is, in what one can only call human ways, richer. Like Beckett's *Godot*, say, compared to *Endgame*.

I should finally note that my discussion goes back and forth over a proportion of the same materials to shed light on the "Ancient Mariner" from different directions: I hope with cumulative effect. The amount of repetition involved has been minimised but a portion remains for the benefit of readers who might turn to different parts of the book with particular interests in mind. For this reason, also, references to Coleridge poems (poem numbers) in the Bollingen *Poetical Works* begin afresh with each new chapter.

1.5 IDEAL CORE OF THE ONION

I have been describing what I do in the chapters that follow, and it might likewise help if I describe what I fail to do, or know I fail to do. As anyone must admit, usually in tears, an onion has no core. As this applies to the "Ancient Mariner," it means one can say a great deal about the poem, and what went into its formation and how it appeared differently to many people at other times and places: in short, a lot of things that fit and that might prove in some way helpful; but the most important thing in the poem—the state of mind reached by its poetry—is beyond explanation. Coleridge emphasises the distinction involved in Chap. 14 of the *Biographia* (*BL* 2:13–18). Given the chaotic circumstances in which that book was put together, it remains uncertain whether the chapter and the two following were written after or before Chap. 13, which contains the famous definition of Fancy and Imagination (and the chapters leading up to it); that is, whether the poem–poetry distinction is *ur*-text or an inserted supplement or link passage.[9] Whatever the case, Chaps. 13 and 14 provide alternative formulations of the same argument. In Chap. 14, Coleridge describes the components of a poem functioning together like a well-organised mechanism, patterns of sound taking priority over matters of sight and so on, emphasising that the result might at the same time not necessarily be poetry. Thomas McFarland rephrases the distinction involved:

> [I]t is my contention that though linguistic manipulation can generate a poem, it cannot generate poetry as such.[10]

Coleridge describes poetry as distinct from a poem, in terms of the poet's mind, as a process of sublimation: a rhetorical tergiversation that affronted twentieth-century critics wary of "the intentional fallacy" and looking for consistency.[11] Regrettable or otherwise, such is the limit of what I can demonstrate in Chaps. 2 and 3 when discussing the "supernatural"[12] dimension of his poem: the quality he later called Imaginative or Touching Reason.

Coleridge wrote an amount of prose that provides plentiful means to furnish his own further explanation. The Order of the Mental Powers diagram, written into blank pages of a German history of philosophy (*CM* 5: 797–98), could be summoned to explain how an ordinary slow reading of a poem, reinterpreted by an Imaginative act, reaches meanings that ordinary understanding does not encompass. Gerald Janzen ("Notebook 55 as Contemplative Coda") has shown how entries in the late "flypaper notebooks"—written in prose but surely poetry according to the *Biographia* definition—represent a calling *of* the soul and *on* the soul to complete the task of reaching God, a dialectical instinct that reaches back into Coleridge's early maturity and perhaps before:

> O Lady! we receive but what we give,
> And in our life alone does nature live.[13]

Such explanations may appear reasonable to philosophers and theologians or may not, depending on their concept of the numinous. Coleridge fudges the issue in the *Biographia* by couching the matter in secular terms—emphasising just the ideality and wholeness of mental activity—although it is quite clear from elsewhere in the book (e.g. the closing pages) that he is writing very much as a Christian. In Chap. 14, he quotes and rewrites stanzas of a late sixteenth-century poem to sum up in alchemical terms how the transmutation takes place (*BL* 2:17). But is his explanation good enough? Can good intentions suffice to turn a poem or literary prose into poetry if they are not good enough to reach heaven?

The question arises, is this not an old chestnut—do the sound patterns know they are expressive?—but it is not the same. The poetic mode of speech perception is easily understood, although the explanation by professional linguists can become complicated. The explanation involves the way patterns of sound within and between words interact with meaning thereby to affect the same meaning. The interaction works by conjunctive and echoing processes so as to supplement the ordinary (understood) meaning of words that remains alive when inflected by the sound. The meaning of "supernatural" in Coleridge's literary discussion (e.g. *BL* 2:66–7) is quite specific and you could say a world apart. It contains not merely echoes that carry a trace of their cause but ethereal sounds that the echoes pick up from a different, outside source. The otherness of their new source is their Imaginative authority; and unless one recognises (allows) this as truth, one could be a deluded enthusiast overtaken by the heat of the moment. Coleridge, writing primarily for himself, always wrote with a particular church in view, and often with an even more particular interpretation of its doctrines, but it does not follow that his appeal is thereby limited. And if this is so, how to explore the challenge he presents in terms that a wider community of readers will understand? the something beyond the merely marvellous that is there to be felt?

The frustrated critic can only offer sober observations: call them comforts. For a start, the "Ancient Mariner" was written during a transitional period in its author's development and differs from shorter, simpler poems written during the following decades that can also be reckoned supernatural in their implications. "Phantom" (**667**) is direct in its celebration of a numinous almost abstract Neoplatonic quality; "The Picture" (**300**) plays with the idea as if it was in part an obsession that could be shrugged off; "First Advent of Love" (**574**) employs a direct reference to Guinizelli's "Al cor gentil" ("gentle heart," modified by Coleridge to "gentle mind") to ensure its larger point is not lost.[14] The list of comparisons could continue, but perhaps the most useful is the verse-letter to Sara Hutchinson

(**289**): a poem of comparable length in which the numinous alternates with a painfully personal situation. This "Letter" is written in the first person and as if to-the-moment: its markedly original and changing stanza form reflects back its author's voice very differently from the Mariner's narrative; it apprehends similar difficulties and fears more completely; the terror of the storm is an outer one (not stalking, hidden, behind); it is able to conceive of a marriage of minds of some sort, with God's blessing; and what remains out of touch, if beyond control, is more imaginable in a more ordinary sense. The presences that lie above and beneath the "Mariner" narrative are intrinsically confused and confusing, uncertain as to the trust they should compel as well as to their place in the scheme of things. Maybe it helps to know that Coleridge's allegiance was beginning to shift at the time the poem was composed, away from Spinoza's intellectual love of God to a more personal faith, without abrogating his earlier commitment entirely. However, all such additional knowledge amounts to little more than a comfort blanket when held against the complex of live, interacting feelings in the poems.

The matter can be approached differently from the perspective of style. The "Ancient Mariner" is distinguished by its unusually small and predominantly simple vocabulary. Half a dozen ordinary words gain a sense of heightened significance, although for no clear intrinsic reason. The stanza form is remarkably regular; and variations from the ballad norm are far less and far fewer than the impression left by different episodes. The accentual beat pulses in a manner that creates a mesmerising effect and yet every scene feels vividly present. When examined closely, the phrasing appears highly wrought, involving repeated patterns of voiced and unvoiced consonants, closed and open vowels, and rhetorical figures like zeugma; yet again the effect of such dense patterning is surmounted by a sense of spontaneous freshness and change. How a relatively limited range of simple resources has been manipulated to produce the predominating effect of mystery is the biggest mystery of all. A poem written with means that are "simple, sensuous, and passionate," succeeding thereby to give pleasure, at the same time reaches towards sense-transcendent values and discovers truth within and beyond the buried self. As Shelley put the sea change, "[w]akening a sort of thought in sense."[15] The situation bequeaths a classic crux: what lies beyond the margin of consciousness escapes shared understanding but is witnessed by every person in the crowd as if they were part of it.[16]

The "Ancient Mariner" makes abundantly clear that such meanings are brought to life and are sustained by sound. In "The Eolian Harp" (**115**), Coleridge describes how sounds made by a material "Lute"—"by the desultory breeze caressed"—become "one intellectual breeze, | At once the Soul of each, and God of All?" (*PW* 1:232, 234: lines 14, 47–48). He adds the question mark because the change to "intellectuality" rests on a supposition ("And what if"). In a manuscript version of the same poem, he writes of "Melodies, | Harmonious from Creation's vast concént?" (*PW* 2:324: line 47.2.4)[17]: again meaning harmony, concord of parts, and probably intending an allusion to "That undisturbed Song of pure concent" in Milton's poem, "At a Solemn Musick," where the word resonates with ideas of ecstatic harmony. As I described in *Experimental Poetics* (113–18), the extraordinary attraction of the "Mariner" for visual artists has resulted in some memorable work that nevertheless serves only to illustrate their starting positions: Gustave Doré's and David Jones's different kinds of religiosity, Mervyn Peake's gloom, Duncan Grant's gaiety, and so on. Although the older musical settings I know are subject to similar criticism—more obstacles than enhancements—the recent collaborations between the poet Susan Howe and the composer David Grubbs are particularly applicable to the complexity of meaning the "Mariner" produces. They provide a model of how undertones and overtones contained in and produced by Coleridge's words might also be enhanced, and I write about this in the last chapter.

Today's common reader may resist the thought that poetry teaches spiritual elevation, even that it is a matter of high seriousness. He or she may nonetheless allow that the explanation I fail to provide is connected with the most important aspect of poetry. A young Irish poet who dodged Trinity College Dublin to become a sailor before the mast and served in the Spanish Civil War on the Republican side put the matter nicely: "[P]oetry—even for an able seaman—is the only way out."[18]

1.6 Neither Sheep nor Goats

I repeat the case for reading Coleridge as an experimental poet, but I realise that to link his name with some of the less familiar names among modern poets—names often associated with minority tastes in writing—might appear odd, or elitist, or even downright perverse. After all, his fame rests on the unusually wide popularity of the "Ancient Mariner," and the poem is embedded in the academic curriculum, so why appear to narrow the interest: to claim possession for another restricted group of readers?

That this is not the point will (I hope) become clear in what follows, particularly in the chapters describing Wordsworth's reaction to the poem. Biographers give most space to the personal differences between the two friends, which is unsurprising since that is the business of their enterprise. In truth, it is remarkable how concealed the deep differences over writing were in the poets' daily dealings. One searches hard for evidence of Coleridge's feelings when Wordsworth treated him badly at the time *Lyrical Ballads* 1800 was published, and for how he felt when he read their shared concerns rewritten by Wordsworth as if in flat rejection. The explanation is, I think, that the two were in total agreement over their relative standing: Coleridge was glad to relinquish whatever claims he had in favour of Wordsworth's ambition to be the great poet of their age, and for himself to continue writing verse for his own reasons. I call his reasons experimental because he turned to verse almost exclusively to explore and compose feelings while he pursued a long-term philosophical agenda in prose. Such being the case, Wordsworth—to create the taste by which he might best be read—had to create a public for his writing, which he did at first very slowly, and then with considerable difficulty, until finally in the second decade of the nineteenth century he began to profit from the fruits of his labours. His initial intransigence mellowed, and he made concessions of a kind and ended with relative fame and fortune, a highly respected literary figure and creator of a landscape to which people flocked. Coleridge the while, who had earlier enjoyed the greater fame, gained a reputation as a lecturer and obscure metaphysician, even while his books were attacked by disappointed former friends and his name surrounded by a miasma of gossip. The purpose of publishing his writing was not so much to gain recognition as to reform public taste on different terms.

Now that all (or almost all) Coleridge wrote is finally in print, the road he chose appears less like a cul-de-sac; and maybe the road Wordsworth chose, more popular at the time, looks a little less impressive. Coleridge wrote more verse than was earlier known and, more importantly, an enormous amount more prose concerning topics that bear on the subject of his verse as well as being of great interest in their own right. He protected what he was writing, during his lifetime, by silence. When he addressed the reading-public, it was often—as for instance in the *Biographia* and *The Friend* (1818)—to discuss the dilemma he faced in writing for readers who found his ideas and manner of expressing them antipathetic: those who wished he would explain his explanations. In his last years at Highgate, it appears that he relaxed somewhat, in the supposition that he personally knew the small audience who sought out his work and found it rewarding, although even then a few complained that they felt an element of reserve on Coleridge's part.

I hope the above can be taken as an even-handed presentation of how things stood, although misunderstandings can still arise when the situation is translated into modern equivalents. Think then of the pairing in relation to two English-language poets of the present times: say, Seamus Heaney as counterpart to Wordsworth and, in the same spirit, Prynne as counterpart to Coleridge. Heaney worked hard to be professional: he understood the risks involved, he worked intelligently to protect the sources of his inspiration from becoming distorted by a devoted public, he won the highest accolades available to him in his lifetime, and his name will be remembered. Prynne has written pretty much for himself and a small circle from the beginning; writing poetry has been separate from his daytime job, which has left him independent of the need to consult reading fashions. It is true that Coleridge read "Christabel" and passed around handwritten copies before it was published; also that he published poems in newspapers and in "Ladies' Albums" for which he was glad to be paid; but, apart from political poems, early and late, he likewise did not write on behalf of any party but himself. The distinction between professional and non-professional is crucial, even when a best-selling author finds that his or her taste coincides exactly with that of their readers, or a non-professional writer achieves public success.

It would be ridiculous to argue that good writing cannot be produced under professional conditions, as the Heaney example illustrates. Likewise the dangers facing non-professional writers are real: the temptation of an isolated narcissism that becomes over-concerned with aspects of technique or simply loses touch with humanity. Neither model is perfect but the point here is that Coleridge did not write poetry with the ambitions of John Keats or Simon Armitage: to become famous as a poet or at least successful enough to support themselves by writing it.[19] Following the "Ancient Mariner" and the Wedgwood bequest, he became a poet on terms that allowed him space to aim closer to the mark than a compromised professionalism would have done (although Robert Frost and Robert Lowell would certainly have disagreed with the way this is phrased). It is in such a sense that I see Coleridge alongside writers like Prynne and Howe, both of whom are now moving towards the end of their careers, publishing with major publishers but still at an enabling distance from the industry. Because that is their fundamental stance, and although Coleridge's best-known poem has found favour with diverse reading groups, I would class it along with all his mature verse as essentially of a minority, alternative or "other" kind. The justification of the term experimental follows. The reading-public is happiest with what it most easily recognises and it does not buy what looks like trouble. It has been very happy with many simplified versions of the "Mariner"—one or other of the multiple strands that make up the poem—and occasional protests on behalf of poems Coleridge wrote afterwards have been largely ignored. These other poems have proved unattractive largely because of the distinctive experimental quality they share with the "Mariner." One could describe the different routes followed by Wordsworth and Coleridge in terms borrowed from a German textual scholar, Klaus Hurlebusch, as, respectively, reception-oriented and production-oriented.[20] The distinction refines on Roland Barthes' much better-known distinction between "readerly and writerly" (French "texte lisible et texte scriptible").

Coleridge's strong antipathy to the demands of the reading-public—a new word in his lifetime—can be used to cast a final reflection on the situation he found himself in as a poet. The difficulty (impossibility) of persuading his critics, to the right and the left of him, that he changed his early political views in good faith undoubtedly contributed, but his sense of separation was exacerbated by the historical context. The times in which he lived saw an expanding mass-market economy of which writing and books were a part.[21] To provide two bizarre examples, the phenomenon of collecting was celebrated by Thomas Frognall Dibdin in *Bibliomania; or Book Madness: A Bibliographical Romance containing Some Account of the History, Symptoms and Cure of the Fatal Disease* (1809) and *The Bibliographical Decameron; or, Ten Days Pleasant Discourse upon Illuminated Manuscripts, and Subjects Connected with Early Engravings, Typography, and Bibliography* (1817), and is exemplified by the life of Dibdin's friend, Richard Heber (celebrated for other reasons in "Virgil Applied" **619**; *PW* 1:1047–48). Collecting turned to hoarding, and when Heber died in 1833, his books overflowed the rooms, chairs, tables, and passages of two houses in London, one in Shropshire, one in Oxford, others at Paris, Brussels, Antwerp, and Ghent, besides numerous smaller hoards in other parts of the Continent. Heber purchased on the principle that a collector needs three copies of any title: one to read, one to lend, and the other to preserve in pristine condition. It is supposed that no one before in history had amassed such a store of choice volumes; they took three years to disperse in a series of auctions across Europe.

Such a pattern of consumption parallels the movement in the arts of the time towards a yearning for the unattainable, a dream of ultimate satisfaction that begins to disappoint even as it is grasped: Romantic *Sehnsucht*, "Heard melodies are sweet, but those unheard | Are sweeter."[22] Keats catered to it wonderfully—and still does—although the Coleridge equivalent of his tiptoe moments are different and closer to Pound's "[f]ormed like a diafan from light on shade,"[23] that is, with meanings that develop into the hinterland of thought beyond sensation. In sum, Coleridge emerged like Blake from a period when modern consumerism, fuelled by artificial need, was fast accelerating. He found a way to write outside it that happened to coincide with a moment when aesthetics began to reach beyond a science of feeling and point towards moral issues. His "unprofessional" view of what he was doing when he wrote poems perhaps reduced their number and the number of his readers but it allowed him to explore broader themes in radically new ways. That is what makes the "Ancient Mariner," where he discovered the means and glimpsed the ends, both so valuable and so relevant.

Talk of consumerism and commodification may be off-putting. If the terminology is antipathetic, think of one writer who naturally fits in and another who finds a way not to: for example, Walter Scott alongside Coleridge. Fitting in may mean being simply companionable, a writer who communicates a sense of shared understanding and easy trust. Not fitting in may arouse uncertainty as to what exactly is being written about and why, a check that enters between the reader and what is being said, making it appear natural to prefer the first kind of writing. It seems more available—more immediately "relevant"—and the other more difficult, more variously "problematic." As Coleridge remarked of Scott's sensationally rapid, widespread popularity: "[w]hen the desire is to be *a* musis, how can it be gratified *apud* musas?—" (*CM* 4:610). By which he meant that significant reading (*"in the company* of the muses") gives and demands something more than mere a-musement (*"away* from the muses"). It follows that the matter of trust—where Coleridge's writing was "coming from"—became mixed up with the political events of his life from early on, and has confused attempts to see it clearly. Rachel Trickett wrote her novel *The Elders* with Wordsworth and Coleridge in mind,[24] displaying the two types of character and their career choices in a modern situation and showing how the Coleridge character was doomed not to attract the majority vote, despite the recognition of his ability. The summary verdict was "[p]erhaps more brilliant but often obscure and certainly not as dependable," as it had been of Coleridge even before 1798.

The distinction between the two kinds of writing remains confusing because, in practice, non-professional writers can adopt professional attitudes and professionals can enjoy fame and fortune uncomplicated by compromise. Successful professionals are by definition more widely known; and there is no reason why non-professionals should be more talented. Hurlebusch's distinction between reception- and production-oriented is therefore only a rough guide to the kinds of poetry at issue. Poems can be written in endless ways. The genus contains many species, separable and comprehensible by judgements based on experience. But, I repeat, what makes any poem poetry is not a matter of majority vote. The answer rests on what Coleridge called, again with reference to himself and Scott, "philosophical" issues (*CL* 5:23–25): in short, fundamental issues of individual intuition and belief.

Notes

1. *Troilus and Cressida* III iii 195–99.
2. The version of the "Ancient Mariner" referred to and quoted in this paragraph and throughout is the first, published in *Lyrical Ballads* 1798 and reproduced in Appendix A with line numbers added. The 1798 title is spelled "The Rime of the Ancyent Marinere."
3. For Warner's tour through Porlock and Lynton to Ilfracombe, see his *Walk* 87–119 esp. For the possibility that Coleridge saw King's "singular edifice" while it was under construction, and how this influenced the writing of "Kubla Khan," see my "King Kubla's Folly."
4. See my *Experimental Poetics* 185 for references to esoteric and exoteric teaching in Coleridge.
5. *Worstward Ho* in *Company, Etc.* ed. Van Hulle 81.
6. "Towards an Open Universe" 137.
7. The anonymously edited "Laureate Poetry Books" *Selections from Coleridge* (Edwin Arnold, 1930) and James Fenton's selection in an untitled author series published by Faber and Faber (2006; in subsequent paperback format included in The Poet-to-Poet Series).
8. I add that it strongly reinforces James Boulger's argument about the Calvinist strain in Coleridge's theological thinking, although it is not

among the late poems by Coleridge that Boulger discusses in his *Calvinist Temper*.
9. Compare Coleridge's earlier attempts to formulate the distinction in *CN* 3:4111 and the reports of his third 1811–1812 lecture (*Lects 1808–1819* 1:217–33). Hazlitt's incomprehension—recorded in the latter—is characteristic.
10. "Poetry and the Poem" 98. McFarland unfortunately never developed the implications of this early, somewhat tangled essay and his interests advanced in other (equally profitable) directions.
11. See in particular Alan Tate in "Literature as Knowledge." Of course, at a more popular level—represented, e.g., by Clyde Kilby at Wheaton College—such difficulties as Tate wrestled with simply did not exist.
12. *BL* 2:6–7 and see ibid. 1:232–33. For the most part, I employ the word interchangeably with "numinous," which is more common in contemporary discussion. Shades of difference are discussed at various points below, not least in relation to Imagination and Reason; and see Chap. 8 below in relation to the Sublime and Sublimation.
13. "Dejection: An Ode" (**293**; *PW* 1:699). Compare *SW&F* 1:383 on "a beautiful object καλον, quasi καλουν," meaning (in a fanciful derivation derived from Plato) "beautiful, as if calling."
14. Chapter 8 below provides more detailed comment on Guinizelli and "First Advent of Love."
15. "Peter Bell the Third" IV 312 in *Poems* 3:116.
16. See on this, for example, Richard Niebuhr's lecture on "William James' Metaphysics of Experience" in *Streams of Grace* 76–112.
17. The printed version prints "concért" (with an "r"). The error was pointed out by Paul Cheshire and appears among the list of corrections on The Friends of Coleridge website (www.friendsofcoleridge.com, under "Poetry & Prose").
18. Ewart Milne's blurb, written by himself, on the cover of his first book of poems, *Forty North Fifty West*.
19. Neither Shelley nor Byron, too, of course, thought of themselves as professional poets, although Byron wrote for money. Armitage, typical of his time, qualified for a position as a university teacher on the basis of his popularity as a professional writer.
20. I apply these same terms to the situation of modern Irish poetry in *N11 A Musing*, which supplies references.
21. See McKendrick, Brewer and Plumb; and, as far as the matter applies to books, the separate publications by Eaves and St. Clair. A plethora of more recent studies has enlarged the field in all directions. For two that concentrate on Wordsworth and Coleridge in particular, see Pfau *Wordsworth's Profession* and *Minding the Modern*.

22. "Ode on a Grecian Urn" in *Poems* 372–73 at 372. For further stimulating suggestions concerning the influence of economics on artistic and behavioural values, see Colin Campbell.
23. Canto XXXVI, following soon after the lines quoted earlier in this chapter.
24. Referred to in my *Experimental Poetics* 198. I have it on Trickett's word that the book has no bearing on the election of an Oxford Professor of Poetry that coincided with the time of publication (as many reviewers assumed).

CHAPTER 2

What Does the Poem Do?

Tell me the Acts, O historian, and leave me to reason upon them as I please… All that is not action is not worth reading. Tell me the What.

William Blake[1]

2.1 Odds

Alice Meynell wrote only two short essays on Coleridge's poems. They focus almost exclusively on the "Ancient Mariner" and largely overlap but they make clear what distinguishes the poem better than any other discussion I know. This is a signal achievement because the poem is full of things that prompt thoughts and feelings moving in many directions. She concentrates her argument in two pithy phrases: the "silly plot" and "exaltation of the senses," the second appearing in her revised version as "spirituality of the senses." By "silly plot" she means not just the contradictions in the story, large and small,[2] but primarily how a tale about the accidental killing of a bird is overwhelmed with entirely disproportionate consequences involving hellish nightmare and the salvation of 200 souls. Modern jargon would rephrase the disjunction as a mismatch between tenor and vehicle, or between concepts and the means used to convey them. Actually, the plot only becomes "silly" if the poem is read as a moral tale, in the way

Wordsworth did and persuaded others to do, forgetting its origins in fun. A further point she makes—about Coleridge being "a non-intellectual poet"—may be taken for journalistic bravado to bolster her central argument. This turns on the disjoin between the relative straightforwardness of the main ingredients that hold the poem together and provide the opportunity for its widespread appeal, and the subtle strains of higher meaning that play at the edges and account for its ever-renewing fascination. She says, "Even the thought necessary for the telling of a story fails him." Others might say that Coleridge cooks his rude ingredients so as to taste like something superior without losing the common touch. Her snap diagnosis nevertheless points the way forward.

Any start should begin with the "silly" aspect of the poem but shorn of the provocation the word suggests. There is nothing foolish about a story that lodges in people's minds with ever-renewing satisfaction. If this is silliness, it is the opposite of stupidity: more like the quality of openness that nonsense poetry shares. It opens a space in which untoward things happen; where the normal world reveals cracks that lead sideways into an adjacent, less anchored frame of thinking. Thomas McFarland described the ubiquitous celebrity that has followed:

> With the exception of the "To be or not to be" speech in *Hamlet*, the "Water, water everywhere" passage in "The Ancient Mariner" may be the most widely recognized passage in the English language, and 'The Ancient Mariner" itself the most universally recognized poem. Certainly there are few, though the age of the cultural prole is upon us, who do not recognize a reference to the albatross.[3]

Meynell's argument insists on the primacy of a feature of the poem that sometimes bemuses adults or that they too easily forget. Proles and children often prove themselves more open to it than their "superiors."

However, as anyone who engages more deeply with the simply pleasurable experience will begin to discover, whether or not they linger afterwards to think about it, meanings begin to attach to the literal sense, meanings that overtake what they thought they were reading, and this is Meynell's second point about the exaltation or spirituality of the senses. She does not explain further, and her words could appear as mysterious and inconsequential as a phrase from a poem by Wallace Stevens: say, the "Nothing that is not there and the nothing that is."[4] In fact, the particular Stevens phrase is apt because it describes the relation between the two aspects of the "Ancient Mariner," which is not exclusive but dialectical or, as Coleridge put the matter, not between contraries but opposites. Spirituality of the senses is at the other end of the spectrum from the qualities that make his poem entertaining, pleasurable, exciting, even foolish, and even disturbing; one might indeed say married to them. Meynell is picking up on the Coleridgean supernatural as numinous: out of the mouth of fools and children come things that transcend earth- and sea-bound characters and events, and connect with experiences that lie beyond ordinary knowledge. She is excused from expanding on what she means because her positive is defined by what she exaggerated as its negative. She saw a numinous value as the true reward pointed to by Coleridge's words, even as it exceeded their reach.

The three paragraphs above map the task of the present chapter, which is first to describe how the poem works, beginning with its basic appeal: its material signs of life. Only when that has been affirmed or recalled is it profitable to look further. Some aspects of technique develop from tendencies observable in Coleridge's earlier writing, other elements are new, a number of both sorts appear to arrive adventitiously; and it is the admixture of these last in particular that makes the "Mariner" the constantly surprising poem it is. It was composed during a significant period during its author's life, on the brink of his discovering the philosopher who took hold of his mind and changed the course of his thinking life. And while Kant's place in the story must wait until the following chapter, enough must be said here to connect what one might call the ordinary literary workings of the poem with the numinous element that Meynell insisted upon: the older, higher kind of silliness that transforms the mundane.

Only the very few can unerringly follow Blake's prescription at the head of this chapter—"Tell me the What"—but it has to be the beginning of a meaningful argument. Discussions that begin with Why and How put the cart before the horse and, though they seem to promise circumspection and reassurance, they cause the reach that seeks to extend beyond ordinary logic to fumble. As Blake goes on to say:

> His opinions, who does not see spiritual agency, is not worth any man's reading; he who rejects a fact because it is improbable, must reject all History and retain doubts only. (579)

Last things share essential qualities with the first and most elementary ones. It is a bold thing to assert, but anyone who disagrees with Blake's words will not understand what goes on in Coleridge's "Ancient Mariner."

2.2 Simply

To concentrate on what is fundamental, then, it is important to be simple: to be reminded of how it was when the "Mariner" was a story in rhyme, for fun or at bedtime; to remember that before it became a text on university syllabuses many of the anthologies in which it first appeared had titles like *Playtime with the Poets* (Longmans 1863) and *The Children's Treasury of English Song* (Macmillan 1875). These anthologies appeared alongside schoolbooks that also included the poem assembled by advanced educationists like Thomas Shorter (Allman 1861), with titles like *The Advanced Reader* (Nelson 1866); and this dual youthful readership preceded a remarkable demand for separate pocket-size editions, frequently with illustrations by children's artists, to be sold as gifts or prescribed for study with introductions and notes by university professors and other "experts" throughout the next fifty years.

The poem opens like a children's story. Not "Once upon a time" but in the same distanced, unthreatening manner: "It is an ancyent Marinere." The characters and places are registered by what they do or where they are. They are not given names; there are simply the mariner, helmsman, pilot, pilot's boy, and hermit. Likewise, the harbour from which the unnamed ship sails and to which it returns is just "home." The situation is presented with no prevarication and everything follows. It may be "silly" to say that killing a bird can change the pattern of the weather and bring down hellish retribution upon the culprit and his mates, but things happen this way in this kind of story. As Coleridge famously said afterwards, it is like the *Arabian Nights* when a date-stone thrown over somebody's shoulder puts out a genie's eye and produces an unforeseen dire result (*TT* 1:272–73): seeming transparency makes explanations redundant until a point is reached when normal assumptions about cause and effect cease to apply. Paradoxically, in such a context, under such a spell, a conventional moral along the lines of "be kind to animals" has a natural place. No matter that the penance exceeds the unwitting crime, no matter that the moral is trite. The admonition is of the same kind as in Hilaire Belloc's *Cautionary Tale*, "There was a Boy whose name was Jim." Jim's miserable fate in the jaws of Ponto the Lion teaches a lesson for life: "always keep a-hold of Nurse | For fear of finding something worse." The child in every reader expects—needs—to find a comforting crumb of the ultra-mundane.

Separate things in the poem are immediately recognisable and understood, yet they hang together in a different—one might say privileged—story-tale way. So there are feelings and situations to which anyone responds instinctively: the exhilaration of starting off on a journey, this being overtaken by the realisation that they have moved into a different world, and then familiar signs by which they take their bearings becoming larger (the sun "over the mast at noon", "the Ice mast-high"), the calling on different senses to respond ("It crack'd and growl'd, and roar'd and howl'd"). Meynell lists them as they come: the sense of sight in the vision of the climbing moon; of hearing in the passage of the spirits singing round the mast; of touch in the stanza when the rain falls "And still my body drank." Other sensations could be added, like the smell of the land as the protagonist pictures the hermit's dwelling-place in "that wood | Which slopes down to the Sea" and the plump cushion on which he kneels to pray:

> It is the moss, that wholly hides
> The rotted old Oak-stump.

The elemental simplicities bind the story to events, and recognised certainties carry it over uncertain waters. Even as the ship leaves harbour, the story contains the comfort of return. The presence of the storyteller promises the safety of a rounded narrative, whatever strange adventures might intervene. The trajectory is as old as the *Odyssey* and, unsettled though it becomes by thoughts of the Wandering Jew who never finds a permanent resting place, the story at least will arrive at a rounded end.

Such simplicities are what complications rest upon. The Mariner's central position in his story is never in doubt. Despite the shifting points of view in which he merges with the wedding-guest and indeed with the teller of the tale, a sense of control is maintained by means of the division into seven parts. And, as the story advances and its complexity increases, the repeated refrain that anticipates or recalls the death of the albatross at the close of so many parts offers a kind of reassurance. These repetitions mark a point of rest in this extra-long ballad (readers today might think of them as pit stops or parking-places, a time for rest). The poem by such means sets up conditions that engage readers completely and yet it treats them with care. It allows a strong element of contradiction they feel as freedom; or call it ventilation that allows a free spirit to enter. Many of the contradictions that twentieth century critics brought to light as complaints or criticisms nest comfortably side by side within their natural home. They do not ask to be reconciled. They are provocations that function as side paths slipping into the depths of the poem.

2.3   Ballad

Most of the features of the "Ancient Mariner" so far described belong to the ballad form. To return to the point where I began and recuperate what lies between, I quote Fenton Hort on ballads at large, written with Coleridge's poem in mind:

> Much of their excellence consists in our feeling that the poet is looking with us at the deeds of his heroes with an equally wondering and interested eye, not articulating his own thoughts (if indeed they take any form in his mind), or wishing to draw inferences or morals, nay, rather dreading the spontaneous action of the understanding, as likely to destroy the charm and reality of the prospect. If a moralizing saw ever is dropped, it is almost always a truism, a saying known to be unlike and utterly unequal to the impulse in the mind at the moment, and *therefore* appropriate, arising from a balance of the felt necessity of utterance and an antagonistic shrinking from utterance. Further, all ballads are symbolical in the entirely true sense in which all history is symbolical, as setting forth deeds representing the inward and external workings from which they spring; and their perfectness in this respect would be destroyed by any intermingling of the things symbolized; they are therefore as transparent as possible, and their whole aim is to set the action before us, believing that to be a better teacher than themselves, and trusting implicitly to the singleness and penetration of our sight. (307)

Two further considerations may be added.

The first concerns the ballad stanza and the peculiar effect it creates in Coleridge's hands. There is little argument about what he was trying to do with it or the way it plays out. His poem continues in the direction he had always written verse, taking metrical experiment no further than in blank verse meditations like "The Eolian Harp" (**115**) and "This Lime-tree Bower" (**156**)[5]; but, within the confines of the predominantly four-line stanza, the same experiment has a different effect. His views on metrical patterning were in one respect conservative: they were what he inherited from the Classical education he grew up with. Otherwise they were radical in both senses: they went back to modify Latin quantity (regularly measured long and short vowels) with considerations of tone derived from Greek accent (rising or falling pitch) in particular.[6] The inherent rhythmic qualities of English (in which stress plays a large part) combine with the latter consideration, particularly in the four-beat rhythm of the rhyming stanza, in verse lines where the number of syllables varies considerably and the position of the beats controls the pace and other values of what lies between them. The controlling factor here is the strong rhythmical pulse that other factors like offbeats and syncopation only serve to vary. Compare the different ways the strong beat pulses within the shorter, rhyming lines of the following stanzas, in each case creating a different overall effect:

> The breezes blew, the white foam flew,
>   The furrow follow'd free:
> We were the first that ever burst
>   Into that silent Sea. (lines 99–102)
>
> Day after day, day after day,
>   We stuck, ne breath ne motion,
> As idle as a painted Ship
>   Upon a painted Ocean. (lines 111–14)
>
> Swiftly, swiftly flew the ship,
>   Yet she sail'd softly too:
> Sweetly, sweetly, blew the breeze—
>   On me alone it blew. (lines 465–68)

Derek Attridge has written well on four-beat rhythm and indeed proposes that it underlies all meters in English.[7] It is certainly easy to understand how it quickly gets into the head of anyone hearing or reading the "Ancient Mariner" and carries the words—propels the narrative—forward. This is the way the poem originated, out of talking with Wordsworth and his sister during a walk; and this is the way it was held in mind as it evolved over several months. No manuscripts are referred to or survive, and the oral characteristics of the poem are corroborated by the way it has impressed itself on popular memory ever since. Equally, the same characteristic encouraged the early use of the poem as a text to learn and to recite: a test of memory and elocution. What makes the poem easy to remember is also what possesses the wedding-guest as he listens to the tale. He, like any listener, is taken into the narrative in a way that has often been described as part-mesmerised and from which he wakes as if from a dream or sleep This is not at all the effect created by the Percy ballads on which Coleridge based his own: he put one feature to work much harder in order to create a particular result. It shares something with chanting rituals, particularly in primitive religions where a regular beat induces a trance-like effect.[8]

Coming at the matter another way, an unusually long story (for a ballad) is projected in uniformly small stanzas, making an impression like a cinema-reel projected at a slower than normal speed. No matter whether the stanzas are considered as units of meaning or of sound, they similarly impress themselves and merge. Images of sight are perhaps more immediately obvious, and these serving to link more widely separate recollections, while the patterning of sounds links more elaborately, with more subliminal effect. When the mind is all ears, it acts like a blind person and sees things feelingly. The effect is contrived in many ways. The first word of a stanza sometimes echoes salient words in the last and the four-line norm is frequently allowed to expand to five or six lines, the latter often in groups, as a mode of adjusting pace; for instance, the 3 five-line stanzas making up lines 259–73 within the context of lines 249–79 that begin and end with six-line stanzas. There are 6 six-line stanzas in Part V, and four more in each of Parts VI and VII, which is significant in light of the changing mood in those parts (see below on the Two Voices). At the same time, many stanzas are linked to one another by identical rhymes, sometimes across a wide span of verses, the "eye" and "ee" rhymes running through Part I providing a good example. This is what literary historians call "romancing the ballad"—a feature that marks the revival of the form in the late eighteenth century—so that the eminent Sigurd Hustvedt, sympathetic though he was to such a development, had to report:

> As a work of art the poem is at the antipodes from the popular ballad because Coleridge himself stands removed at an Antarctic distance even from so apparently sophisticated a ballad writer as the the author, whoever he was, of the classic *Edward*. (98)[9]

Coleridge's version of making music with the anonymous form distinguishes his ballad from others that followed during the nineteenth century, often in schoolbooks in which another later ballad was bound.[10] In my early days, the "Mariner" continued to be set for rote-learning alongside Southey's "The Inchcape Rock" (1802) and Macaulay's "Horatius" (1842), and even as a reluctant pupil I felt the different orchestration of sound: how the unearthly notes of the "Mariner" strike deeper. This feature has attracted elaborate musical settings (the earliest, by John Francis Barnett in 1867, was reprinted in whole or part many times during the century) as well as stage readings and adaptations (notably by Michael Bogdanov in 1984). One must, however, quickly add that these are more homage than attempted enhancement: a recognition of musical or dramatic qualities a later admirer's work seeks to match in quite other ways, not to displace.

Growing more familiar with the poem, one begins to see, as one has perhaps already felt, that there are patterns in these linkages: groupings of stanzas within each of the seven parts that build or diminish in various ways, and mirror or echo similar movements elsewhere. The motivating principle is simple: the rhythm of the way of telling is modulated to the tale being told, at the stage it is at. Take the following examples: Coleridge restricts the grammatical structure within the boundary of 147 individual stanzas out of a total of 151, and the two places where he breaks the rule are significant. The first occurs in the dialogue between the Two Voices at the beginning of Part VI (between lines 422 and 423), where the Second Voice points to the relation between the ocean and the moon before he goes on to explain it. And one should add that immediately following (at lines 427–30), the brother-voices split a single stanza between them. The second instance occurs at the point when the Hermit speaks at the beginning of Part VII (lines 565–66): the gap between stanzas separates a predicate from its subject, requiring a smart skip to connect the meaning. The point is the decided difference in the quality of the surrounding verse that the conjoined stanzas register. In Part VI, the aerial dialogue articulates the force that drives the action—the return home of the boat by the polar spirit beneath the water—in a manner not heard before. The regular beat is lighter and so becomes more even, and the voices are pitched several tones higher than the surrounding norm, the effect of which is to make strange with the acoustic and lift the dialogue above the level of the action in a directly physical way (in a staged-reading it would be spoken from a balcony). In Part VII, the Hermit who speaks also occupies a place outside the main action. His world is quite different from any other in the poem—in particular, different from that of the Two Voices in the air—and the difference is communicated in a way which brings into prominence images uncharacteristic of the poem so far:

> "The skeletons of leaves that lag
>   "My forest brook along:
> "When the Ivy-tod is heavy with snow,
> "And the Owlet whoops to the wolf below
>   "That eats the she-wolf's young."

The change in the predominant rhythm and way of telling in these two instances registers an important complication in the working out of Coleridge's ballad, which reveals itself further as one becomes more inward with the poem.

2.4 Words

The second point concerns words. It is quite evident that every line has been worked over with care, its sound-elements bevelled and arranged to fit into place alongside other words around it, to the extent that one might wonder if this is artifice for the sake of artifice. Kenneth Burke's short essay, "On Musicality in Verse: As Illustrated by Some Lines of Coleridge," marshalls an array of compelling illustrations of sound-figures constructed on patterns of voiced and unvoiced consonants and the reversal of open and closed vowel sounds. He points in particular to chiastic arrangements, and musical augmentation and diminution (see also Seronsy). Did the more confined space of the rhyming ballad line encourage Coleridge to articulate sound more clearly, make it more pointed and antithetical? Features such as "leonine rhymes" (as in "We were the first that ever burst") doubly fold over sound and sense; modifications can then shift the emphasis from the end of the line ("Ne shapes of men ne beasts we ken"), or make the end fall more heavily ("The Ice did split with a Thunder-fit"), or speed up the process described by the line ("Whiles all the night thro' fog smoke-white"). The ballad stanza falls naturally into two parts and the process of augmentation and diminution within individual lines contrives in little what whole stanzas do by rhyme, especially when they are extended. The purpose achieved keeps things moving, seven times over, without getting bogged down in the mix, and one might surmise the poem was for Coleridge a playground of experimentation. He never put so much metrical variety into another single poem, at the same time absorbing this variety so the result appeared natural.

The natural simplicity is important because, if artifice was the whole truth, the poem would sink under a carapace of artistry; like Des Esseintes' unfortunate tortoise that dies under the weight of its jewelled shell in J.-K. Huysmans' novel, *A rebours*. Sound is inseparable from sense, and Katharine Wilson (300) makes an important point when she notes:

> The poem is dominated by a few words which come over and over again with an effect unlike the echoes of any other poem. The same threads weave its texture from beginning to end.

Apart from "eye", all those listed by Wilson are entirely predictable in a mariner's story ("sea," "sky," "ship," "sail," "sun," "moon"). They recur at crucial moments to sustain the sense of a particular world and it is likely that Coleridge revised each of the seven parts separately to reinforce the connections. They are noticeable but not intrusive: neither symbols (apart from the Sun and Moon, which are symbolical in a self-cancelling way), nor quite leitmotifs (because any idea or feeling they recall is too general by itself to be any kind of a theme). They are notably devoid of the kind of historical and literary nuances that resonate through "Kubla Khan" (**178**). Such simplicity produces a notable crispness of presentation; familiar elements are repeated and echo in clear air.

Some words and phrases are in themselves so singular as to cause a little jolt of surprise: "glittering eye," for example,[11] and the word "skip" that occurs only once (line 16) but pops up in its place in a way memorable in its own right ("Or my Staff shall make thee skip"). Just as various sounds predominate in different parts (different kinds of "i" sounds—"eye"/"sky," "kin"/"din"—predominate in Part I) to be picked up later (for instance, at the close of Part VIII), so some unusual words (most notably "albatross") are repeated with particular effect. Two words, "fear" and "dread," ordinary enough but less so than "eye, sea, sky" and the rest, appear late in the poem (line 452) and are then repeated (line 489); and the postponed entrance followed by the closeness of their repetition endows them with a particular power. Both were important words in Coleridge's poetical vocabulary from the beginning as the opposites of Hope and Joy. They are conjoined with the idea of shipwreck in "Dura Navis" (**3**; *PW* 1:5–7) and "dread" appears on its own in important contexts in "Religious Musings" (**101**; *PW* 1:177) and "The Destiny of Nations" (**139**; *PW* 1:286). The word "fear" is repeated five times in eight lines at the opening of Part IV of the "Mariner," following a cluster of words with which it rhymes in the spectre-ship episode of Part III (most notably the homophone "Pheere" in line 180), and it joins with "dread" in Part VI in a stanza everyone remembers:

> Like one, that on a lonely road
> Doth walk in fear and dread,
> (lines 451 et seq)

The coupling describes the mariner's reaction to the chthonic powers that drive his ship forward, after the Two Voices in the air have spoken, and to the moment (line 489) before the seraph-band leave the dead crew and the ship goes down in a maelstrom on its arrival home. The mysterious heavenly powers are something irrational beyond supplication.

The qualities of "fear" and "dread" that enter are of a different order from any emotions encountered before, and for this reason I argue that the poem is less about crime, punishment, and expiation—as it has too often been taken to be[12]—than a story of wonders and hardships endured that, at a late stage, discover a deeper level of guilt and fear. One might compare the presence of Long John Silver in *Treasure Island*, a book that has much in common with Coleridge's poem, not least its narrative shape.[13] The difference is that Silver haunts Jim as a physical presence: horrible though the sound of his tapping wooden leg is, it is a thing attached to a person. The feeling that comes to haunt the Mariner, his auditor, and his readers—and therefore presumably the author—is visceral: wholly intangible and below the level of consciousness. It cannot be grasped so as to be repelled: in order to be shriven, it must be confessed (articulated). The stanza in which "fear and dread" entered together into the poem is completed as follows:

> And having once turn'd round, walks on
> And turns no more his head:
> Because he knows, a frightful fiend
> Doth close behind him tread.

A later notebook entry supplies a gloss Coleridge never published; indeed the feeling behind his words made it hardly necessary:

> It is a most instructive part of my Life the fact, that I have been always preyed on by some Dread, and perhaps all my faulty actions have been the consequence of some Dread or other on my mind/from fear of Pain, or Shame, not from prospect of Pleasure. (*CN* 2:2398 f 127)[14]

2.5 Shape

The movement of Coleridge's poem is varied, then, and may even be described as uneven. It opens fast, with rapid changes of perspective and pace until the ship crosses the line; the next move into a polar landscape goes outside space and time in a way that continues when the ship moves back up into the tropics, where extreme conditions otherwise reverse. The sensations of extreme cold and heat are the same, as Coleridge afterwards asked Davy to explain (*CL* 1:556–57). In locales of ice here, there, and all between, and of the sun bloody and afterwards flecked with bars, the principal adventures happen: the killing of the albatross, the blessing of the water snakes, and the Mariner's release. After this, there is only the homecoming, and yet this occupies three of the remaining four Parts. The proportions are unconventional; the Nostos is oddly protracted. Does this have anything to do with the fear and dread that enter Parts VI and VII and modify the overall tone of the incomplete conclusion?

In Part V, after the Mariner revives, along with the dead crew who begin to move the ship onward again, there is a change of mood and vocabulary:

> Sometimes a dropping from the sky
> I heard the Lavrock sing;
> Sometimes all little birds that are
> How they seem'd to fill the sea and air
> With their sweet jargoning.

New words enter the poem along with the odd grammar and off-rhyme and the following stanzas continue to add them: "flute," "angel," "song," "mute," "pleasant." They are configured in a different sort of music, and an oasis of sound forms:

> A noise like of a hidden brook
> In the leafy month of June,
> That to the sleeping woods all night
> Singeth a quiet tune.

They look forward to the world on dry land that the Hermit inhabits: "that wood | Which slopes down to the Sea," though this later description is significantly fraught with images of cold and violence:

> "When the Ivy-tod is heavy with snow,
> "And the Owlet whoops to the wolf below
> "That eats the she-wolf's young."

And more than this, Part V contains an anticipation of the well-known conclusion of the poem as if it had once intended to end at this point:

> Never sadder tale was told
> To a man of woman born:
> Sadder and wiser thou wedding-guest!
> Thou'lt rise to morrow morn.[15]

While the poem is being read or listened to, such a slight bother of anticipation and repetition does not feel out of place. The progress hitherto has been one of shifting directions and surprises; a mobile aggregate recalling Coleridge's interest in the fluid, integrating flight of starlings called a "murmuration" (as nicely discussed by Peter Anderson). A change in the style in Part V introduces the Two Voices, who shepherd the action into a kind of supernatural world different from any encountered up to that point. Alternatively, does the passage in Part V contain the trace of a conclusion that was overtaken while Coleridge hurried on to pick up with a new project ("Christabel" **176**)? Are its features, if not intended, a remnant of first thoughts that were never tidied away? I will come back to When and How in later chapters. Blake's imperative "What" is meanwhile pressing.

I am inclined to read the foreshadowing of the ending in Part V in relation to the words "fear" and "dread" that enter the poem in the surrounding context. The poem—like all the verse Coleridge wrote with few exceptions—is consciously prompted by feeling, not ideas (*CL* 2:961), and he might have said of the "Mariner" as a whole, "I see it feelingly" (*King Lear* IV vi 150).[16] The temptation to remember the narrative as a collection of scenes is overwhelming but, more important, they are sustained in their place by the oxygen of emotion; attempts to realise the scenes as pictorial illustrations vary widely, and most of them fail. Everything that came into it—the memories of voyages documented by Lowes, the echoes of recondite sources recorded by Beer—came this way. Being composed in the head, the poem led the poet as often as vice versa, leaving him to steer it as best he could. Its jostling progression is like Rimbaud's "Bateau ivre" (drunken boat poem), a disturbed advance towards a destination that is less important than the journey.

2.6 Pictures

The "Ancient Mariner" has always attracted illustrators because it tells its story in a series of pictures. It was published on the eve of a fashion for literary texts interspersed and decorated with new forms of illustration, and there are by now more than fifty separate illustrated versions of the poem; that is, not counting collections like W.M. Rossetti's 1871 edition for Moxon's Popular Poets which contains illustrations by Thomas Seccombe and sold in tens of thousands of copies.[17] It provided considerably greater scope for invention than Wordsworth's poems, which on the whole require detailed knowledge of particular landscapes; and more even than its rival among late nineteenth-century illustrated gift books, Edward Fitzgerald's *Rubaiyat of Omar Khayyam* (1859–1889), which outsold it at the time but whose popularity declined as fashions changed.[18] However, despite the justified celebrity of many of the "Mariner" artists, they may all be said to fail for reasons made clear by Coleridge himself when he commented on the first that were made:

by David Scott, shown to him in 1832 and published in 1837.[19] He tactfully explained that pictures of the surface narrative are merely decorative when they ignore the invisible components that drive what is seen. "My eyes make pictures, when they are shut," he wrote in *A Day Dream* (**629**; *PW* 1:1070); and he repeatedly castigated "that despotism of the eye" (*BL* 1:107), "that Slavery <of the Mind> to the Eye" (*CM* 3:138), "the LUST OF THE EYE" (*OM* 85). If a visual artist is to encompass what the text holds, he must—like any reader—make an imaginative leap beyond the superficies of description into the action of the poem as it works through by means of meter and other devices. He must find a way to project the Mariner as a person who is younger than David Scott's "grey-beard Loon" within the story and, at the same time, an old man when he tells it: a feat that can only be accomplished by a protean literary form commensurate with the visual contradiction. Maybe, if Coleridge had anything in mind, and since he is unlikely to have imagined anything like twentieth-century abstraction, it was something like the coarse woodblock illustrations that allowed a whole rookery to fly out of Tom Hickathrift's beard in the tales of his youth (*BL* 2:68). Sven Berlin (1997) is one of the few who has explicitly tried to work according to Coleridge's prescription, although I fear his effort sadly falters.[20]

The point is easily misunderstood. Coleridge is a supremely pictorial writer, as his attraction for artists abundantly proves. The "Ancient Mariner" was written at a time when his visual sense had been sharpened by contact with the Wordsworths, particularly Dorothy: "her eye watchful in minutest information of nature—and her taste a perfect electrometer" (*CL* 1:330–31); his notebooks, in particular, are filled with detailed recordings of appearances.[21] He was also a sympathetic and intelligent friend of painters and their patrons, with knowledge of art from the makers' point of view.[22] Why relegate descriptive illustration—in effect what most artists attempt to do with his poem—to a lower place? The answer is that his poem contains no static points of rest: even the opening crackles with the energy that will unfold a familiar scene into a less familiar one and set in process events that will not close down when the narrative ends. Memorable moments do not last: as the poem builds towards them, they already contain what makes them reverse and turn inside out; release from pain opens into another kind of adventure; the return home is a discomfiture. The poem offers "pictures" galore, but they are carried by sound. The separate meanings of words touch when they are sounded; grammatical positions are smudged and thereby become reactive and alive. Any one word stands in relation to others in the same line and stanza, and to other instances in other situations elsewhere, so that any one picture that fixes in the mind (understanding) is literally an abstraction, an incomplete paraphrase. When a separate picture is made of what is happening, the action and its affect is stilled, is frozen. Prose meanings—references to the sun and moon, and so on—shift, even reverse, as they are moved by the life of the whole.

The attraction of artists to this poem in particular is therefore a great irony. As with the attraction of filmmakers to the novels of Jane Austen, they fail because the life of the original lies in words and they prioritise pictures. Of course, artists do not fail entirely: Duncan Grant's colour is there to be enjoyed, Mervyn Peake's pain to be shared, if that is what the book is opened to see, although other artists can fail totally if they have nothing to give. David Jones made up his own text of the poem from bits and pieces that Coleridge never published as a whole,[23] and might be forgiven for so doing or might not. Without dismissing the possibility of an Imaginative pictorial accompaniment, in Coleridge's sense, I suggest that more attention be given to typography if visual presentation is to mean anything. It is a peculiar irony that some of the most ambitious and distinguished "visualisations" line up alongside texts that are ugly and even difficult to read. Having the whole text set in italic is a particularly frequent misfortune to befall the "Mariner": is it because of a misguided tribute to the out-of-the-ordinary? A half-way lunge towards gothic script? At the same time, there are a few printed versions that deliver the text in ways for which I for one feel deeply grateful. Bruce Rogers (for Oxford University Press, 1930) sets a classic standard but is not alone. With reference to the "Coleridgean" argument about illustration sketched here, the way the text reads on the page deserves as much care and attention as the interpolation of images by other hands. And the pictures embodied in words on the page are no ordinary pictures: they change shape, depth, and value as they enter the mind.

Coleridge later spoke of his verses as Sibylline Leaves, as if they floated free like the images in Shelley's "To a Skylark."[24] They were never so: his mature verse defined itself as an attempt to steer emotion on the wing, balanced by a sense of what lies below. Josie Dixon, in the essay cited above, argues that the special quality of catching description in motion that one finds in his earlier poems and notebook-prose was later lost: the old story of imaginative decline, but I think not. Coleridge wrote less verse after the "Ancient Mariner" because he had less need to do so, but this was always on the incorporative principles that the poem helped to discover. I imagine him in agreement with Susan Howe's thought that "[m]aybe the nature of a particular can be understood only in relation to sound inside the sense it quickens.. ... Sound is sight sung inwardly."[25]

2.7 Mix

As I have suggested, I am not convinced by the view of the "Ancient Mariner" as an evolving sequence of crime, punishment, and reconciliation; the protagonist passing through successive phases of self-realisation (involuntary shooting, blessing water snakes, biting arm and shouting out, etc.). The phases are presented as completely as they are understood, but they follow at angles to each other like a discrete series of numbers in mathematics; that is, as George Oppen famously remarked of the poems in his first book, like the stops on the East Side (New York) subway.[26] No one vision is imposed on the whole, and I think it is entirely possible that lines that are often quoted as a key to the poem—

> Instead of the Cross the Albatross
> About my neck was hung

—were born of an accident.[27] Coleridge succumbed to the easy internal rhyme, and it might have encouraged him to think he had finished with the story Wordsworth had given him when the albatross fell off—which he had not. There is no reason to believe he thought of the killing of the bird in the same way as Wordsworth did, as specially symbolic of a crime against nature, nor of the bird as later generations have (following Baudelaire's "L'Albatros") as somehow symbolic of poetic imagination. In a similar way, it has proved easy to be distracted by the ethereal tone of the voices in the air. They counteract the forces of fear and dread, they assert the highest values in the poem at a stage when they are most needed, but they remain none the less spooky visitants rather than persons in the story.

The energy generated by the poem is not to be earthed (grounded) in material forms: linkages of sounds and images establish a condition equivalent to the numinous. Echoes and mirrorings everywhere connect words like the sides of prisms, tangentially and momentarily. Rowan Williams writes about such linkage under the heading *cynghanedd*, as it were a style of underrhyming, most obvious in writers in the Welsh and Irish languages (132–33), although reproducible in English. It is important how it happens: one might feel that Dylan Thomas and Hopkins sometimes strain for effect, rubbing damp sticks together to make a spark, or that William Barnes and Austin Clarke are not above cheering themselves up by indulging their skill. Sometimes the spark that reaches from earth to heaven moves in the reverse direction so that, as in many poems by Henry Vaughan, it is all over in the first line; sometimes a poet wants to wrap him or herself in a cloud of unknowing sentiment, as it seems to me Eliot does in passages of *Four Quartets*. Coleridge's epiphanies are threaded through the texture of his writing, like Joyce's in *Ulysses* and even more obviously in *Finnegans Wake* but, when they come together as in the episode when the water snakes are blessed, they are witness to something beyond a portrait of artistic mastery: the senses merge and, so merging, suggest the quality of the dimension beyond themselves. They differ radically from Wordsworth's episodic "spots of time," in which the bodily senses tend to be "laid asleep" in order to "become a living soul."[28] Coleridge's numinous spreads and corruscates are full of *enérgeia*. The all-over effect that Andrew Lang called "euphrasy" (eyebright) comes across as a wakening, enlivening sparkle.[29] Coleridge had employed the technique in poems before the "Mariner," but not raised to such a pitch.

Unfortunately, the numinous can morph downwards as well as upwards. It is alive and works on the edge, so that twinkle can without warning turn into threatening gloom. Meynell did not mention such a possibility, perhaps judging that a welcoming introduction should point out what raises, not depresses, the spirits. The poem suggests one is the obverse of the other; the two guiding voices are the counterparts to an undercurrent that is sheer power, devoid of value. It is a quality in the poem that Coleridge discovered—or confronted more directly than ever before—as he wrote, enabled by the writing itself. One might reckon that he soared so high and discovered by surprise the depths below, their unwanted appearance containing fear and dread. In subsequent poems, as such feelings became more familiar, they became the dull, despondent ache from which so many other poems begin; the condition that poetry must surmount if it is to move towards the light. I do not mean to suggest that Coleridge's earlier poems are exempt from gloom. "Lines on a Friend, Who Died of a Frenzy Fever" (**85**) in 1794 describe feelings in terms that anticipate the "Letter" to Sara (**289**) in 1802. Simply that, after the implications of the "Mariner" sank in, the feelings became a different order of "Dejection" (see **293**).

It is important to recognise that the numinous dimension of Coleridge's style that I have been at pains to gloss has its own specifically Christian signature. When the edges of words touch in the mind, they have already reached as far as Understanding can go: the Reason they reach towards in poetry is, ultimately, "pure Transparency" (**575**; *PW* 1:995: see further Chap. 8 below). So much could also be said of—and has indeed been said by—modern writers for whom God is dead and all poetry is consequently, in some way, elegiac. The idea of the numinous, in twentieth-century mythological and psychoanalytic perspectives, understood the "Mariner" as a textbook example of a return to the Great Mother; and gained a widespread secular meaning.[30] For Coleridge, by contrast, whose faith wavered only for a few years during youth, the relation is live even when problematic. The wedding-guest of his poem may end "a sadder and a wiser man" but its author forever looked forward in Hope, as many of his later poems describe and celebrate. I will return to this matter in the next chapter.

2.8 So What

There are three points to emphasise now and to be returned to later. First, the "Ancient Mariner" began as a light-hearted joke: it contains the joke but was open enough to embrace much else. The parody dimension provided the space to discover a darker dimension that came into being side by side with the transcendental one. While it might appear odd to call a poem as carefully worked over as this one "improvised," loose beginnings propelled it into existence and the same freedom from restraint still buoys it up. If it had advanced more completely under stricter control, one might speculate that the supernatural dimension would not have enlarged in both directions (both positive and negative) and the poem would have remained a mere moneymaking exercise. The degree of adventitiousness left Coleridge's mind open to discover things he barely suspected he knew and might have preferred not to know; and so the result remains unpredictable, astonishing, and inhabited by frights and horrors.

Second, Lang suggested that writing the *Rime* discovered for Coleridge a *cupitor impossibilium*, an eagerness for things impossible.[31] The poem was not preplanned and the result is certainly not as coherent as "Christabel," but it could well be said to be the richer for being thus. Joseph Skipsey demurred at Swinburne placing the later poem first, insisting at length on the variety of qualities possessed by the popular "Mariner." He cited the way its qualities "glide so stealthily into the mind" and "take possession of the soul." He asserted that there is

> no poem of which we are so utterly without a prophecy, much less a forerunner; and no poem of which we have had, in the remotest degree, a blood relation or legitimate successor.[32]

There can be no argument with the points he makes. The poem is Coleridge's most celebrated poem for good reasons: the broad range of readers to whom it appeals and its coming together in a way that does not overdetermine the various ways in which it can be enjoyed. Skipsey's second point, uniqueness, again describes a quality that is usually (automatically) open to challenge but is in this case true. The poem has left its trace in the work of other writers from Wordsworth and Keats onwards, but there is nothing like it *au fond*. Skipsey's "in the remotest degree" is no exaggeration.

The third point returns to the matter of the numinous: in Meynell's terms, the poem appeals to senses that not only are exalted but become spiritual. Now, while it is relatively easy to show how our senses are manipulated by literary means, it would seem impossible to demonstrate how they reach beyond the perimeter of consciousness. Words may point to it but they cannot communicate it. Such higher qualities may be available to those prepared to make the same leap of faith, but what do they say to others? Are they stopped short? A conditional "as-if" would surely not suffice. The answer waits on further discussion but for the moment one must insist that, whatever about the non-negotiable dimension of Coleridge's faith, his poem is not exclusive property. Two centuries of literary history prove it is alive to readers of different faiths and of no faith at all.

Notes

1. "A Descriptive Catalogue, No. 5: The Ancient Britons" in *Writings* 579.
2. A trivial example is the bassoon in a story set in a time before the instrument had been invented. At the opposite end of the scale, the ship appears to return via the Northwest Passage (unless round the Cape of Good Hope), which was waiting to be discovered and (long after Coleridge died) turned out not to exist. This latter "contradiction" will prove to be significant in the discussion that follows.
3. "Foreword" to *The Road to Xanadu* xiii.
4. "The Snow Man" in *Collected Poetry* etc. 8.
5. Purves 79–94 provides charts based on metrical analysis, comparing the "Ancient Mariner" with most of Coleridge's poems from early days onwards. He strongly contests the "sudden emergence" of a new style of writing.
6. "English Hexameters" (**185**; *PW* 1:527–30) provides an example; and, for further commentary on the same, see esp. *CM* 1:671–72.
7. *Rhythms of English Poetry* and *Poetic Rhythm: An Introduction*.
8. Edward Snyder was one of the first to compare Coleridge's poem with others in this respect. For a modern study of "Kubla Khan" along the same lines, see Tsur.
9. In this respect, it is significant that Louise Pound, the distinguished folklorist and authority on American ballads, edited a notable selection of

Coleridge's poems for Lippincott's Classics in 1920 that included excellent observations on the handling of narrative and related features of the "Ancient Mariner." At the present day, it is more necessary to say more about matters of sound.

10. Gall and Inglis began this conjunction with an oft-reprinted *Poetical Works of Thomas Campbell and Samuel Taylor Coleridge* in a single volume; at about the same time they brought out their mass-market edition of Wordsworth's *Poetical Works* in identical format (1857). Houghton Mifflin brought out an annotated schoolbook pairing of the "Mariner" with Campbell's "Lochiel's Warning" in 1895, after which the "Mariner" was paired with James Russell Lowell's "Vision of Sir Launfal" by three different publishers from 1898 onwards. Other combinations followed.
11. While the word "eye" connects with the mesmeric effect of the Mariner's tale, it connects with the theme of several contemporaneous Coleridge poems as I remark below in Chap. 3, note 31.
12. House, e.g., in his eminently sensible Clark Lectures 84–113.
13. And, I might add, the presence of Stevenson's "black spot." For Coleridge on the "dark cold speck at the heart," see *AR* 24; and variations of the same in *CN* 2:2454, 4:5275.
14. The personal matter is pursued, in particular, by Miall in his hypertext essay "Coleridge's Albatross."
15. Wilson 322–23 and 327 also remarks the "more ethereal music" of these parts.
16. Nicely glossed by Miall "I See It Feelingly."
17. Moxon figures are given by St. Clair 716. The Coleridge Moxon was subsequently reprinted by other publishers (e.g. Collins, Ward Lock, Griffith, Farren, Okeden, and Welsh). The otherwise excellent survey by Klesse is limited in its coverage of illustrated collected editions.
18. Chapter 7 enlarges on this story of illustrated editions. Fitzgerald's poem, of course, never circulated widely as an annotated text for study.
19. See *TT* 1:273–74 and further references in my *Experimental Poetics* 115–16. I see now that Sophie Thomas's "Poetry and Illustration" makes the same point in a useful extra context, at 363–66 particularly.
20. I write from the point of view of those whose primary interest is in the poem. The illustrations are reviewed by Beare and Kooistra.
21. Well described by Dixon's "The Mind's Eye."
22. Again well described by Woodring's "What Coleridge Thought of Pictures" and by Knox's "Coleridge and the Arts."
23. Chapter 6 below supplies details.
24. See Meynell's succinct comments on the poem in her *Poems by Shelley* vi–vii.

25. "Vagrancy in the Park." Stevens' late poem "The Course of a Particular" previously entered Howe's discussion.
26. Letter to Rachel Blau Du Plessis, 4 Oct. 1965, in *Selected Letters*, 121–22 at 122.
27. Wilson 309 makes the same point: "I should imagine Coleridge thought of it to get 'cross' and 'Albatross' into the closing stanza."
28. "Tintern Abbey" in *LB* 201. See also *Prelude* (1850) VI 600–01; Norton Critical Edition 216–17.
29. "Introduction" to *Selections from the Poets* xxxix.
30. They began with Bodkin *Archetypal Patterns*, were developed with considerable sophistication in others like, for example, Sewell *Orphic Voice*, and are reviewed from a mainly non-literary point of view by Casement and Tracy in *Idea of the Numinous*.
31. "Introduction" to *Selections* xxv.
32. "Prefatory Notice" to *Poems of Coleridge* 22–23.

CHAPTER 3

As a Poem of the Imagination

> Wherefore with leave th' infinite I'll sing
> Of Time, Of Space: or without leave; I'm brent
> With eagre rage, my heart for joy doth spring,
> And all my spirits move with pleasant trembeling.
>
> Henry More[1]

3.1 Return to Source

The *Biographia Literaria* is central to the emergence and centrality of the term Imagination in twentieth-century literary criticism. How this came about is described in Chap. 7, and my present interest is in Coleridge's thinking at the time Imagination emerged as central to it, originating in his and Wordsworth's poetry immediately before and particularly after the "Ancient Mariner" was finished in March 1798. There is a discrepancy here, between their thinking at this time and the retrospective account of it provided in the *Biographia*, which is something many critics failed to appreciate after the fortunes of that book revived. The account written in 1815–1816 is a reconstruction much affected by the exigencies of the moment of writing, as were the attempts to unwind its inconsistencies more than a hundred years later again by Lowes, Richards, Robert Penn Warren, and others, and a helpful start is to set aside the mismatch and return to source.

The main interest of twentieth-century literary critics and philosophers became Imagination as creativity, and in this respect as a justification of the humanities as a whole. Albert Levi's *Literature, Philosophy and the Imagination* (1962) and Mary Warnock's *Imagination* (1976) are representative samples of how the *Biographia* was incorporated into a discussion that moved from Hume and Kant to Gilbert Ryle and Sartre, back and forth across the Atlantic. In this context, two particular issues in Coleridge's discussion in Chap. 13 occupied students and teachers: first, the difference between Primary and Secondary Imagination, and the usefulness of Coleridge's formulation; and second, whether the difference between Fancy and Imagination was to be construed as a difference in degree or of kind. Discussion of the first issue, it seems to me, was stymied by Coleridge's statement that Primary Imagination is "a repetition in the finite mind of the eternal act of creation in the infinite I AM" (*BL* 1:304): how to keep God (usually a specifically Christian God) out of the neutral space of classrooms and critical analysis. Discussion of the second issue was bedevilled by the assumption that the difference between Fancy and Imagination had to be at the level of technique, as it has to be when the Secondary Imagination is not privileged by the way Coleridge makes it echo the first. Disputants for the most part silently, if not blindly, avoided, or stumbled over, these questions while they found themselves led round in a circle by the argument in the following chapter (*BL* 2:14–18) that the definition of what a poem is depends ultimately on what makes a poet. Self-set limitations of the newly interpreted "practical criticism"—an ideal of the "objective correlative" and the anathema of the "expressive fallacy"—forced a different meaning on Coleridge's distinctions; indeed, restrictions on the way poetry works and can hope to succeed.[2]

The openness of the *Biographia* to various interpretations is obvious: it contains several arguments and levels of argument bundled together under difficult circumstances, as it has always been prudent to recognise. Leslie Stephen's observation in 1888 still stands—it was "put together with a pitchfork" (3:355)—and it would be prudent not to take it as the summation of Coleridge's thinking on any subject without considering the factors bearing on his statement. To start over again, the word Imagination does not occur in his earlier writing in any special sense:

Fancy recurs very much more frequently, for the most part in conventional ways, although once, and significantly, in a contribution to Southey's *Joan of Arc* describing "Preternatural agency" that fed forward directly into the "Ancient Mariner."[3] The following year (1796), the word Imagination was employed in "Religious Musings" (**101**) to describe a similar process of artistic creation:

> But soon Imagination conjur'd up
> An host of new desires, with busy aim.
>   * * * * * *
> Hence the soft couch, and many-colour'd robe,
> The timbrel, and arch'd dome and costly feast. (*PW* 1:183)

And so the word began on its way to becoming what it was by its next appearance in his verse: "My shaping Spirit of Imagination!" of the "Letter" to Sara in April 1802 (**289**; *PW* 1:688). It thereafter became an important term in Coleridge's critical vocabulary, one that had evolved in half a dozen intervening years of discussion with Wordsworth with a powerful special meaning that attached to that relationship, and with markedly decreasing frequency (in isolation) following publication of the *Biographia*.

Thus, following two important letters concerning the nature of poetry written to William Sotheby in July 1802, Coleridge drew together his thoughts on the difference between Fancy and Imagination for the first time. He connected the distinction to the difference between Classical mythology and the Biblical prophets, the first at best involving

> Fancy, or the aggregating Faculty of the mind—not *Imagination*, or the *modifying*, and *co-adunating* Faculty. This the Hebrew Poets appear to me to have possessed beyond all others—(*CL* 2:865–66)

Of course, part of what Coleridge wrote was not new; his father said similar things about the Hebrew poets thirty-five years before, and was not himself original.[4] In the meantime, as Coleridge told William Godwin, "Wordsworth descended on him, like the Γνῶθι σεαυτόν from Heaven; by shewing to him what true Poetry was, he made him know, that he himself was no Poet" (*CL* 2:714). The last issue is crucial. Coleridge's thinking about Imagination not only evolved in conversation with Wordsworth, with admitted differences of opinion, but took place alongside a sense of how his own powers differed from his friend's. Put differently, he was just as concerned to define a quality in his friend that he himself lacked, or possessed in a way connected with his own anxiety. The dialogue continued as Wordsworth wrote his poem to Coleridge (eventually titled *The Prelude*) in stages, to which Coleridge responded in verse in January 1807 ("To William Wordsworth" **401**). But fundamental issues remained unclear until Wordsworth wrote at length on Imagination and much else in the Preface to his 1815 *Poems*, and Coleridge felt obliged to reply, at even greater length, in what began as the preface to his *Sibylline Leaves* and ended as a version of his literary life. The prominence of Imagination on Wordsworth's terms—like the discussion of verse in terms of appropriate diction instead of metrics, rhythm and sound—set the agenda Coleridge followed; and this pulled awry what he might have written independently to introduce his own poems.

The trouble with the book he published in 1817 is not only due to the way it came together during a period of great personal distress. Wordsworth, who required answering, had moved ahead of Coleridge as a professional poet while Coleridge had moved into deeper areas as a thinker. The implications of his view of Imagination had for him become far more complicated and difficult to separate from unresolved circumstances of his life. Indeed, in outline, one might wonder if they had advanced much beyond the time the "Mariner" was written: I mean, at the basic human level that determined all else. It is a fact not often remarked that both texts, critical and poematic, describe a similar problem in a decidedly similar manner that both fail to solve. The ostensible plot of the *Biographia* centres on seventeen years, from the time Coleridge left Ottery for Christ's Hospital to 1798, when *Lyrical Ballads* was published. And these are folded over—and interpreted by—the seventeen years from 1798 to 1815, when Coleridge's understanding of earlier philosophical issues (involving Hartley and Association, etc.) clarified. The overlapping chronological planes merge and the present interferes with the past. For instance, the serious business of canvassing for *The Watchman* is made fun of (*BL* 1:179–86), which affects the "main plot" in the same way the Wedding Guest is affected by the story he is being told (or, one might add, the "guileless Genevieve" in the poem "Love" **253** finds herself re-enacting the story being told to her). The "Mariner" bequeathed unanswered questions that the prose argument of the *Biographia* still could not solve, and Coleridge found himself forced to patch over borrowed sources (his notes on Schelling) that he had not fully absorbed. There are patent non-sequiturs. How seriously can one take a chapter based upon a sequence that progresses from admitted digression and anecdotes, to an exhortation on the ambition to become an author, to excuses for omissions in what follows? On what ground do the insights gained by Imagination stand? How to know if they are delusory? How to prove when they are true? How to control access to them so they do not veer into nightmare?

If Coleridge thought he had an answer to Wordsworth's version of an argument they once shared, he was wrong, as he later admitted (see *BL* 1:304 note). He might indeed have realised almost at once, before the *Biographia* was published, because he rephrased the argument about Imagination and Fancy in terms of Symbol and Allegory in *The Statesman's Manual* (*LS* 29–31; and see *Lectures 1808–1819* 2:99–103); and did so in a way that sticks closer to his discussion of the language of prophecy in *Biographia* Chap. 14, with which one supposes he had hoped to recover from the confusion in which his overdependence on Schelling had landed him. Symbol and Allegory attracted the generation of modern critics following those who took up with Imagination and Fancy and were looking for an Anglo-American version of French *symbolisme*, but they found the task equally difficult and it was quickly turned on its head (deconstructed). Coleridge did not secure the place of Fancy and Imagination in relation to each other until the time he formulated an "Order of the Mental Powers" referred to in Chap. 1 above. Imagination here is based upon the enlightened Understanding and connects with Reason, a region of truth at the edge of human comprehension. Fancy connects a separate lower stage of Understanding to the world of Sense (*CM* 5:797–98). In a related note in Tennemann, made at another time, Coleridge added his tectractic explanation of how the Christian Trinity complements the equation, to make its highest point (Reason) not simply a Kantian or Neoplatonic *Ding an Sich* (It is) but a living Godhead (I am) (*CM* 5:798–99). The focus of Coleridge's attention shifted from making to contemplation during the course of the 1820s, and an altered vocabulary gave Imagination a less prominent place than Reason.

If the above recursus teaches anything, it is that the problems Coleridge discovered in the writing of the "Mariner" were philosophical and psychological by turns, and revisiting the circumstances of the poem in the *Biographia* brought no solution. It proved to be simply a reminder formulated at a time when his spirits were at their lowest ebb. The search for an answer recovered and continued, improving as it shifted ground, unceasingly until his dying day. It was in part inhibited and goaded by the awareness that his argument about Reason and Understanding (and

Imagination and Fancy) rested on "an inward Beholding" (*AR* 223–34), containing truths difficult if not impossible to share with those not already in possession of them. At the same time, the poem always remained important because it first brought him to the brink of discovering what he could say about what is and ought to be; to an awareness of depths within himself he had previously not known. No previous poem had drawn so deeply and widely on his emotional resources, given him greater need to pursue further research and consecutive logical thought. As he had written to John Thelwall a twelvemonth before he lost himself in composing it:

> I feel strongly, and I think strongly; but I seldom feel without thinking, or think without feeling.... My philosophical opinions are blended with, or deduced from, my feelings: & this, I think, particularizes my style of Writing. (*CL* 1:279)

Ironically, the task of putting together the "Mariner" cut deeper than before simply because it went on for so long on such a free rein. It uncovered the idea of Imagination at its most urgent and diverse. The poem as first published preserves the working of Imagination live, not obscured by partial and ultimately unsatisfactory answers (glosses). The way Coleridge came to understand the difference between prose and poetry in *Biographia* Chap. 14 anticipates Kierkegaard's by-now hackneyed assertion: "Life can only be understood backwards; but it must be lived forwards."

3.2 Sensible and Intelligible Worlds

The definition of Imagination in the *Biographia Literaria* Chap. 13 served as a convenient locus from which twentieth-century critics and philosophers found a profitable *point de départ*, but as far as Coleridge was concerned, the definition was an interim, seriously flawed statement. It progressed beyond the beginnings of his concentrated thinking on the subject in 1801–1802 with the aid of an ill-conceived over-reliance on Schelling that he quickly regretted. While the mistake perhaps prompted him to come sooner to a more balanced conclusion on matters that had long remained undecided, this eventual conclusion made more sense in the context of philosophy and religion than as literary criticism. If such an interpretation is correct, it makes more sense to turn to the poem that began the philosophical journey than to be distracted by the unresolved discussion that interrupted it, and to take note of its philosophical implications. Chapter 2 described how the "Ancient Mariner" is a poem on the brink of meanings that hover at the edge of words. The dimension is beyond dream or magic—although these words are often applied—and is better called transcendental. It transcends understanding and cannot be justified in any other way.

There are signs at the time the "Mariner" was written that Coleridge was both engaged with Berkeley's version of idealism and equally aware of its opponents' criticisms. Poems as early as "Imitated from Ossian" (**55**) conjure with the idea of a mirrored persona defining his identity via an invariably female counterpart[5]; and the theme continues through the decade, varying aspects of need and validation all the time in tune with Berkeley's fundamental proposition, *esse est percipere*. Coleridge was not above making fun of the trope and "Lewti," initially positioned in the *Lyrical Ballads* volume, is a good example: it is as much a parody of his own verse as an adaptation of Wordsworth's youthful original.

> Oh! that she saw me in a dream,
> And dreamt that I had died for care!
> All pale and wasted I would seem,
> Yet fair withal, as spirits are! (**172**; *PW* 1:461)

Berkeley remained seriously in favour enough to become the name of his second child, born in May 1798, but by this time Coleridge was on the brink of discovering other, more permanent intellectual guides in Germany. Kant's transcendental argument overturned the simple idealist position that to be is to be perceived on the grounds that an existent cannot be perceived as it actually is because time and space are already (a priori) forms of perception. Whether Kant simplified Berkeley's argument, or whether or not this makes any substantive difference, is a matter of dispute. The important thing is that Coleridge moved on decisively from Berkeley when, in March 1801, he was able to announce he had "completely extricated the notions of Time, and Space" and simultaneously "overthrown the doctrine of Association, as taught by Hartley" (*CL* 2:706 and cf. *CM* 3:966).

Hartley is, alongside Berkeley, an important figure behind the "Ancient Mariner," similarly positioned as the representative of a body of ideas that had attracted Coleridge for a considerable time and yet towards whom, even before writing the poem, Coleridge began to feel stirrings of unease. His theory of association connected with an instinctive tendency in his mind towards a sense of bodied nature that sat uneasily with total Platonic abstraction; his mind was never entirely happy with that "pure intense irradiation" of mind, "with its own internal lightning blind," which Shelley imputed to him.[6] One must instead understand it alongside his defence of personal feeling as the basis of poetry in the Preface to his 1796 *Poems* and alongside his commendation of Walter Whiter's *Commentary* as a guide to reading Shakespeare.[7] The association of ideas not only connected the meanings of words: it traced currents of feeling in verse by melding sound and sense into a whole of which every part spoke its contribution. At the same time (as Coleridge understood Hartley, at least), the individual's place in such streamy processes was largely passive, selfhood absorbed within a material process. The processes of nature swallow individuality, a kind of pantheism in which *natura naturans* melts into *natura naturata*: everything composes an all-encompassing, immanent God. It was a philosophy that gained considerable support during Coleridge's lifetime, and to which he was instinctively drawn, but over which controversy had erupted in Germany following Jacobi's *Briefe über die Lehre Spinozas* (1785; 2nd enlarged ed.1789) and which Coleridge sought to learn from.

It is unclear whether Coleridge could follow German intellectual discussions in detail before he enrolled at Göttingen in early 1799, but he returned the following summer certainly more able and informed. Before that time, he undoubtedly relied on his friend in Bristol, Dr. Thomas Beddoes, who gave what appears to be the first account in English of Kant's theory of knowledge in the *Monthly Magazine* 1793 and an almost complete English translation of *Zum ewigen Frieden* in the same journal three years later.[8] However, if Coleridge was at first reliant on conversation and a small number of English translations and abstracts, he was certainly in a position to read Kant in Latin. Kant's inaugural dissertation of 1770—*De Mundi Sensibilis atque Intelligibilis Forma et Principiis*—was available; and Coleridge referred to and quoted from it at various points later in his life (*BL* 1:288–89, *CL* 4:851, *CM* 2:612, *CM* 3:318–19, *Logic* 243–44, etc., *SW&F* 1:805).[9] The second of these references is a letter of advice to a beginning student; and the fourth is a marginalium on Kant's *Vermischte Schriften* where, following high praise, Coleridge claims the *De Mundi* "contains all the main principles" of Kant's First Critique, "often more perspicuously expressed." He continues:

> the former work should always be studied & mastered previously to the study of the Critique d. r. V. & the works that followed it.—The student will

find it a better auxiliary than 50 Vol of Comments, from Reinhold, Schmidt, Schultz, Beck, Tieftrunk, &c &c &c.—

These two references in particular suggest Coleridge could have found the dissertation useful before he read Kant's writing in German, and the earliest possible reference to it has been dated December 1800–January 1801 (*CN* 1:887). This is likely and there is good reason to suppose he read Kant's dissertation earlier still.

De Mundi argues on behalf of an intelligible or intellectual world beyond the sensible one; or as Coleridge came to say, a world that can be *apprehended* and is no less real because it cannot be *comprehended* (e.g. *CM* 4:302, 6:82 and 86, etc.). Kant came to the distinction via the mathematical problem of transeunt action, in which he parted company from Leibniz, for whom movement through space was aggregative, and joined forces with Newton for whom such action was continuous (fluent). This is particularly significant in that Coleridge's father took the same side in the argument over the mathematical study of change (calculus) that reached a pitch in England (and Devonshire) in the years following Berkeley's *The Analyst* (1734).[10] These strands come together in the letter Coleridge wrote to Thomas Poole in October 1797, a month before he began work on the "Mariner," in which he conjured up a memory of his father on a dark winter-evening walk telling him the name of the stars and impressing on him the size of the heavens and how all appeared still and yet was still moving. And how this only confirmed something he felt he already knew, his innate sense of the vast:

> I never regarded *my senses* in any way as the criteria of my belief. I regulated all my creeds by my conceptions not by my *sight*—even at that age. (*CL* 1:354)[11]

He had been prepared to think thus by reading fairy tales and of giants and genies, and continued:

> —Those who have been led to the same truths step by step thro' the constant testimony of their senses, seem to me to want a sense which I possess—They contemplate nothing but *parts*—and all *parts* are necessarily little—and the Universe to them is but a mass of *little things*.—

Kant came to the same conclusion in *De Mundi*—formulating it in a less personal, less anecdotal way—before he sat down to the ten years of silence during which he put together his first Critique. The only real difference is that Coleridge probably understood the insight Neoplatonically (i.e. as a positive recognition that brought the unknowable world to life)[12] and poetically (with promise that he might reach towards it with words) whereas Kant was already very conscious of the further dimensions of thought necessary to join this world and others. The letter to Poole is justly celebrated, and Coleridge returned to describe the same star-gazing experience on many later occasions: for instance, in a notebook entry of 1804 (*CN* 2:2151), a marginalium on Boehme's *Aurora* (*CM* 1:576), the conclusion of the *Biographia* (*BL* 2:247–48), and the close of Fragment 2 of *Opus Maximum* (*OM* 210–13)—which some see as the true close of that late project.[13]

If the giant hand of Kant had not taken hold of Coleridge before he went to Germany, then, he could have felt its touch. Stanley Cavell, too, would argue from the same position that the "Ancient Mariner" is a study of Kant's two worlds: "I am not saying that when he wrote his poem he meant it to exemplify Kant's *Critique of Pure Reason*, merely that it does so." As a philosopher, Cavell is concerned that "the region of the thing in itself, below the line,... cannot be *experienced*,... *logically* cannot be brought to knowledge." And he goes on to relate it to Romantic themes of "the origin of consciousness, hence self-consciousness, hence of guilt and shame" (40–49). Whatever his very similar doubts about such a train of thought spiralling beyond control, Coleridge appears to have it very deliberately in mind when he ceased working to improve the "Mariner" in order to pursue the topic it discovered for him by beginning "Christabel." I therefore suggest four additions to Cavell's diagnosis. (1) Cavell's image of the line between two worlds might also be understood (as it is very profitably by Peter Cheyne) as analogous to Plato's allegory of the Divided Line in *Republic* 509d–511e. (2) Coleridge understood the line dividing the understandable world of sense and the world beyond as not regulative (like Kant) but permeable (like a veil?), the threat of the latter being as invasive as it could at other times be regulative (comforting). (3) Coleridge connected "delirium, confounding its own dream-scenery with external things, and connected with the imagery of high latitudes"[14] from long before (1795), when he read Granz on the Laplanders; and he likewise connected superstition with equatorial temperatures (the West Indies and Africa, which he read and heard about in relation to the slave-trade), the point being that hellish cold and hellish heat are equidistant from the medians where they balance. They are equivalent polarities of unformed chaos, of possibly Godless *tohu bohu*. (4) Wordsworth's remark that Coleridge delighted to call the Mariner "the Old Navigator"[15] significantly lays emphasis on the course he steered, which reverses the magnetic value of the geographic poles (and takes him home by a course impossible on a map). Coleridge uses the imagery of the Arctic (drawn from voyagers searching for the Northwest Passage, like Thomas James) and applies it to the Antarctic, replacing the positive with the negative pole: a primal upturn from which the action flows. This draws on traditional associations of the Arctic with darkness and evil spirits,[16] and Coleridge's modification of the tradition by having his spirit from a land of mist and snow carry the Mariner's ship somehow *safely* home by the mythical "Juan de Fuca route" described by Samuel Purchas. Such bewildering reversals animate Coleridge's concept of polar opposites as they are felt on the pulse, a source of delight and dread. The conflicting, reversing energies that surround the passive protagonist make up a world of sense in which he is lost. The Two Voices that accompany him home are real, aspects of a power that is beyond Understanding and a fortiori overheard, not heard. Exactly how this was so became less an accepted obstacle and increasingly a more positive part of his thinking. At this point, one other factor needs to be added to what I have written thus far: religion.

When Coleridge began writing his poem, he was on the brink of becoming a Unitarian minister at Shrewsbury, where Hazlitt heard him preach. By the time he had halfway finished the poem, he decided instead to accept an annuity of £150 a year from the Wedgwood brothers and to dedicate the following years of his life to pursuing intellectual interests in Germany. The change of career does not mean a change of mind: merely, a more congenial and practicable way to pursue the interests that allied him to Unitarianism in the first place.[17] Hartley's *Observations on Man*, which supplied him with a theory of association, was a foundational text in the Dissenting Academies; Joseph Priestley and the circles in which he earlier moved provided a model of unrestricted intellectual inquiry; the radicalism of dissent following the Feathers Tavern Petition (1772) made the young Coleridge automatically a fellow supporter. Indeed, one could go back further, before he encountered (sought out?) William Frend at Cambridge, and cite his father's friendship with the Presbyterians at Ottery.[18]

In due time, Coleridge came to think earlier heroes like Hartley and Priestley as conceptually wrong and morally hazardous; that the existence of a personal God involves a different guiding principle from Spinoza's intellectual love; that the different teleology involves a different kind of epistemology. Politics were mixed up with theology, of course, and apocalyptic hopes for a new heaven on earth of the first two editions of his *Poems* (1796, 1797) were in process of giving way to the muted domestic statements of the *Fears in Solitude* volume of 1798.[19] He continued none the less to share a number of Dissenting attitudes to the end; not least, the insistence on examining the text of the Bible rationally like any other book, so that when his reflections on the same were published posthumously as *Confessions of an Inquiring Spirit* (1840) it was condemned for infidelity and the controversy rumbled on for decades. Circumstances are such that one must consider his religious position in the poem as, like his political and philosophical ideas, in transit and part of a wider loosely evolving pattern. He might not have believed in Christ as Redeemer but the "Ancient Mariner" contains signs that he was on the brink of beginning to understand the need: notably, how the Will is essentially corrupt.

The direct references to late medieval religious superstition, combining with the legendary superstition of sailors, are inconclusive, but what of the specific attention paid to the cross around the Mariner's neck that the albatross displaces, dropping off when he blesses the water snakes? Is the cross more pointed in a Unitarian context where the Atonement and crucifixes are less meaningful? What of the Mariner/Christ figure drinking his own blood at line 152 in light of Priestley citing Averroes on the sacrament: "no sect so foolish and absurd as that of the christians, who adored what they eat"?[20] Is Coleridge, in a poem that began as something of a joke to be submitted to the *Monthly Magazine*, aiming it also at its Unitarian editor John Aikin? The possibility needs to be taken seriously by any who press hard for the Mariner's "fall and redemption," not least because Coleridge took such matters so seriously as not to take communion for thirty-three years following Cambridge.

This may serve as a fitting possibility to end a discussion of ideas in the poem. The "Mariner" contains real traces of where Coleridge's serious thinking had been and was travelling to, in a mix that is all the more vibrant for being largely unpremeditated. Hartley's Associationism is an evident background for the style, but so too is an incipient awareness of a transcendent meaning at the edge of poetry. Meanings beyond words are a fraught business because they cannot be shown (proven); those who do not hear can only be adjured to listen more closely. No wonder Coleridge's discussion of Imagination in the *Biographia* is distracted to the point of being confused; no wonder he was hesitant about what his poems are pointing to. All one can say is that, if the *Biographia* embodies thoughts in commotion at a later stage of his journey towards Kant, a knowledgeable reader of his poem might have foretold—from the quality of the poetry as much as from the buried allusions to Neoplatonic sources—that what is transcendental in Kant would eventually become a constitutive reality (not merely regulative) for Coleridge.

3.3 Touching Reason

This last matter joins with questions about the "spirituality of the senses" raised by Alice Meynell in Chap. 2 and contained within my suggestions concerning Kant on sensible and intelligible worlds along with Neoplatonic influences on Coleridge's reading of Kant. It is not enough to say, what is true in Coleridge's (later) terminology, that the "Ancient Mariner" is an Imaginative poem that reaches towards and touches Reason. The present book is about the way a poem is written—does what it does—and I presume readers want an explanation in those terms. I will put my comments in the form of comparisons.

There are what one could call two "epiphanic moments" in the "Mariner": the blessing of the water snakes in Part VI, after which the albatross fell off and fell like lead into the sea; and when the ship moves on in Part VII, driven by a force below and manned by four times fifty dead sailors. This follows a pattern traceable in Coleridge's blank-verse poems from the "The Eolian Harp" (**115**) onwards, where the second epiphany in various ways improves or enlarges upon the first.[21] In the present instance, the improvement is from a condition of isolated stasis, marked by silence, to a communal action accompanied by heavenly music. In terms of a two-part progression, the contemporaneous "The Nightingale" (**180**; included in the second issue of the 1798 *Lyrical Ballads*) provides an interesting analogy. To gain a further understanding of what is happening, one might also compare such epiphanic moments in Wordsworth's poems. In this respect, "Tintern Abbey" is modelled on "Frost at Midnight" (**171**) in particular; and the pattern is continued in poems as different as *The Prelude*, with its twin-peak structure of crossing the Alps through the Simplon Pass in Book 6 and the ascent of Snowdon in Book 12. As I touched on in the previous chapter, Coleridge's moments are crucially full of movement, colour, sound, "streams of grace" (*AR* 71); Wordsworth's of stillness, permanence, and silence, when the "light of sense goes out." Wordsworth's "spots of time"[22] also most often occur as single moments following moments of high physical tension after which the bodily senses relax, identity is swallowed by a sense of wholeness; whereas the same numinous quality in Coleridge's writing diffuses itself across the span of what he is writing and consciousness is never entirely lost. Instead of a plain construction built to support a towering conclusion, Coleridge's sometimes intricately modest, often domestic, narratives are threaded and covered with spangles all over. "Frost at Midnight" holds a particular interest in this respect. Coleridge first borrowed a very Wordsworthian "spot of time" to encapsulate his vision of his child's future as a boy among the Cumbrian lakes and mountains and later trimmed off his own very different (Coleridgean) ending to make it in effect a more Wordsworthian poem.

The lines Coleridge trimmed are as follows:

> Like those, my babe! which ere to-morrow's warmth
> Have capp'd their sharp keen points with pendulous drops,
> Will catch thine eye, and with their novelty
> Suspend thy little soul; then make thee shout,
> And stretch and flutter from thy mother's arms
> As thou would'st fly for very eagerness. (*PW* 1:456 note, 2:572)

The style shares a good deal with the intricately interwoven epiphany passages of the "Mariner." Two of the few passages in Wordsworth that match this glitter over everything are from "Resolution and Independence" and the near contemporaneous beginning-part of the "Intimations Ode," in both of which Wordsworth appears to have Coleridge very much in mind. Compare also the "trembeling" lines by Henry More that stand as epigraph to the present chapter.

"Intimations Ode" was influenced by Plato's doctrine of anamnesis, although scholars disagree over exactly how, and Wordsworth did not care enough to explain in detail. This leads on to a second author with whom to compare the numinous quality in Coleridge: Shelley, who of all his young contemporaries admired Plato most. Shelley's sense of the ideal he was striving for—"Pinnacled dim in the intense inane"[23]—was more consciously abstract than that of either Wordsworth or indeed Coleridge. It was more firmly anchored to Greek textbook sources and also less actually critical of Plato's philosophical position. Coleridge's sense of the numinous trembled in a realm surrounded by philosophical doubts and qualifications; it was at the same time more enriched equally by Neoplatonic sources and later fellow travellers; and most of all it was inhabited by a personal God whom Shelley rejected. Their statements on this last matter appear side by side in Coleridge's "Hymn before Sun-rise, in the Vale of Chamouny" (**301**) and Shelley's reply to the same in "Mont Blanc." The pairing is more than a simple confrontation between believer and non-believer. It is interesting principally because of Coleridge's relative failure to communicate the beatific assurance conveyed by the scene he has described. As critics observe,[24] he appears to fumble uncertainly at a crucial moment of his concluding prayer. For one who held the poetry of the Psalms and the Hebrew prophets in such high esteem, this might seem odd. Many reasons have been suggested; most often his embarrassment that he was never at Chamonix and had appropriated his narrative from a poem by Frederike Brun. I do not believe this explanation is adequate: he admitted his dependence frankly at the time he showed the poem to friends, and it was just as much a device to avoid treading on territory Wordsworth was making his own. I would suggest that, among other things, Coleridge was self-conscious because of his sense that he was addressing God as a person, not as an idea; and throughout the larger part of his life he found communal worship problematic, particularly within the Anglican community (remaining socially and intellectually more at home with dissenters of one kind or another).

A third comparison, closer to present circumstances, can be made with Wallace Stevens, who has already been quoted several times. Stevens's poems continually reach out beyond the circumstances he is writing in to a world of Imagination that is elsewhere or lost in the past. Poems cannot contain it but they can make its absent quality felt.

> The poem must resist the intelligence
> Almost successfully. Illustration.[25]

Such lines assume Coleridge's argument: Imagination points to a world of truth that can be apprehended, even if not comprehended. This truth is not rarefied, as it characteristically appeared to Shelley; nor associated specifically with one place, or kind of place, as for Wordsworth. Nor is it an already lost cause or fiction defined by a negative: a mere "suspension of disbelief" to be approached, as by Stevens, with stoic gaiety. It involves a living personëity (e.g. *CM* 3:520), and Coleridge's angels announce themselves with a comforting sense of warmth or in the form of someone he knows. See for example his poem "Phantom" (**347**), which, as so often, centres on Sara Hutchinson and to which, on one occasion, he added the following comment:

> This abstract Self is indeed in it's nature a Universal personified—as Life, Soul, Spirit, &c. Will not this prove it to be a *deeper* Feeling, & of such intimate affinity with ideas, so to modify them & become one with them (*CN* 2:2441).

Coleridge often quoted the Classical tag "actus purissimus sine *potentialiate*" (e.g. *CL* 2:1195) with the emphasis on the last word, but everything about his mature conception of God is dynamic. As Gerald Janzen wrote to me (13 May 2015), on the edge of strict heresy though this may be, everything about God for Coleridge *matters*: his developed thinking about Reason is different from Plato's static changelessness and Kant's and Schelling's pure act. It is equally different from what Reason means when God is dead or celebrated (as also sometimes by Stevens) as carnivalesque act.

Thus, plentiful examples can be found in Coleridge's later writing that celebrate Reason as he understood it in the "Order of the Mental Powers." It is nevertheless a power "which passeth all understanding" (AV Philippians 4:7) and, while he appreciated Dante's attempt to communicate it in the *Paradiso* (**575**; *PW* 1:995, quoted in Chap. 8 below) he was equally aware of how poetry only "partakes" of such vision or is "the same Power in a lower dignity" (*LS* 30, 72). In his own case, humbly, he emphasised the fragmentary glimpses of Reason afforded by an Imagination that rested on limited Understanding and how the element of selfhood particularly necessitated further compromise. His epiphanic moments are trembling, ambiguous and dispersed, often clouded or seen through obstacles: in "The Three Graves," through "close thick leaves" (**155**; *PW* 1:348); in "Alice du Clós," through "The Lattice of her Bower" and the blossom of a May-thorn (**655**; *PW* 1:1100, 1101–02); just as in the "Mariner," the sun appears through bars like "a dungeon grate" when Death and Life-in-Death catch up with the protagonist. At the same time, he held to Shakespeare's belief that, in poetry among the shadows, the air "is full of noises, | Sounds and sweet airs, that give delight, and hurt not,"[26] and without such music the silence would be deafening. This, and just this, is what the "Mariner" is about.

Meanwhile the poem bequeathed some more immediate poetic tasks to be undertaken.

> I wrote the "Ancient Mariner," and was preparing among other poems, the "Dark Ladie," and the "Christabel," in which I should have more nearly realized my ideal, than I had done in my first attempt. (*BL* 2:7)

3.4 Consequences

The consequences of the two poems that followed were long lasting, in different ways, and I will take "Christabel" first. The "Ancient Mariner" is unusually long for a ballad and Coleridge worked it over and over again for a long period in his head. The process opened portals of discovery and, at the same time, vistas of uncertainty; and his next project was consciously more specific. His aims were (one must surmise) to examine more closely the sense of being haunted by sin; how blameless (or near blameless) innocence can become contaminated through no fault of its own; also, the way, if any, that such a sense of sin might be redeemed. Hölderlin laid down the challenge in his famous hymn, *Patmos* (1802):

> Wo aber Gefahr ist, wächst
> Das Rettende auch
> (But where the danger is, grows
> also the rescue/remedy).

The sense of a "fall" is not as objectively presented in "Christabel" as in the "Mariner"; it is connected more firmly to a sense of sexual shame (Life-in-Death and the spoiling of an occasion of Romantic marriage being the only hints in the earlier poem); there is mention of a "guardian spirit" but the situation is more domestic, less overtly cosmological. The solution appears to be the same in so far as it is passive. The unwitting protagonist is helpless to defend herself against her sense of violation or to recover from it alone, and her recovery will involve an ideal marriage or reconciliation of gendered opposites: "by grace" one might say. In short, "Christabel" as first conceived maps both the problem and the answer: "my strength is made perfect in weakness" (AV II Cor 12:9). How does an individual guided by inner feelings embrace (accomplish) that truth? When Coleridge returned to the poem to add Part II, his narrative moved into a world of daylight happenings that left behind the language of his starting-point.[27] Part I had whirled its reader into the frosty centre of a plot; the protagonist is isolated and crosses the line into the castle where "it" happens and nothing is the same thereafter: she wakes up to a changed world. "It" is everything and nothing; the point is—despite the hints of vampirism and sexual assault—that it defies understanding.

So much for the argument that followed Coleridge's clearer awareness of his aims; or, put another way, of the aims the "Mariner" uncovered in part. What of the different means he employed? The images and pictured situations (cold and warmth, the threshold moment) are less important than matters of sound. "Christabel" works its way by means of lines that for the most part contain four beats across a span measuring a much more widely varying number of syllables (between four and fourteen). They are grouped into stanzas or paragraphs of between two and twenty-six lines, for the most part in couplets but also in other rhyme schemes: for instance, aabbcdcdaa and ababccabab, and also a significant number of lines that do not rhyme.[28] As I explained in Chap. 2, the "Mariner" advances in ballad stanzas, predominantly a8, b6, c8, b6; or (better) four beats alternating with three beats with varying numbers of syllables and extra lines (and rhymes) that extend the length of stanzas up to five or six lines (and up to nine in later versions). It is easy to over-interpret the obvious differences, and Coleridge might have added his 1816 preface hoping to deflect interest from vampirism towards technical matters, but it is no less true that he was more self-conscious about what he was doing in the later poem. The "Mariner" does not depart far from the model of Percy's *Reliques*, and the devices it employs and their effects continue an already established practice. However, the strong forward momentum of the shorter stanzas and pull of the narrative appear to work against his inclination to linger and go deeper. The different quality of sound in Parts V and VI bear out this suggestion—they reach a limit of difference that caused him to begin afresh—and he repeatedly asserted that the "Christabel" metric was designed to register subtle shifts of feeling. A greater "sweetness" and fluency of versification, as he noted of Spenser, places the reader in a different "mental space" (*Lects 1808–1819* 2:409–10; and see 1:289).

It would seem, then, that in the process of writing the "Mariner" Coleridge found the narrative too wide-ranging: that his story of action and physical marvels, with its succession of reversing scenes, distracted him from the theme he had discovered. What holds the attention of the common reader inhibited the author from pursuing the deeper theme. Frances Ferguson puts it thus:

> [T]he difficulty of the poem is that the possibility of learning from the Mariner's experience depends upon sorting that experience into a more linear and complete pattern than the poem ever agrees to do. For the poem seems almost as thorough a work of backwardness—or *hysteron proteron*—as we have.[29]

Beginning "Christabel," Coleridge fixed on the emergent theme and his means of dealing with it became more specific. Longer, variously rhyming paragraphs were better suited to describing his new protagonist's predicament; they moved more slowly and sinuously and cut deeper.

The story of his later adjustments to the spectre ship in the "Mariner" Part III illustrates the incipient difficulty and the solution it prompted. The episode presumably earned its place as a parody of fashionable Gothick—a send-up of pure thrill, detached from any personal concern—but this only left it the more open to occurrence: to take on a burden of extra, deeply personal anxiety. Who are, what are, Death and Life-in-Death? They were not named until the gloss was added in 1817—indeed, the latter figure at first appears "far liker Death than he"—although the difference in gender was strongly emphasised from the beginning. Why was the stanza-length description of Death (lines 181–85) dropped when the gloss was added? If it was to complete the pruning of Gothick elements begun in 1800, why not then? Donald Ault's preface to Martin Wallen's "Experimental Edition" of the poem suggests some pertinent answers (xi–xii). He draws attention to the game involving dice, the echo of the witches in *Macbeth*, and how in 1817 Coleridge wanted the later stanza describing the woman's mate (lines 195–98) struck out; as indeed it was in 1828. He points to Coleridge's evident concern to make clear which of the two figures won the game, to a possible overlap with the theme of vampirism in "Christabel," and even to suggestions of a ghastly primal scene. In short, he suggests Death and Life-in-Death comprise a vision of Coleridge's dead father and his mother who was still alive and whom he blamed for his sense of damaged personality (his own life-in-death). It could indeed be so, and Ault could have added that Coleridge must often have wondered about the events that led up to the birth of his oldest brother Jack, with all the subterfuge and repressed feelings that involved.[30] The appearance of the ship carries reverberations like his vision of Geraldine undressing; and in *Sibylline Leaves*, the woman in line 189 becomes a "Night-Mair" figure: a mare of the night or succubus. The ship of death—"a little speck" or "certain shape" (lines 141, 144)—became an ineradicable stain, a seal of more intense entrapment and not just isolation. The episode, sometimes regretted as an interruption, discovered the theme on which his most deeply personal thoughts subsequently turned.

"The Ballad of the Dark Ladiè" (**182**), begun at about the same time as "Christabel," remained a fragment of fifteen stanzas. It happens that the ballad in Percy's *Reliques* that so influenced the metric of the "Mariner," "Sir Cauline," also interested Coleridge for its story. The protagonist is stricken with love for a princess; he is at first unable to articulate it but, when he eventually finds his love reciprocated, he finds himself condemned to a love that dare not make itself known. His plight involves the proof of love mixed up with identity, separation, and sadness in which the healing power of the princess named Christabelle is nevertheless asserted; and the ballad ends with the death of the two lovers. The two extant scenes of the "Dark Ladiè" reflect the same narrative of a love that fails the Berkleian promise that to be is to be perceived. In the first scene, the Lady is described anxiously waiting for her betrothed lover, Lord Falkland, who eventually arrives; in the second, a dialogue between the pair (slightly confused by the lack of quotation marks in its latter part), the Lady's considerable anxiety over her lover's dilatoriness in wedding her becomes apparent: does he really intend to do so? Despite naming his poem as a ballad in the title, and keeping the abcb rhyme scheme, Coleridge extends the length of his second lines to match the first and third. The rhythm then runs continuously across these first three lines before the fourth (rhyming) trimeter brings each stanza to a close in varying ways. The effect is of a series of heavier, less mobile tableaux than one finds in traditional ballads.[31] The first scene portrayed is notably statuesque, the second is dramatically developing and, whatever surrounding material was jettisoned, the extant stanzas elucidate a predicament completely, even if they leave the narrative unfinished. In this, and in other ways, "The Ballad of the Dark Ladiè" provided a model for "Christabel," stripped of the supernatural element that Part I of the latter carries forward from the "Mariner."[32]

While later poems by Coleridge recur to images in the "Ancient Mariner"—"To William Wordsworth" and "Constancy to an Ideal Object" (**357**) are often cited—such echoes are less relevant than two poems descending from the "Dark Ladiè." The first version of the poem "Love" appeared as an Introduction to the "Dark Ladiè" when the two poems were first published together in December 1799. It provided a narrative that helped make sense of the 1798 fragment; and, revised, it became the story within the story of "Love" when this was published alone. The 1799 Introduction replaces the original suggestion that the knight deliberately deceived his mistress with a situation closer to the "Cauline" original, and this is modified further in the separate "Love" version, where both lovers are too bashful to declare their love frankly. So the story mutates until the telling of the story brings about a mutual release; poetry makes evident what words cannot say directly and effects a resolution. Or perhaps not. Elements of the "Love" story remained in loose solution in Coleridge's mind—reappearing in phrases in other poems and notebooks, in a state of not complete decidedness, still unsettled by the "powers beneath" that moved the Mariner—and Coleridge's final comment came in "Alice du Clós," which he worked on through the 1820s: see below Appendix B. The knight is a deceiver but his lady is both innocent and, as things stand, complicit in deceit; when truth is suppressed, disaster strikes. Their life on earth is not long enough to close down the questions raised.

Finally, to a poem probably written about the same time as the "Mariner" was finished and "Christabel" and the "Dark Ladiè" were begun; indeed some would date it even nearer to the time "Love" was written in 1799. Coleridge never linked "Kubla Khan" (**178**) with any of these poems, but the reading public has from the time of its publication thought of it as one of his famous trio of mystery poems or poems of pure Imagination. "Kubla" is quintessentially a poem haunted by a dream that is both wonderful and dangerous, out of this world and threatening; and the question that follows is whether it is possible to grasp such dream in waking life, an action hedged with imperilment. I am one of those who think the poem is complete as it stands; this in the same way as "Christabel" and the "Dark Ladiè" are, and the "Mariner" is paradoxically not. Many elements of their style are shared by "Kubla Khan" but balanced in a different way. In particular, "Kubla" is not questing, probing: it makes a contained statement, however one chooses to unpack it. It is a poem that draws directly on historical allusions; its implications are more about art than about metaphysics and psychology. It poses a question about writing at the level of the other two mystery poems but gives this question prominence and leaves it open on the table. The Preface added in 1816 merely encourages identification with the fallible author, which downplays the status of the question even as it makes it public.

Coleridge meanwhile applied himself closely to the pursuit of metaphysics in his prose and left verse for personal questions that resisted permanent answers.

"Christabel" and "Kubla Khan" have been held in special esteem at different times and will doubtless continue to do so. The "Ancient Mariner" marks the beginning of Coleridge's second career as a poet and will always enjoy a wider, more varied audience. "Moved onward from beneath," it succeeds in transforming personal vacillation into a poem that strikes a chord in the minds of children and *poètes maudits* alike.

NOTES

1. *Democritus Platonissans* sig B1^v. The limitation of More's statements, as Coleridge noted in *CM* 3:913, is that he "was a poetical philosophist, who amused himself in calling Aristotelian abstractions by the names of Platonic ideas, but by no means a philosophic poet, formed in the life-light of a guiding Idea."
2. I hope it is clear that I am writing about the interpretation of Coleridge and formation of critical attitudes in the earlier part of the century. Magisterial and discriminating surveys of Coleridge on Imagination from an historical point of view, published in the later part of the century, are provided by Engell *Creative Imagination* and McFarland *Originality and Imagination*.
3. In *Joan of Arc* (1795) II 1–140, based upon Coleridge's reading in Leemius and Crantz. The apostrophe to Fancy begins at line 280 (**110**; *PW* 1:210–16 at 214 specifically) and was taken forward to "The Destiny of Nations" (**139**; *PW* 1:285). The connection between these sources and the "Mariner" is glossed by Lowes 93–102.
4. See my *Coleridge's Father* 23, 318–21, 327, etc.
5. Discussed in my *Experimental Poetics* 53–54; and see 143–44 on "Lewti."
6. "Letter to Maria Gisborne" lines 203–05 in *Poems* 3:452. One might add that Coleridge always took particular delight in the more colourful figures in the Platonic tradition, like Giordano Bruno and Jakob Boehme.
7. On Coleridge and Whiter, see *CN* 3:3762 and note. I assume (as Coburn inexplicably does not) that Coleridge refers to Whiter's *Specimen of a Commentary on Shakespeare* (1794), which advertised itself as based upon "the association of ideas." See also *CM* 1:607–08 (a marginalium on Boehme).
8. Details and further commentary are supplied by Class 28–29, 98–101, etc.

9. The first person to draw attention to Kant's dissertation in relation to Coleridge was, I believe, MacKinnon. See subsequently Pradhan 103–07.
10. *Coleridge's Father* 152–53, 231–35, etc. Coleridge found himself on the side of Leibniz, against Kant, in his reading of the latter's *Metaphysische Anfangsgründe* (*CM* 3:269–303), but that was on grounds other than mathematics.
11. I should add that there is a good deal of self-fashioning in the series of autobiographical letters of which this one forms a part. See Shepherd's "Where first I sprang to light"; also my *Coleridge's Father* 50 fn3.
12. See, e.g., the note he made while he was in Germany "To procure & read Mirandula de Ente et Uno" (*CN* 1:374), the snippets of which he copied down bear on the same theme (cf. e.g. *CM* 1:574).
13. Janzen's magnificent "Tale of Two Samuels" is surely the final word on the collocation of texts involved, although, again, it is important to acknowledge the original experience as described may embody a fictive dimension: cf. *CM* 3:341–42, which also invokes the memory of Poole's too-conventional respect for such images of "super-superlative Sublimity."
14. De Quincey 2:145 reporting Coleridge's plan for an unwritten poem.
15. Isabella Fenwick "Notes and Illustrations of the Poems" (1843) in *Prose Works of William Wordsworth* ed. Grosart 3:16.
16. See Dante's description of hell in *Inferno* XXXII and Milton in *Paradise Lost* II 587–95, and compare the Mariner's admission, "And I had done an hellish thing" (line 89).
17. The Wedgwoods were Unitarians, Coleridge continued in his preaching duties (such as they were) at Bridgwater and Taunton through the summer of 1798, and he continued a nominal Unitarian through 1803, probably up to February 1805. References are supplied by Piper "Coleridge and the Unitarian Consensus." Piper's chapter "Biblical, Natural, and Gothic Symbolism in *The Ancient Mariner*" in his *Singing of Mount Abora* 43–59 argues for a Unitarian presence in the poem that one must assume is handled with a degree of detachment.
18. Frend was the first Fellow to sign out Coleridge's borrowings from the Jesus College Library: see my "Coleridge's Borrowings." John Coleridge even selected a prominent Presbyterian, William Evans, as one of his son's godparents (*Coleridge's Father* 488).
19. A process of change succinctly described by Paley *Apocalypse and Millennium* 91–153. See also Kitson's "To Milton's Trump."
20. *Corruptions of Christianity* 2:58. Coleridge borrowed the volumes from the Bristol Library in March–April 1795: Whalley "Bristol Library Borrowings" 119.
21. Discussed in my *Experimental Poetics* 58–61, etc.

22. *Prelude* (1799) I 288; ibid. (1805) XI 257; ibid. (1805) XII 208; Norton Critical Edition 8, 428 and 429, respectively.
23. *Prometheus Unbound* (1820) III iv 204: *Poems* 2:611.
24. Sally West's *Coleridge and Shelley* 86–98 is specially recommended on this matter.
25. "Man Carrying Thing" in *Collected Poetry and Prose* 306.
26. *The Tempest* III ii 133–34.
27. As already intimated, I hold to the view that "Christabel" Part I is a complete poem which Coleridge might have thought of extending only after he rejoined Wordsworth on his return from Germany. See further in Chap. 5.
28. That is, with end rhymes; several rhyme in other ways within the line.
29. "Coleridge and the Deluded Reader" 250.
30. The circumstances of Jack's birth, upbringing, and exile are described in my *Coleridge's Father* 188–90, 393–94, 406–08, etc. They involve what might be construed as the entrapment of Coleridge's father, who was already engaged to be married, by a much younger, four months pregnant, Anne Bowdon.
31. Compare the nearly contemporaneous "Story of the Mad Ox" (**177**), where lengthened ballad stanzas with two rhymed lines move forward in a predominantly regular meter.
32. I should add a point on the play on "eye/ee" sounds that joins the three poems (discussed in my "Contemplation in Coleridge's Poetry") and thereby connects to the incipient theme of self-consciousness. It could well derive from the West country pronunciation of "ee" for "ye," thereby making a corresponding play on "I" and "you" and connecting with the theme of unstable identity running through early poems like "The Complaint of Ninathoma" (**51**), "Imitated from Ossian' (**55**), "Absence: A Poem" (**60**), and onwards to "Lewti" (**172**), etc.

CHAPTER 4

Wordsworth as Collaborator and Contributor

...take no pains to contradict the story that the L.B. are entirely yours. Such a rumour is the best thing that can befall them.

William Wordsworth[1]

4.1 SEEDS

There is much more to be said about Wordsworth's part in making the "Ancient Mariner." The poem was the last in a sequence of three (namely, following "The Three Graves" **155** and "The Wanderings of Cain" **160**) that the two poets began writing together and it formed the lead poem in their collection of *Lyrical Ballads* when this appeared anonymously. No matter that all three attempts at collaborative writing failed and that the shared volume contains poems of widely different kinds: the further differences that time uncovered will form the subject of Chap. 5. Meanwhile, a comparison of the two poets' converging and diverging aims and methods up to September 1798 can throw further light on what has been said thus far.

The first two attempts at writing a poem together failed for different but connected reasons. In the first instance, Coleridge attempted to continue and complete a poem begun independently by Wordsworth and likewise abandoned his attempt when, one might say, he swerved off the other side of the road. It is commonly assumed that Wordsworth had begun in the hope of pursuing ideas about guilt that had been building in his mind through previous poems, and found that his narrative had ground to a halt. Coleridge picked up the challenge and took the ideas forward in a direction of their own, in a way disturbing to them both. As a result, "The Wanderings of Cain" was planned in another way from the start, based upon an agreed outline (drawn up by Coleridge) to be finished with no room for second thoughts in one session at the same table. Coleridge completed his portion, but Wordsworth found himself unable to write more than a few words, and so this project also remained unfinished. The repeated failures raise the question: what was the interest which drew them together but on which they found it impossible to collaborate, and why, then, did the third attempt (the "Ancient Mariner") succeed? Was it because, although Wordsworth contributed a little more at the beginning, he quickly withdrew, leaving Coleridge to finish the poem in his own way? If so, Wordsworth soon found himself writing his own transposition of essentially the same narrative ("The Idiot Boy") and writing a spate of poems at a tangent to the route Coleridge discovered through the process of writing (i.e. "Christabel" **176** and the other poems discussed at the close of the last chapter). Why did the agreement to disagree happen as it did? What made the "Ancient Mariner" the catalyst it proved to be?

Other poetical enterprises play a part in this story. Both poets were separately engaged in writing full-length plays before Coleridge took up Wordsworth's "Three Graves." Wordsworth had in hand *The Borderers*, involving a Iago-like protagonist, Rivers, and themes of guilt that biographers have associated with his earlier affair with Annette Vallon,[2] while Coleridge had *Osorio*, pursuing similar themes further in the direction of remorse and expiation. Wordsworth set his play aside when it was rejected by Covent Garden, but Coleridge took forward two extracts from *Osorio* to *Lyrical Ballads* under the titles "The Foster-mother's Tale" (**152**) and "The Dungeon" (**153**). The first of these is a brief and haunting life story of "A pretty boy, but most unteachable" that reverberates with curious overtones of Coleridge's own mythologised sense of himself; the second, more simply, describes a life cut off from healing nature. Both of them can be connected with aspects of the "Mariner," as can "Lewti" (**172**), a rewriting of a poem Wordsworth wrote as a schoolboy. See, for example, the "little cloud" "of palest hue":

> Onward to the Moon it passed.
> Still brighter and more bright it grew,
> With floating colours not a few,

> Till it reached the Moon at last:
> Then the cloud was wholly bright,
> With a rich and amber light! (*PW* 1:459)

The image initiates a striking moment of hope, which at that same moment floats away: "Its hues are dim, its hues are grey—." The comfort it offers is unstable, potentially deceptive, mirroring such visions of truth in the ballad, although here in the lyric hitched to a narrative of ostentatiously adolescent feeling. Coleridge included only one poem from among those he wrote in the months after finishing the "Mariner"—namely, "The Nightingale" (**180**)—when he was forced to withdraw "Lewti" (**172**) to preserve the anonymity of the volume (see *PW* 1:457, 516 notes). Why "Frost at Midnight" (**171**) was not automatically included is another question to which I return below.

The conclusion of the "Ancient Mariner" coincided with a breakthrough moment in Wordsworth's career. Part VII of the ballad ends with echoes of the poem he was writing at the time, *The Ruined Cottage* (see *PW* 1:413 note), and the two friends ended their poems with a similar moral, Wordsworth already varying his to "a *better* and a wiser man" (my italics: see *PW* 1:419 note). It is a challenging difference, not least when Coleridge's ending is born in mind, and it sets the mood for the positive spirit that Wordsworth struck in the quatrain poems that poured from him during that Alfoxden spring. He took inspiration in "the hour of feeling" (*LB* 96) to celebrate the harmony he saw and the joy it contained:

> The birds around me hopp'd and play'd:
> Their thoughts I cannot measure,
> But the least motion which they made,
> It seem'd a thrill of pleasure. (*LB* 116)

This celebration is quite unlike Coleridge's description in "The Nightingale," of a mysterious "gentle maid" in a moonlit castle wood:

> And she hath watch'd
> Many a Nightingale perch giddily
> On blosmy twig still swinging from the breeze,
> And to that motion tune his wanton song,
> Like tipsy Joy that reels with tossing head.
> (*LB* 68; *PW* 1:519–20)

Here the words "wanton," "tipsy," and reeling" sound an unambiguous note of danger, a "giddy" or disoriented loss of control.³ The aesthetics of passive openness and unsteered association had become problematic for Coleridge while at the same moment Wordsworth's rising confidence in the same laid down a challenge. After the two failures, their collaboration on the "Mariner," from which Wordsworth quickly withdrew, succeeded by accident to become the foundation of a New School of poetry; or so Wordsworth could have thought when he paused to take stock in March 1798. Hence the moment of panic when he was about to advance the experiment—or rather, his version of it with further explanation—a stage further in December 1799: see the epigraph to the present chapter.

There have been various attempts to show how the poems comprising *Lyrical Ballads* 1798 form a balanced whole.⁴ *Au contraire*, the volume strains to hold together and that is part of its joy.

4.2 Early Collaboration

"The Three Graves" is, as I said, Coleridge's attempt to continue a recently abandoned Wordsworth text, presumably copied for him by Dorothy Wordsworth following his visit to Racedown in summer 1797.⁵ Wordsworth's contribution derives from a German ballad by G.A. Bürger, translated by William Taylor as "The Lass of Fair Wone," and published in the *Monthly Magazine* in April 1796; it is also connected (e.g. through characters named Edmund and Mary) to some even more fragmentary lines he wrote which are known to the Cornell editors as the "Greyhound Ballad."⁶ The relationship between these several materials remains conjectural: for instance, whether the parts of the transcript are separate or meant to be read as a sequence, or whether the "Greyhound Ballad" stanzas are the beginning of a separate venture. Stephen Parrish interpreted the situation to show Wordsworth fixing on German Gothick imagery (the graves, the toad, the thorn) and becoming absorbed in the idea of a curse living in the mind of his narrator, the sexton (a theme developed further in "The Thorn"); this is contrasted with Coleridge's continuation, where the events recounted "are meaningful in themselves, not for what they reveal about their describer."⁷ I am not persuaded: Coleridge appears to me to give the narrator an equal importance in his continuation in verse, and in the prose note introducing the published text. Again, continuation may be a misleading word: Coleridge can just as well be described as writing the same over again, that is, beginning at the point where Wordsworth began instead of following where he left off; which could well explain why he returned to perfect his effort in spring 1798,[8] before abandoning it altogether in favour of "Christabel" and the related ballads.

Coleridge's part in "The Three Graves" is full of resonances that find an echo in the "Ancient Mariner." The troubled narrator discovered in a churchyard and the blocking out of the sun referred to in the previous chapter are examples. The introduction of the Commination Prayer into the Ash Wednesday service, which "Our late old Vicar, a kind man," much regrets (*PW* 1:341), is a reminder that curses can rain down from above as well as rise from below; or, more personally, the figure of the mother-possessed might well have prompted the figure of Life-in-Death, if Donald Ault's surmise holds true (again see the previous chapter). However, much as Coleridge was interested in morbid psychology, I suggest he was equally interested in the possibilities of the ballad stanza, which he took much further. He expressed high approval of the language of "Sir Cauline" in Percy's *Reliques* to Wordsworth during January 1798 (*CL* 1:379), and Lowes (331) records the reappearance of much of it in the "Ancient Mariner." Significantly, that word "ee" for "eye" also carried into Coleridge's part of "The Three Graves" (line 289: *PW* 1:348), the part that forms an ambiguous epiphany before Edward's lurch into the realisation "I have torn out her heart" where the poem ends. Thus, although Coleridge made the subject, in Wordsworth's words, "too shocking and painful, and not sufficiently sweetened by any healing views" (*PW* 1:336 note), its interest lies equally in the different way the authors handle the ballad stanza. Wordsworth's stanzas are all in regular meter and do not extend beyond four lines; Coleridge's contain an amount of trisyllabic substitution, six of his stanzas extend to five lines, and two of them to six lines. The movement of his verse is more pliable as befits his perception of the subject matter and one can observe him moving towards modifications that his later ballad narrative was to take further: proportionally twice as many expanded stanzas and doubled offbeats. It is as if he willingly retrieved Wordsworth's discarded experiment and what he found of interest came to hand when he embarked on his own longer poem in the same meter.

"The Wanderings of Cain" began as a conscious attempt, a few months after Coleridge took over "The Three Graves," to complete a shared project by beginning together. Perhaps the Biblical prose among Wordsworth's working-manuscripts—divine imprecations and curses that possibly prompted Coleridge to introduce his reference to the Commination

Prayer[9]—encouraged them to write it in prose. Coleridge suggests they had in mind to imitate a prose translation of Salomon Gessner's *Death of Abel*; and they possibly entertained thoughts about the Biblical brothers in relation to his own familial situation, just as thoughts of his own mother hover in the background of "The Three Graves." Whatever the case, they hoped to complete their task in a single sitting. Wordsworth was to take Canto 1, Coleridge Canto 2, and whoever finished first would take Canto 3 (*PW* 1:359–60). The immediate inspiration followed a lengthy walk to Lynton, where the Valley of Rocks gave them a primordial setting and atmosphere, but only Coleridge's portion was written and (very much later) published. The two surrounding portions were never begun. A rough plan exists, which appears to divide the project into three parts (*PW* 2:495–96) but these do not bear a clear relation to each other, and the fair copy of the Canto Coleridge prepared for publication in 1809 does not match any of them. The situation is tangled, to say the least, and it would be unwise to go beyond some general observations.

The extant portion by Coleridge (*PW* 1:361–65) involves three characters. First, Cain, Adam's eldest son, who murdered his brother Abel because (as Coleridge put it) "he neglected to make a proper use of his senses," is a haunted, suffering Mariner figure. He is indeed the agent—the person who caused the action—but the emphasis is on an encounter with his innocent victim who—surprisingly—is equally tormented. This second character, Abel, is dead and appears only as a haunted spirit ("a Shape"). The third character is a child named Enos, by which one would suppose him to be the son of Adam's third son, Seth (AV Gen 4:26). However, Coleridge gives him a place in the narrative where he functions as Cain's guide and intermediary with the dead Abel and is thereby equivalent to Cain's son whose name is usually given in English as Enoch (e.g. AV Gen 4:17). The change of name is significant in that it associates Coleridge's character with the Generations of Adam (or genealogy of Jesus in AV Luke 3:23–38) and bears on the supreme innocence of his character, which is severely tested. It also links with the child Coleridge who was conscious of having been born, like Enos in AV Gen 5:6, to a father in legendary old age.

Only a few lines of the rough draft (*PW* 2:495, lines WP19–23) correspond—and loosely—to the published text. There is proportionally less emphasis on the dependence of father on son, and the child is never actually named. The important feature here is the habitation of the dead Abel by a devilish spirit who then pursues the vulnerable (guilty) Cain.

This Abel *faux* persuades Cain first that God is severe and unforgiving, and then to burn out his eyes, and later reappears and almost tricks Cain into sacrificing his son. The melodramatic close involves the true Abel "sail[ing] slowly down" alongside the archangel Michael to save Cain and the child from further ruin; the original conception, all through, implicitly lays as much stress on the redemption of Abel as of Cain. The published version, with its apologetic preface and concluding verse lines describing an innocent boy-child "plucking fruits, | By moonlight, in a wilderness" (PW 1:360), would seem to want to override this theme; although at the close of the same verses, multiple echoes of Christabel lingering alone at night in the forest, and in her chamber with Geraldine with "no loving mother near," also resonate with portent.

What can be said, then, other than that Coleridge made a simpler public statement from a hastily assembled, tangled set of notes? First, at all times, the adult characters are broken, tortured figures moving across a landscape as desolate as the wide, wide sea of the "Ancient Mariner." Second, Abel in his despairing undead state, suspended in a kind of purgatory, still tormented by Cain and apparently forsaken by his creator, also complicates any simple understanding of crime and redemption: the division between perpetrator and victim breaks down. The action sketched in the draft is tumultuous and apocalyptic, calmer in the published text, but the latter nevertheless contains clues to what drove Coleridge's original thoughts. The odd denomination of Enoch as Enos, simply by making one pause to think, also triggers thoughts of the apocryphal book of Enoch that connect not only with Coleridge's interest in the location of Paradise in Ethiopia, and "Kubla Khan" (**178**),[10] but also with Gnostic traditions of Enoch and the Watchers: the fallen angels who had intercourse with the daughters of men before the second Fall of Adam and Eve. The Shape (Abel) in the published text declares that "The Lord is God of the living only, the dead have another God" (lines 117–18). Enos lifts up his eyes and prays (like the "Mariner's" Hermit), but Cain rejoices at this revelation and twice asks for more knowledge of "the God of the dead" (lines 125–26, 140–41). Why? The answer would appear to be, linked to what I said before, that Coleridge has in mind the Hermetic-Gnostic tradition as he gleaned it at Christ's Hospital from Pico della Mirandola's *Apology* (1487), where Pico talks of two kinds of gods and magic, black and white.[11] This is not a far cry from the Two Voices that preside over events in the "Mariner" and the mysterious undercurrent that drives them forward from beneath.

In short, the valley at Lynton, that desolate spot on the Exmoor tourist trail, elicited notions of mythic figures of a Gnostic first Fall from Grace in which perpetrator and victim merge and God's will is difficult to understand. The clearer this becomes, the more obviously it was primarily Coleridge's project: Wordsworth, willing to contribute, was left staring at a near-blank sheet of paper and so the incomplete scheme was set aside with a laugh. Despite the muddle, it is revelatory for two reasons. It made unmistakably clear to Wordsworth the ferment of arcane resources that were circulating in Coleridge's mind, going back many years to his schooldays (the idea of a double fall is present, for example, in Boehme): this is a short time before they set off to visit Lynton again and mapped their project to write a ballad together. On the second occasion, Wordsworth took care to lay a clear story line at the setting-out. He had also learned to withdraw and bide his time when Coleridge began to run away with the story, and instead continued with his own projects in hand. He waited for Coleridge to finish before attempting to think out what he himself would have done with the same topic. On Coleridge's side, what part of his contribution to "The Wanderings of Cain" is not reflected in the "Ancient Mariner" later surfaced in a different way in "Christabel," as many have noticed. For a start, his new protagonist's name is made up of Christ and Abel.

4.3 The Third Attempt

The "Ancient Mariner" was planned on the spur of the moment to defray the expenses of a walk along the coast from Stowey. When the plans for the ballad quickly began to elaborate, Coleridge instead sent the *Monthly Magazine* three sonnets "attempted in the manner of contemporary writers," signed Nehemiah Higginbottom (**158**; *PW* 1:355–57). The ballad began as a similar light-hearted gesture; indeed, just as much a parody of a contemporary fashion as the sonnets mocked the idea of a "Coleridgean school." Charles Lamb saw the point of the ballad if not of the sonnets: "I call it a right English attempt, and a successful one, to dethrone German sublimity."[12] Other readers in the next generation like the Cambridge undergraduates Derwent Coleridge and Thomas Babington Macaulay were aware of this element of fun[13]; so were parodists like George John Daire (1841) and later writers in the burgeoning Victorian tradition of nonsense verse: for instance, Edward Lear in "The Owl and the Pussycat" (1871) and Lewis Carroll in "The Hunting of the Snark" (1876).[14]

This dimension of the "Mariner" was altogether forgotten when it became an examination text bound with (a particularly favoured companion) James Russell Lowell's "The Vision of Sir Launfal" (dual-title editions in 1889, 1898, and 1906, reprints from half a dozen publishers) which was only partially retrieved when Hunt Emerson's comic book version appeared a hundred years later (1989).

The object of the original parody is more evident in the first (*Lyrical Ballads*) version of the poem, where the curious spelling as well as border-ballad style makes very clear the authors' target. Their poem began less as an exercise in early balladry than a send-up of the current revival of the same. Wordsworth had long been interested in Taylor's translations of contemporary German ballads, and G.A. Bürger's *Lenore* (1774)—English translation (by Taylor) in the *Monthly Magazine* 1796, followed by five more translations, including one by Walter Scott—left its mark on this poem and others (for instance, "Hart-leap Well," discussed in Chap. 5). Coleridge, meanwhile, had reviewed Matthew Lewis's *The Monk* for the *Critical Review* in 1796 (*SW&F* 1:57–65), remarking that the poetry it contained was the better part; and the debased supernatural remained in his critical sights when he reviewed two more gothic novels for the *Critical* in summer 1798 (*SW&F* 1:79–82). The difference between real and fake gothic is crucial. Indeed, the two poets' particular interest in the most "revived" (i.e. rewritten) ballad in Percy's *Reliques*, "Sir Cauline," was possibly, from the beginning, an interest in what was fake. Edmund Blunden quoted stanzas from Chatterton's "The Dethe of Syr Charles Bawdin" as a close parallel to the "merry Minstralsy" entering the marriage hall[15]:

> Before hym went the council-menne,
>   Ynne scarlett robes and golde,
> And tassils spanglynge ynne the sunne,
>   Muche glorious to beholde.

Blunden did not make the point that Coleridge often parodies himself when he writes in a style he is growing out of. It was an enabling position for the latter to assume, as he had already proved to himself and continued to do later.[16] As the manner, so the story. The protagonist is hedged about with dubiety; he is a grey-beard loon, an outsider, a weirdo at a wedding feast. There is every reason not to take an old navigator who gets lost seriously, that is, until the story he tells becomes involving in itself.

The special relevance of the "Ancient Mariner" beginning is that Coleridge had little reason to take the project seriously until he was drawn into working it out. The accidental circumstance gave him the opportunity to range more widely and deeply among his own resources than any other project he had previously embarked upon. Another aspect of the same is undoubtedly the greater interest Wordsworth took at the beginning; or better say, from the very beginning and for not long after that. Possibly the dream of "a skeleton ship with figures in it" told to Coleridge by their Stowey friend John Cruikshank, and passed on in conversation to Wordsworth (Dyce 185), connected with the latter's recent reading of Shelvocke, whence came the shooting of the (originally black) albatross.

These elements together supply the central action, to which Wordsworth added the navigation of the ship by the dead men and two stanzas that are equally important, the first near the beginning of Part I:

> He holds him with his glittering eye—
> The wedding guest stood still
> And listens like a three year's child;
> The Marinere hath his will.

And the second that opens Part IV:

> "I fear thee, ancyent Marinere!
> "I fear thy skinny hand;
> "And thou art long and lank and brown
> "As is the ribb'd Sea-sand.

The word "eye" introduced in the first of these stanzas occurs more than any other in the poem (eighteen times, to be exact) and—combined with repeated words like "bright," "glitter," "fixed," "still," and "trance"—makes up a pattern of images spread across the meaning of the whole poem. The second stanza here, in which Coleridge narrowed Wordsworth's contribution to the last two lines, might seem less significant: perhaps a footnote on the peculiar striations on the beach at Kilve, of which Wordsworth was particularly fond. However, as Lane Cooper argued,[17] just as the earlier stanza contains the clearest suggestion of the primary psychological trait of the Mariner, so the second gives the clearest picture of his outward appearance. In short, there is a strong argument to support the view that Wordsworth was instrumental in establishing a basic ground plan before the poem was begun. Cooper calls it "a manageable plot," something

Coleridge was wont to forget when he forged ahead on his own. It carried Coleridge through to a conclusion that he might not otherwise have attained, although naturally not to Wordsworth's entire satisfaction.

The joint process of gathering together and mapping out appears to have lasted several days, even perhaps a week or more. Dorothy Wordsworth, in a fragmentary letter dated 20 November 1797, refers to an eight-mile walk to Watchet a week after the first plans were laid on the walk to Lynton: "William and Coleridge employing themselves in laying the plan of a ballad."[18] It is unclear when Wordsworth separated "from an undertaking upon which I could only have been a clog."[19] He also told Alexander Dyce (185) that he "had a very small share in the composition of it" beyond the initial contribution of separate incidents because "the style of Coleridge would not assimilate with mine," and so one assumes Coleridge continued alone from the time Wordsworth was in London seeing to his play between early December and the beginning of January 1798. He told Cottle he had completed a version in 340 lines by 18 February (*CL* 1:387); and Dorothy Wordsworth recorded that Coleridge came to dinner on 23 March, bringing the finished version which presumably approached very near the published version of 658 lines.

The development of the poem during the five-month period when it came together is clear, at least in broad outline. Initial discussion with Wordsworth set the parameters of a rounded voyage structure, with a strong protagonist moving through central scenes. Wordsworth probably encouraged the framing narrative, set in the churchyard, and possibly bequeathed the shadow of a "hunt narrative" evident in the fragmentary "Greyhound Ballad." At the same time, Coleridge came with earlier abandoned projects still in mind, like his project for a sequence of "Hymns to the Sun, the Moon, and the Elements" (*CN* 1:174 f 25); his reading in the exploration of "high latitudes" and the Gnostic tradition[20]; his interest in metrical experiment and loosening the bounds of prosody as then understood; and all the personal concerns that made his understanding of (for instance) the inheritance of guilt different from Wordsworth's, as their previous attempts at collaboration made clear. Luckily, this time, the narrative outline was able to contain the divergent elements that poured into it. It even survived to accommodate the expansion during the last month of composition that almost doubled the length of the whole. This was achieved by planting what is in effect a subplot into the Mariner's return journey that left the main story unaffected, but nominated the forces that move it from above and below and made clearer (if not altogether clear) why the homecoming is complete in name only.

This last matter is the point. While Wordsworth probably felt he had set Coleridge on a course that would succeed, the "Ancient Mariner" may be said to succeed best on account of its very incompleteness. Coleridge's contribution to "The Three Graves" turned on the same subject—"A haunting in her brain" (*PW* 1:345, line 210)—but its treatment was more simply pictorial, scenic; a world of neighbourly visits on mossy tracks, and preoccupied walks "fast down along the lee" (line 138); the sound of rain on the church roof and bells heard in a holly dell beside a brook, and where the teller of the tale is an old gravedigger. The meter and rhyme do not stray much beyond conventional norms; the pace of narrative is brisk and decisive. The narrative breaks off but only when it contains everything the poetry has suggested. Like "Christabel" Part I, it has the satisfaction of a balanced torso. Conversely, the Mariner's narrative rounds to home but leaves all it has encompassed still afloat. The magical world it inhabits is outside familiar space and time, and the haunting in the brain resonates in a larger atmosphere. The more elaborately worked-over style appeals not only to the sense that *appears* to the eye of the mind but equally to the *sound* of sense, a sound that can be intimated by whispers, echoes caught from chance associations.

Similarly with regard to "The Wanderings of Cain," which bears particularly on Coleridge's expansion of the end part of his poem: Wordsworth's sense of a curse brought down on the man who slew the albatross evidently did not reach as far back as Coleridge's, in which causes are elusive to define and more problematic to resist. A far more complex psychology is at once presumed, with feelings stemming from unseen and unheard depths, and the suspicion or part-knowledge that others have wrestled with the same thoughts and feelings since the beginning of time. "The Wanderings of Cain" is a jumble of recherché sources that picture duality in the godhead, theologically unsound but wise because they speak to human needs and picture truths that were lost upon the knowing.[21] The "Ancient Mariner" gives better expression to these forces from the beginning, as soon as the ship crosses the line; and the allegorical presentation in Parts V and VI of these "bottom-winds" as Coleridge afterwards called them (with reference to the Northern lakes: *CL* 5:23) is a less distracting, more integrated, means of signalling them than allusions to heterodox legend. The ballad altogether provides an open context for the issues that clog the annotations of twentieth-century scholars. It keeps deep matters at the edge, and above and below, in a poem that can be enjoyed by schoolchildren. It encompasses thoughts that are indeed "painful," but readers less close to the writing than Wordsworth only come to them in due time.

4.4 A Different Direction

While Coleridge was writing and rewriting his ballad, Wordsworth was finishing his major blank-verse poems, *The Ruined Cottage* and *The Pedlar*. This important moment coincided with news that the Alfoxden lease would not be renewed, and the moment of release and uncertainty stimulated Wordsworth to new powers of composition. As Dorothy wrote on 5 March 1798:

> His faculties seem to expand every day, he composes with much more facility than he did, as to the *mechanism* of poetry, and his ideas flow faster than he can express them.[22]

The outpouring of lyric poems in a new style accompanied various discussions with Joseph Cottle for book publication of earlier writing and settled on a joint volume of the two poets' new material during April–May. Hazlitt read a number of the poems when he visited Coleridge towards the end of May, after which Cottle took the bulk of the material for the new book back to Bristol. "Tintern Abbey" was written and added after the Wordsworths made their short tour of the Wye (c.10–13 July); there was a last minute substitution to preserve anonymity; and publication took place in mid-September, just days before Coleridge and the Wordsworths sailed from Yarmouth for Germany.

The new poems written by Wordsworth between early March and the end of May 1798 formed the core of the new collection, but earlier verse was retrieved and revised to swell their number. "Lines left upon a Seat in a Yew-tree" date in part from schooldays at Hawkshead, and "The Female Vagrant" derives from the then-unpublished *Salisbury Plain*. Considerable care was taken with the overall arrangement, as several commentators have shown. For example, James Averill suggests ("Shape" 398–99) that the opening lines of "The Foster-mother's Tale" are positioned (at *LB* 53–54) so as to connect with the "Ancient Mariner" that comes before it—"It is a perilous tale!" and, later, "'Tis a sweet tale"—and Maria to whom the tale is told is "sadder and wiser" for hearing it. It is another story of crime and punishment, a second version of the Mariner's moonstruck travels, and the dangers of guilt and misdirected imagination are strongly set forth. Read in this way, Maria's naive protestation—"this strange man has left me | Troubled with wilder fancies"—further undercuts the artificiality of the previous Gothick pastiche. The next (third) poem, Wordsworth's "Yew-tree," presents another traveller who is lost because he feeds exclusively on visionary views, though this is a poem of rest, not travel. The parody of picturesque feeling, which is particularly evident in the opening lines, is a kind of "scorn" or "pride": they are words that crop up in the context of Coleridge's "Dark Ladiè" and "Love" (**253**) as born of, and the necessary counterpart of, timidity.[23] So the volume advances through to the end. It is possible that "The Idiot Boy" was intended to serve as conclusion at the time Cottle took the manuscripts to Bristol before the late arrival, "Tintern Abbey," replaced it. It matches the "Mariner" in length, the parallels between the two poems are elaborately contrived, and it is the only other poem in the volume with a separate title page (*LB* 147).

Two poems Wordsworth wrote in March–April 1798—"Lines Written at a Small Distance from My House" (*LB* 95–97) and "Lines Written in Early Spring" (*LB* 115–16)—are superficially similar in tone and manner yet their differences are subtly telling. The first is a dialogue contained in the mind of the speaker. In the setting, which is "the first mild day of March,"

> There is a blessing in the air,
> Which seems a sense of joy to yield.

He urges his sister to join him with the child in their care out of doors in a day of "idleness":

> Love, now an universal birth,
> From heart to heart is stealing,
> From earth to man, from man to earth,
> —It is the hour of feeling.

The second, beginning "I heard a thousand blended notes," is a shorter first person meditation on a speaker's similar surroundings, framed by a concluding reflection:

> If I these thoughts may not prevent,
> If such be of my creed the plan,
> Have I not reason to lament
> What man has made of man?

The stanza form, situation, and general idea of both poems are the same, yet the first is altogether more insistent as it urges on others to share in what it describes; the second describes the world surrounding simply as it is, but steps outside to wonder at the consequences of ignoring it. The loss caused by remaining indoors or with books in the first instance is personal; in the second instance, despite or equally because of the quieter more meditative tone, it involves a "creed" that affects humanity at large.

A similar point can be made by two poems written in a much more complicated stanza form: "Goody Blake and Harry Gill" (*LB* 85–93) and "Simon Lee, the Old Huntsman" (*LB* 98–104), which are both in regular 8-line stanzas rhyming ababcdcd. "Goody Blake" has 4-feet lines with an extra syllable in the first line (4½ feet); "Simon Lee" also has 4-feet lines, but with shorter lines in lines 4 (3 feet) and 8 (3½ feet). It also has feminine rhymes in lines 6 and 8. The stark statistics measure a quite different way of telling. For a start, the rhymes in each poem divide the stanzas into two but the first half of the stanzas in "Goody Blake" are off-balance, set tumbling by the extra syllable, which contrasts with the more solid arrangement of sounds in the second half. While it is possible to follow the story by reading only the second half of each stanza, the first half contains more of the speaker's responses: he or she asks questions and exclaims, reports dialogue. The result is that a reader's perceptions travel through the narrator's understanding to come up time after time against hard fact. Compare this with the effect of the emphatically divided stanzas in "Simon Lee," where the second half dangles off the first—a sort of trailing commentary on a previous statement—though the speaker spreads his voice through both parts. The impression made is of a concern that continually fails to follow through. The narrator is directive and participant but admittedly, in the end, inadequate. In "Goody Blake" the circular pincer movement of the narrative encloses the reader in the curse. In "Simon Lee," the reader is implicated in the pathos of the speaker's willingness to assist and failure to cure. Each poem combines a sociopolitical argument with a critique of differently inadequate responses to the same.

Two more sets of deliberately paired poems—placed following one another at a different point in the volume—pursue the same themes further by implicating the reader even more deeply. "Anecdote for Fathers" (*LB* 105–09) and "We Are Seven" (*LB* 110–14) are dramatic encounters between adults and children, at cross-purposes over fundamental human truths. "We Are Seven" is the milder: the moral is at the beginning; a dialogue with a chance-encountered little girl punctures adult condescension. There is a hilarious display of well-meaning egotism from which the child is instinctively protected. "Anecdote for Fathers" turns the irony more sharply back upon the speaker. He is more demanding, as a father he assumes a right to be, and the more he insists on an answer the more he fails to understand that his question is a non-issue. The child's lack of concern thereby becomes a criticism of the speaker's insistence: a satire on the cut-and-dried expectations of the adult world. The subtitle is stark: "shewing how the art of lying may be taught." Children are not born corrupt; they are made so by a lying world.[24] The stakes are raised higher in a continuous pair of poems based on encounters real or imagined between Wordsworth and Hazlitt in late May 1798—"Expostulation and Reply" (*LB* 183–85) and "The Tables Turned" (*LB* 186–88)—perhaps sent on to Bristol after Cottle left Alfoxden. Wordsworth placed them first in *Lyrical Ballads* 1800 (when he demoted the "Mariner" from first place to last), a tacit declaration that they represented his sense of what was most worthwhile in the volume as a whole. On the one hand, they set out in almost expository terms the "general argument" so many poems rest upon; but, by varying the stress pattern in line 2 of the last two stanzas of "Expostulation," which carries forward to all eight stanzas of "Tables," the pair become one whole. William becomes an expostulator in his turn, first echoing Matthew's words and then replacing them with concrete images lacking before, and thereafter progressing into a philosophising mode with a newly fostered assurance—and humour.

I should mention "The Thorn" (*LB* 117–32) because its subject matter, length, and formal complexity define it as a poem of considerable importance to its author. The curse is taken forward from "The Three Graves" and becomes centred on images of the hill, the pond, the thorn, the woman, a "spot," and an unchanging cry, "O woe is me! oh misery!" In the same way, the intricate numbered stanzas[25] construct repeated, predictable, refrain-like rhythms among the wind and beneath the mountains and stars. The shifting point-of-view makes a double occasion—the thorn and its story, and the effect of this conjunction on another mind—and it remains uncertain which one is primary. Wordsworth's poem matches the "Ancient Mariner" in its concern with something not understood, a protagonist condemned to relive her trauma, but with an odd literalness or stiffness that remains puzzling as much as moving. The poem reads its readers while they read and to that extent (only) they inherit the problem (the curse) it conveys. "The Idiot Boy" is a more obviously designed and satisfactory "answer" to Coleridge's poem, although an insufficiently serious one, and I will come to that matter shortly.

4.5   AND SUDDEN SURPRISE

It should be evident that the division of labour sketched in Chap. 14, *Biographia Literaria*—between one partner contributing poems that began with the supernatural and the other with things of every day (*BL* 2:6–7)—is a retrospective simplification and even misleading. If one begins with the poems, one observes Wordsworth reworking a less spooky supernatural, a more questioning credulity. When he added a note to *The Thorn* in 1800, for example, it was to describe the narrator as an old sea captain "prone to superstition." Then, in "Goody Blake and Harry Gill," the supernatural is given a sociopolitical turn consonant with poems like "The Female Vagrant," "The Last of the Flock," "Old Man Travelling," "The Complaint of a Forsaken Indian Woman," and "The Convict": all of which, in context, make Coleridge's "The Dungeon" very much more like them. One could continue to list differences of attitude but more significant is the difference of style. Wordsworth's diction is closer to the older ballads in its plain directness, the evenly observed pictorial stance, while his metrics move in a very different direction from Coleridge's in the "Mariner." They are altogether more regular, many of the shorter poems are in common or hymn meter,[26] very often building these simple blocks into longer more complicated stanzas, as I described above with reference to "Goody Blake" and "Simon Lee." "The Thorn" is the prime instance. What is striking is the way such simple means of vocabulary and sound are under control and manipulated in such a confident—nay, challenging—way: the same means that close like a trap on innocent readers of "Anecdote for Fathers" and "We Are Seven."

Wordsworth's buoyant stance, turning the tables on those who picked up *Lyrical Ballads* with expectations that it would conform to the fashionable verse of the time,[27] is exactly what excited the young Turks. Whereas their elders—including Southey and the anonymous neighbours and acquaintances reported by Mrs. Coleridge—could not see the point, Hazlitt and others found "the unaccountable mixture of seeming simplicity and real abstruseness"[28] was a life-changing experience. The Advertisement to the volume describes the majority of poems as "experiments" (*LB* i), but the "Mariner" presents a different challenge. Although it likewise began in parody and very possibly the moral stanzas towards the close were inserted as bait for the wrong readers, it came, via confrontation with the supernatural numinous, to involve the ambiguity of deep feelings (their visceral attraction–revulsion) and ideas about how to be saved. The parody element remains present as a ghost and—as in "This Lime-tree Bower my Prison" (**156**), another journey out and back—Coleridge maintains a slightly humorous attitude towards his protagonist. His most important contribution did not so much play tricks with the false taste of the reading public as search, by technical means involving sound, for meanings obtainable only by experimental means. Given this difference, which is ultimately profound, it was a problem for Wordsworth how to balance Coleridge's contribution: in effect, how to bring the volume to a fitting close.

Wordsworth's first choice appears to have been "The Idiot Boy." It contains traces of Taylor's translation of "Lenore" that fed into the "Ancient Mariner," and might even have been begun at about the earlier time (November 1797). It follows the same journey as the Mariner towards the unknown, accompanied by expectation and hope, alternating with blame and panic. There is likewise a central vision "of no unlikely thought," a dream within a dream of the protagonist "hunting sheep" (*LB* 171–72), followed by a return home and reconciliation. A reader follows the fluxes and refluxes of a mother's mind; the neighbour Susan Gale is cured by becoming concerned for others; the Idiot Boy, though central, has as little character as the Mariner; but nothing is serious for very long. For the most part, it is unadulterated fun. Wordsworth wrote a matching poem that, very deliberately, avoids nightmare. It makes the same point, it traces a similar journey, but the heart of it is simple innocent openness: "just Johnny," solitude but also "glee." It is a complete burlesque answer to the serious problems and anxieties that haunt Coleridge's poem, but in every other respect no answer at all. Wordsworth was particularly proud of it,[29] but also surely aware that it was not consonant with the bulk of the shorter, sharper poems that accompanied it. In my judgement, the problem of seriousness at the close of the volume weighed on him more heavily than matching Coleridge's opening poem in a way that would be clear to all. In an attempt to deal with the problem he wrote *Peter Bell*, which one might consider a recasting of matters contained in "The Idiot Boy," and which is much more directly linked with the "Ancient Mariner" through its Prologue. Hazlitt read the early draft of *Peter Bell* along with the *Ballad* poems before Cottle removed them to Bristol, so it might still have been under consideration in June–early July 1798. In the event it was obviously too large and serious an "answer" to Coleridge to be hurried. It was published, much worked-over and separately, in 1819, and "Tintern Abbey" appeared in the *Ballads* instead.

"Tintern Abbey" makes such a fitting end to the volume that it is hard to realise the boldness of Wordsworth's move. He answered the "Ancient Mariner" with a poem written in a heightened blank-verse style that has moved considerably beyond the poetry that preoccupied him up to early March 1798. His new poem celebrates with authority the expanded confidence that the shorter poems embody but does this with reference to a then-unpublished poem by Coleridge, "Frost at Midnight": unpublished, one must suppose, because it contained elements of which Coleridge was not quite sure. "Tintern Abbey" ignores the challenge of ending the collection with a poem that in some way engages with or responds to the poem that opened it. Instead, it picks up from the impetus of the poems that come between and supplies an ending of another sort altogether. There can be no question of its success. One poem matches the other in its strength, and although the strength is of different kinds, they are profoundly characteristic of each author. How "Tintern Abbey" achieves this is nonetheless worth pausing over because it throws light on the processes of Wordsworth's reasoning.

"Frost at Midnight" was written during the last month of Coleridge's work on the "Mariner," indeed it might be seen as an offshoot. The connection goes beyond the unusually spelled and carefully chosen title-word "*Rime*," which can mean "frost" as well as "ballad."[30] "Frost at Midnight" positions itself for its larger part in the country-village equivalent of a polar region, where its isolated speaker has strange dreams; the dreams are of the past and ambiguous in various ways: fragmentary and with unspoken dangers at their edges, for instance, the jinny in the sparking fire and the fairy world connected with the Ottery church bells. The poem advances with a borrowed promise of a better childhood for Coleridge's sleeping infant son, and night moves into sunlit morning as the cold and darkness are overtaken. It is important that the poem Wordsworth knew continued beyond the poem Coleridge revised, in lines that sparkle as they do in other Coleridgean epiphanies (*PW* 1:456 note, 2:572). I quoted the lines in the previous chapter to compare with similar moments in the "Mariner" and other poems. They complete a sentence that began ten lines before and the transition from conditional tense ("whether") into the simple future ("will") makes the prophecy more certain, more particular, and more joyous. Elements of description that were listed separately in the earlier part of the sentence here merge, and sounds bounce off each other likewise. Perhaps Coleridge was uncertain, and was later persuaded he had gone too far. He pruned the lines before the poem was republished, as he said, to strengthen the sense of a rondo (*PW* 1:456 note). This is a Wordsworthian solution applied to a different kind of poem, and from that point of view an unarguable success, but whether the solution makes a better Coleridgean poem is a moot point.

Meanwhile, what Wordsworth did in "Tintern Abbey" is to take the basic structure that "Frost at Midnight" shares with other poems written previously by Coleridge, and turn a poem about the same *feeling* at different times and in different places into a poem about the same *place* at different times with different feelings, the gap between the two occasions measuring his own advance.[31] In place of the poet Coleridge hoping to learn from the innocent child Hartley—that is, beginning anew—Dorothy follows in the wake of William in a poem celebrating achievement: the growth of a poet's mind. Coleridge's poem about Imagination, the "Mariner," is magnificently balanced, though not answered, by Wordsworth's blank-verse statement: the issues raised by the "Mariner" are overridden rather than addressed.

"Tintern Abbey" confidently rejoins society, opens a path to the future, on Wordsworth's terms. It builds on Coleridge's hesitancy to publish "Frost at Midnight," either separately in a newspaper or outside the joint collection. Given its later popularity, one may wonder why he held it back only to apply it to political ends in the *Fears in Solitude* volume, published after the two friends had left for Germany. The revision of the ending may hold the key. A year and more after their return, the "Ancient Mariner" changed both its appearance and its position in the expanded *Lyrical Ballads* of 1800 that carried Wordsworth's name on the title page, thus opening a new phase in their relationship. Coleridge's collaborator became the reader and critic by whom he was most directly influenced, while Coleridge saw the same collaborator's poetry on its way to becoming the standard by which his own poetry would be judged. To complicate things, as the epigraph to this chapter indicates, Wordsworth's growing confidence still needed reassurance, and indeed material support.

Notes

1. To Coleridge, 24 and 27 Dec.1799: *Letters: Early Years* 273–81 at 281.
2. In the context of this paragraph, it is relevant to note that one of Wordsworth's important sources was William Godwin's novel, *Caleb*

Williams, whence derives Coleridge's name (Falkland) for the "villain" of "The Ballad of the Dark Ladiè" (**182**).
3. See my *Experimental Poetics*, 51, 59, 72, 73, 98–99, and so on.
4. Averill "Shape of *Lyrical Ballads*"; Freistat "The 'Field' of *Lyrical Ballads*"; Shepherd "Integrity of the 1798 *Lyrical Ballads*."
5. Her transcript is reproduced with minor variations of punctuation and spelling in E.H. Coleridge's edition of *Complete Poetical Works of S. T. Coleridge* (1:269–75: see *PW* 2:464 note). The Cornell *Early Poems and Fragments* edition includes only the holograph material from which the transcript derives.
6. The Bürger connection and Taylor's translation are discussed by Jacobus 224–29 and 284–88; for the Greyhound Ballad, see Wordsworth *Early Poems and Fragments* 835–41.
7. *Art of the "Lyrical Ballads"* 110–11.
8. Early editors—namely, Hutchinson *Lyrical Ballads, 1798* 258 and E.H. Coleridge (ed.) *Complete Poetical Works* 1:267—were led into dating the continuation thus on the basis of the fine spring weather.
9. *Early Poems and Fragments* 858.
10. See Beer *Coleridge the Visionary* 124–25; also Drew *India and the Romantic Imagination* 158, 175. One might also note that the book of Enoch was of particular interest to writers whom Coleridge's father read: for instance, William Whiston on Josephus and Francis Lee in his *Dissertations*.
11. Or, as Beer *Visionary* 114–24 suggests, the two Egyptian gods of the afterlife, Anubis (in his canine form) alongside the more benign Osiris, who were in Coleridge's mind at the time. Modiano adds several further interesting details in "Historicist Readings of *The Rime of the Ancient Mariner*" 283–96, although in the context of a different overall argument.
12. To Southey, 8 Nov. 1798: *Letters* 1:142.
13. "Introductory Essay" to *Poems of S. T. Coleridge* xl–xli.
14. Christina Rossetti's "Goblin Market" (1862) is another poem written professedly for children whose fantasy logic contemporary readers like Mrs. Charles Eliot Norton instinctively traced back to the "Mariner." Sewell's *Field of Nonsense* makes a strong case on behalf of such writing as a bridge between the Romantic and Modern periods in the English tradition.
15. Introduction to *The Rime of the Ancient Mariner* v–vii; Chatterton 166–67.
16. Compare the use of antique style as a distancing qualification in, for example, "The Pang More Sharp than All" (**412**). The manoeuvre is discussed further in my *Experimental Poetics*, index s.v. "burlesque."

17. "The Power of the Eye in Coleridge" and "Wordsworth's Conception of the 'Ancient Mariner'" in his *Late Harvest* 65–95 and 96–100, respectively.
18. *Letters: Early Years* 194.
19. Fenwick "Notes and Illustrations of the Poems" (1843) in *Prose Works of William Wordsworth* ed. Grosart, 3:17.
20. The latter, perhaps beginning with Boehme and Pico at Christ's Hospital, enlarged with his reading of Joseph Priestley (*Lects 1795* 195–202). His later views were publically often dismissive, although they could be different in private (e.g. *CM* 4:258–59, 5:624–25).
21. *CN* 3:4449, *CN* 5:5624–25, and *TT* 1:34–36 express Coleridge's later position as theologian. His annotations of Boehme better register his gratitude for keeping the heart alive in his head.
22. *Letters: Early Years* 200.
23. See *PW* 1:606, 608 and Chap. 3. See also *CM* 1:560–61 on scorn.
24. Rousseau and Godwin's point exactly. Simpson offers pertinent reminders of the political implications of these paired poems in his *Irony and Authority in Romantic Poetry* 39–41 and "Public Virtues, Private Vices."
25. O'Donnell *Passion of Meter* 62–63, 130–36 explicates their dynamics with a sure hand.
26. O'Donnell 136–55 reiterates and expands on the point of difference.
27. As described by Mayo. Jordan reviews and gives references to contemporary reactions to the volume in his *Why the "Lyrical Ballads"?* 103–27.
28. "Mr. Wordsworth" in *The Spirit of the Age* (1825); *Complete Works* 11:87.
29. See his spirited defense to John Wilson, 7 Jun 1802: *Letters: Early Years* 352–58.
30. First pointed out by Arden Reed "The Rhyming Mariner and the Mariner Rimed."
31. I borrow phrases from a lecture I gave twenty years ago: "New Light on Wordsworth's Coleridge" 14.

CHAPTER 5

The Shadow Cast by Wordsworth

...we begin to suspect, that there is, somewhere or other, a *radical* Difference [in our] opinions.

S.T. Coleridge[1]

5.1 THE PAIRING

Three general considerations should be borne in mind as the story of the Wordsworth–Coleridge relationship advanced beyond the publication of *Lyrical Ballads* in September 1798 and different emphases became the cause of disagreement. First, Coleridge's general debt to both William and Dorothy, brother and sister together.

Coleridge's debt to Dorothy's acutely sensitive response to natural detail has been mentioned several times. Norman Fruman remarks that it may be odd to think that such receptivity could be learned but cites George Whalley in support, who was "struck by the general absence of vivid sensory images" in Coleridge's verse before the Wordsworths moved to Alfoxden in July 1797: "Very little evidence of an exceptional sensibility breaks the opaque surface of a multifarious but received poetic manner."[2] This is true in a sense, and to add to the examples given by Whalley, one might add the opening of "The Eolian Harp" (**115**), dating from 1795, where Coleridge is more concerned with the eye seeing than anything seen.³ Things change very soon after the Wordsworths became neighbours: the closely noticed landscape of Coleridge's continuation of "The Three Graves" (**155**), the stand-alone details in the "Ancient Mariner" like the "noise...of a hidden brook" and the "skeletons of leaves," then "The One red Leaf, the last of its Clan" of "Christabel" (**176**), and so on. Wordsworth at the same time was possessed by a deep understanding of Coleridge's powers, and quickly afterwards came to perceive how they were connected to his weaknesses; that is, of Coleridge's ability to see and communicate "the light that never was on sea or land" and of the "fiends" that plagued him so. Perhaps he was the only person in the world who understood so much of him at the time the "Mariner" was written. Four years afterwards, when he wrote "Resolution and Independence," his view was even clearer. The hare "running races in her mirth" and followed by a rainbow mist that "[r]uns with her all the way, wherever she doth run" is a perfect image of the Coleridgean Imagination and its counterpointing by "fears, and fancies," "Dim sadness, and blind thoughts." Wordsworth even uses Coleridge's word, "dejection" as the opposite of "delight," and sets against such oscillation his stoical image of the leech-gatherer:

> We Poets in our youth begin in gladness;
> But thereof comes in the end despondency and madness.⁴

More generally, Coleridge owed a debt to Wordsworth simply for being what he appeared to be from the moment he came to know him: "a great man," "a very great man—the only man, to whom *at all times* & in *all modes of excellence* I feel myself inferior—," "The Giant Wordsworth" (*CL* 1:327, 334, 391). He bought into the idea of Wordsworth's greatness totally. Even before they became well acquainted, he had named him as one "whom I deem unrivalled among the writers of the present day" (*PW* 2:329), and as his ideas about the creativity of the mind were emerging, he was convinced that Wordsworth would be able to embody them in the great epic poem of their time. While the belief that he contributed to Wordsworth's self-belief relieved him from any grand ambitions he might have entertained for his own poetry, encouraged him to use verse to explore his own emotional states regardless of the need to create and hold a public audience. And, of course, respect went the other way: Wordsworth was dependent on Coleridge for ideas, for an idealist metaphysics that he probably did not entirely understand or, if he did, did not think he needed in its entirety. It made for a curious interdependence: call it that, and not a marriage of minds. It irritated supporters of both parties, at the time and later: for instance, in different ways, Coleridge's old school friend, Charles Lamb, and Wordsworth's great-great-great nephew, Jonathan Wordsworth. What Wordsworth himself did not understand of Coleridge's ideas was certainly at odds with his temperament.

The second general consideration to be borne in mind follows from this first: the different sense of themselves as poets. Both were suspicious of what Coleridge was to call the reading-public, Wordsworth perhaps the more stridently in early days and the more conventionally later. His ambitions from the beginning were large, he self-consciously sought to be recognised as an original voice, and this influenced the way *Lyrical Ballads* came together. The choice of title was deliberately fashionable but the contents were designed like a Trojan horse, to surprise and overtake unsuspecting punters. Wordsworth's contribution, far more than Coleridge's puzzling ballad, whose parodic dimension was soon obscured by changing fashion, divided the sheep from the goats among their readers. This was the New School of poetry when Francis Jeffrey named it such in the *Edinburgh Review* and that was parodied in poems like "The Barberry-tree"[5]; and a paradox lies therein. Wordsworth, who was more assertive of his own originality as a writer than Coleridge, turned out to be far more conservative in respect of style, in verse and in prose: the difference between the two poets' handling of meter and rhyme as described in the previous chapter is striking. Coleridge, more thoughtful about the choice of language to be used in poetry, was actually the more radically original in other respects: going back to understand how sound can be measured and thinking forward afresh. Both were wary of and indeed estranged from the popular readership that confronted them, but while Wordsworth largely came to terms with the people who bought his books Coleridge remained continuously "different" or "other" to the very end. The difference is repeated in their handling of the supernatural. Coleridge's broken narrative has a quality of nonsense poetry—anything might happen as in the *Arabian Nights* where a genie can start up out of a fire-grate— and Wordsworth takes him at his word in "The Idiot Boy," where nonsense words encapsulate the story. For Wordsworth, the numinous was a tremendous blank, a more conventional sublime: the light of sense goes out. For Coleridge, it was live and personal: earlier with deeply troubling dimensions, later a relationship underpinned by complex thoughts about the persons of the Trinity.

The third consideration can be described even more briefly: the danger of retroactive over-interpretation. Coleridge's quiescent acceptance of Wordsworth's treatment of his poem is sometimes puzzling and the means by which the pair expressed disagreement is sometimes oblique. The explanation to be borne in mind all the time is that Coleridge suppressed what was vexatious; he bought into Wordsworth's own myth of self to the end of his days, and never gave public expression to the painful feelings that drove his public statements. The fact is simply stated but centrally important. It is also why the present next stage in the story is so relevant to the "Ancient Mariner." The issues raised by Wordsworth's treatment of the poem after it was first published bear directly on Coleridge's view of what he had written and possibly on his subsequent alterations. And again, the Wordsworth connection—as they both knew it and as it continued following Wordsworth's death—laid the foundation of Coleridge's reputation and even still influences the way his poems are read now.

5.2   Welcome to Town End[6]

The evolution of the 1798 volume described in the previous chapter is the record of a takeover. Wordsworth's new-found, aggressive even while fragile, confidence in his abilities did not immediately fix on the partner with whom he began the volume. The failure to proceed very far with *Peter Bell* is a sign he was unsure how to mark out the territory over which they disagreed but "The Idiot Boy," followed by the late insertion (substitution?) of "Tintern Abbey," became statement enough. There were already other signs. For example, the 1798 Advertisement that stated baldly "The majority of the following poems are to be considered as experiments" interprets the style in which they are written very much in terms of language—"the language of conversation in the middle and lower classes of society"—which is known from other sources to have been very much Wordsworth's preoccupation, while Coleridge was much more concerned with matters of sound. As Lane Cooper pointed out, the author of the Advertisement also showed a disposition to separate the authorship of "The Thorn" and the "Ancient Mariner" (distinguishing one from another by lower- and upper-case letters), as if to make the latter poem something different from the majority.[7] Coleridge took the trouble to answer Wordsworth on his own terms in *Biographia Literaria*, which suggests a prearranged division of labour and that the critical difference between them might rest entirely with language, but as Richard Bradford noted

(50), even as he did this, he made a subtle distinction between the plan that "was agreed" and what "Mr. Wordsworth, on the other hand, was to propose himself as his object" (*BL* 2:6–7). In short, whatever difference existed at the beginning continued, becoming both clearer and more complicated, throughout the following years.

The eighteen months preceding the second edition of *Lyrical Ballads* was a confusing time for Coleridge. He returned home from Germany in July 1799 and was busy with family obligations and picking up with old friends like Tom Poole and Southey. He travelled north to meet the Wordsworths in October, where he first met Sara Hutchinson at Sockburn, and returned to London in late November, where he applied himself to political journalism and translating Schiller's *Wallenstein* trilogy. William and Dorothy meanwhile settled into Dove Cottage; Coleridge visited them there in April–May 1800, and returned to Bristol with the beginnings of a new edition of *Lyrical Ballads* for Cottle to print and Longman in London to publish. In the next two months (June–July) he decided to rejoin the Wordsworths in the north and settled with his family in Greta Hall, Keswick, all the while assisting Wordsworth with revising and writing new poems, arranging them and proofreading. The new edition was published in two volumes in late January 1801 under Wordsworth's name. It included Coleridge's earlier poems plus one other, *Love* (**253**), but without the Introduction that accompanied it when it had earlier been published in the *Morning Post*: all these poems described as by "A Friend." However, the new edition was fundamentally different from the first.

Although Wordsworth complained and remained anxious for his reputation, the first edition of *Lyrical Ballads* had not sold badly. Indeed, he was already entertaining thoughts of a second edition in June 1799 in which the "Ancient Mariner" might be replaced with "some little things" of his own "which would be more likely to suit the common taste," his supposition being that "the old words and the strangeness" of the ballad "have deterred readers from going on."[8] His decision to publish "a second Volume of Lyrical Ballads, & Pastorals" to add to the first followed nine months later, during Coleridge's first visit to Dove Cottage, on the understanding that Coleridge would provide practical help (*CL* 1:585). Coleridge obliged when he returned to Bristol and London, the arrangements were in place by early June, and from then on he was intimately involved, although—it must be stressed—wholly on Wordsworth's behalf. He cannot therefore have been entirely surprised that his own contribution was marginalised, but the new edition certainly surprised and upset old friends like Charles Lamb (Marrs 1:266).

The major change in Volume I was to open it with Wordsworth's lengthy, argumentative preface, followed by the most assertive pair of his quatrain poems, "Expostulation and Reply" and "The Tables Turned," and then to rearrange the following shorter poems to give continuity to the Wordsworthian opening. At the same time, Coleridge's poems (plus "Love") were dispersed through the sequence in a way that diminishes their effect, postponing the "Ancient Mariner" to appear in penultimate position so as to conclude as before with "Tintern Abbey."[9] The "Mariner" was considerably revised and in many respects, one might argue, improved. The particular Gothick dimension of parody was lessened by normalising many of the spellings, which could be defended since the fashion it targeted was already half-forgotten. Some transitions are smoothed and minor improvements made, which may well outweigh whatever was lost. Even the subtitle that was added—"A Poet's Reverie," which some assume to be some kind of demotion—has a justification in Coleridge's special vocabulary and probably had his approval. The major surprise, and I suppose outrage, is the long note Wordsworth added to the close of the volume listing four "great defects" of the poem:

> first, that the principal person has no distinct character, either in his profession of Mariner, or as a human being who having been long under the controul of supernatural impressions might be supposed himself to partake of something supernatural: secondly, that he does not act, but is continually acted upon: thirdly, that the events having no necessary connection do not produce each other; and lastly, that the imagery is somewhat too laboriously accumulated. (*LB 1800* 1:[214])

The issues Wordsworth touches upon are vital, but the tone is dismissive as if formulated by a truculent Dr. Johnson. The act is insensitive, and not least following Wordsworth's assurance on the same page that the author of the poem was "himself very desirous" the poem should be suppressed and that such readers as may be pleased with it, or any part of it, "owe their pleasure in some sort to me." One can only conclude that Coleridge in a depressed state of mind knew what was happening, and agreed to it for Wordsworth's sake, and that Wordsworth at one point became embarrassed and confused. The note was omitted in the next (1802) edition.

The story gets worse with "Christabel," which was once intended to be part of the second volume but was, in decidedly odd circumstances, omitted altogether. As I described in Chap. 3, it grew directly from Coleridge's experience of writing the "Mariner," and from references later in Germany one must assume that a version of Part I was finished during the summer of 1798 (Carlyon 1:138–39). Part II includes references to places and persons in the North and it is quite possible that Coleridge began it along with the development of a second volume of *Lyrical Ballads* when he visited Grasmere[10] or when he settled at Keswick, even perhaps at Wordsworth's prompting. The mode of supernatural—"witchery by daylight" (*TT* 1:410)—is noticeably different, as every reader notices. Whatever the case, Dorothy Wordsworth records that Coleridge read the completed Part II at Dove Cottage on 4 October. It was received with delight, and there was a second reading—given even more praise—the following day. However, the day after that (6 October) a firm decision was made (apparently in Coleridge's presence) not to include the poem and instead to publish it separately alongside *The Pedlar* (which never happened). This sequence of events must be understood alongside a note sent by Wordsworth to Cottle, seemingly unknown to Coleridge, three weeks earlier (15 September), instructing him not to proceed with the printing of "Christabel," even if the type had been set, and giving no reason.[11] Longman was then informed and the remaining months of 1800 were a flurry of rearrangement and insertions. "Michael" entered the new volume as its finale on 18 December, delaying publication into the New Year, and Wordsworth excused the extra trouble as follows:

> A Poem of Mr Coleridge's was to have concluded the Volumes: but upon mature deliberation I found that the Style of this Poem was so discordant from my own that it could not be printed along with my poems with any propriety.... I therefore, since my last letter, wrote the last poem of the 2nd Volume.[12]

That "Michael" is an extraordinarily good poem—bringing fitting closure to a volume that opens with "Hart-leap Well" and "The Brothers"—nobody will gainsay; but it must be conceded that Wordsworth took a lot for granted from his friend and faithful helper.

Wordsworth was obviously concerned to present his most recent poems as "new" in the sense of distinctive and original, and not to have that quality obscured by any admixture. This inflects his use of the word "experiment" throughout the new preface and his emphasis on the poems being founded "upon a theory professedly new" for Longman.[13] It embodies a sense of defiance, of being at odds with the spirit of the age, that arose in the spring of 1798 and would persist for a few more years. As I said at the beginning of this chapter, Wordsworth and Coleridge were writing "new" poetry in different ways for different reasons that became confused in the minds of their young first admirers like De Quincey and Hazlitt. A good many sentences, indeed paragraphs, in Wordsworth's preface begin with a conditional: for example, "If in this opinion I am mistaken I can have little right to the name of a Poet" (*LB 1800* 1: xiii–iv). They are carried by a defiant assertiveness, a fragile egotism. Some blame Wordsworth's behaviour in the whole affair for sending Coleridge into a spiral of drug dependency; others construe Coleridge's critique in the *Biographia* as deriving from "pain" and "hatred."[14] But the interesting fact is, Coleridge suffered his friend's thoughtlessness, assisted the revised plans without outward complaint, and dissociated himself from his friend's manner of proceeding only much later in subtle and circuitous ways. The poems he wrote in the wake of the "Ancient Mariner" were written for himself, along different lines, while he concentrated on his grand philosophical project, his magnum opus.

5.3   Counterstatement

Wordsworth's unease with the "Ancient Mariner" is implicit in his failure to respond to it satisfactorily within the 1798 volume, or rather in his response via quatrain poems and other rhymed and blank-verse forms ending with "Tintern Abbey." The same unease is inscribed in the way he treated the "Mariner" and "Christabel" in the enlarged edition of 1800. Although Volume 1 is rearranged to suit his sense of what is original in his poems, Volume 2 was written and put together from a more firmly held position gained in the course of settling into Town End. The volume comprises a counterstatement in verse at a level Coleridge received from nobody else, and it came from someone Coleridge thought the greatest poet of his time. The first three poems of the second volume—"Hart-leap Well," "There Was a Boy," and "The Brothers"—continue the dialogue over the "Mariner" in particular and also with "Kubla Khan" (**178**); "Christabel" had become a raw issue during 1800 that was perhaps best ignored. The three new Wordsworth poems signal a process from which many more great poems were to come during the next few years but which was raw at the start: two of them ring with both upset and discovery that their author found difficult to accommodate before he further adjusted the way forward. There is an intimate interconnection between these two—"Hart-leap Well" and "The Brothers"—the latter having been begun first and the former helping it to completion. "There Was a Boy" goes back to Wordsworth's first months in Germany and the origins of *The Prelude*. Positioned between the other later-written poems, it indicates the taproot underlying their fresh shoots of inspiration.

"Hart-leap Well" is based on a story William and Dorothy heard on their journey to settle into Town End in December 1799, a trance-like moment William recorded in *Home at Grasmere*. The regularly rhyming four-line stanzas tell the story twice over. Part I describes the end of a chase in which a deer's valiant death is celebrated by a hunter, Sir Walter, who builds a memorial in its honour; Part II gives the same story as the speaker heard it much later from a shepherd. Part I is a story of destructive pride and self-satisfaction; Part II, in which the speaker explains the shepherd's sympathy for the slain deer, overtakes the tale of cruelty and vanity with one of suffering and feeling for "Nature":

> One lesson, Shepherd, let us two divide,
> Taught both by what she shews, and what conceals,
> Never to blend our pleasure or our pride
> With sorrow of the meanest thing that feels. (*LB 1800* 2:13)

There are echoes of Bürger's ballad "Der wilde Jäger" (available in Scott's translations as "The Chase" and "The Wild Huntsman") in Part II, that is, of the haunted and demonic; and the chiastic structure created by the addition of Part II converts this into something more positive: in fact, into something like "The intimation of the milder day | Which is to come, the fairer world than this—" that William and Dorothy experienced on their original journey.[15] So much is clear, and, if the hunt narrative also contains echoes of the "Ancient Mariner" and the slaughter of an innocent albatross, reducing such an event to a mean and tawdry thing, so the ending quoted above faintly echoes and alters Coleridge's close.

There is an ambiguity in the lesson Wordsworth's speaker draws, and it could also be applied to the "Mariner" directly. The lines could be read to mean "Let the two of us divide (share) this (different) lesson" or "Let this one lesson divide (separate) us two." Julien Temple's film *Pandaemonium* assumes that Wordsworth's exclusion of "Kubla Khan" from the 1800 volume helped destroy Coleridge's faith in his own creativity and pushed him into drug-addiction: an assumption one does not need to make, although Coleridge was forever silent over "Kubla" and he might have assimilated the poem into his hurt over the "Mariner" and "Christabel." On the other hand, one does have to ask why Wordsworth introduced such obvious echoes of "Kubla" into the Part II description of the "Pleasure-house" Sir Walter constructs on the spot where the deer died. Notable discussions of Wordsworth's poem record such echoes in passing,[16] but, I repeat, they require to be taken into a full account. The place of "murder" is where Sir Walter dreams of entertaining his "paramour"[17] and the monument to himself is manifestly selfish indulgence. The corresponding figure in "Kubla Khan" is destructive and ambiguous, but nothing like this, nor as petty as the ruins of Part II imply. The date when "Kubla" was written is uncertain, but Tim Fulford makes a strong case for the poem being not only in Coleridge's mind during August–September 1799 but in Wordsworth's during December, when "Hart-leap Well" was written, and even suggests that Coleridge's first encounter with a copy of Purchas's *Travels* was at Dove Cottage in the following months.[18] There are references to "Kubla Khan" existing in some version or another before Coleridge returned from Germany, and it is indeed possible the text was on the table while the make-up of the new *Lyrical Ballads* volume was debated. Whether it was or not, the way the allusions enter "Hart-leap Well" comprises a blunt response to Coleridge's ambivalent protagonist, his predecessor with "no distinct character," and to poetry that aims to speak of anything other than, plainly, "what we are, and have been." Sir Walter is a hollow hero, his construction is a sham without mystery, and the local shepherd's wisdom is the only true comfort for a broken heart. Whatever is left of this haunted chase is dispelled in a real-life, open-air encounter with reality.

"The Brothers" is based upon a story Wordsworth and Coleridge heard in their walk through the Lake District in November 1799. The narrative in regular blank verse moves through three phases: the opening paragraphs introduce "a homely Priest" and his wife in front of their cottage, the priest commenting on tourists in general, and a particular stranger in the nearby graveyard; then the stranger engages the priest in conversation and is told the story of two brothers, Leonard who went away to sea and James who stayed and died as the result of an accident; the final paragraphs briefly describe the departure of the priest and that of the stranger (who by now, it has become clear, is Leonard revisiting). The story ends with Leonard:

> That it was from the weakness of his heart,
> He had not dared to tell him, who he was.

This done, he went on shipboard, and is now
A Seaman, a grey headed Mariner. (*LB 1800* 2:45)

The poem is ambitious, resembling "The Thorn" in its restless changes of point-of-view. The priest softens from one who is complacent and quick to judge to someone far more hospitable; Leonard—who is introduced as cautious, and then anxious following his conversation with the priest (which repeats what we are told of him from another point of view, thereby fixing attention on his response)—relinquishes the purpose for which he came. Thus the teller of the tale develops a degree of understanding, but only adequate to record what he sees. The scope is wide—it embraces satire on tourists, humour at the expense of the priest's complacency, strong social commentary concerning the poverty of shepherds and the depopulation of the countryside—and Wordsworth at one point contemplated using it to open the volume.[19] In the event, he placed "Hart-leap Well" before it almost as a key. The shorter poem was written quickly in the course of writing the longer one; and it is put to use as a simplification, a sketch that clarifies the direction in which the larger poem is going.

Allusions to Coleridge are just as entangled in the longer poem as they are in the shorter one. The grey-haired Leonard of course is the Old Navigator—more so in terms of the larger movement of the story than he is the Wordsworths' brother John, who contributed only incidental details—and the description of the calenture, to which Wordsworth attached a footnote alluding to William Gilbert (*LB 1800* 2:22), corresponds to the vision of water snakes in the "Mariner" Part IV. There is an allusion to the heart's tongue at Holford Glen that appears in "This Lime-tree Bower" (**156**) and in Dorothy's *Alfoxden Journal*, and, to take a different tack, it is important that Leonard was added to the story with which Wordsworth began (for which see *CN* 1:540 ff 35ᵛ-35). Leonard's story shares a good deal with that of the unnamed Coleridgean protagonist of "The Foster-mother's Tale" (**152**), the extract from *Osorio* included in the 1798 *Ballads*, whose supposed death among "savage men" is exactly the fate assumed to have overtaken the protagonist of the play. The two poems end on a similar note (compare the lines quoted above with *PW* 1:332–33); and even Leonard's failure to speak his name to the priest is surely an allusion to an intimate Coleridgean theme—"Yet Love wants courage without a Name!" (**655**; *PW* 1:1103)—that extends back into his past as far as his inability to declare himself to Mary Evans.[20] Frances Ferguson sums up the matter as follows:

"The Brothers" (along with the very different "Hart-Leap Well") represents a poetic alternative or rebuttal to "The Ancient Mariner."[21]

She is correct to emphasise that the critical, referential dimension of the poem is as important as the positive values Wordsworth desired to assert. He was able to communicate those values—concerning place, rootedness and human transience—more clearly a year later in "Michael," which he placed at the end of the volume. "The Brothers" meanwhile works—again and characteristically—in a particularly wounding way of which he was probably unconscious. It left his Brother Bard praising it as "that model of English pastoral, which I never yet read with unclouded eye" (*BL* 2:80fn), which in turn leaves one wondering about the spirit in which he read.

"There Was a Boy" was drafted (in the first-person) as Wordsworth began to write what became *The Prelude* soon after he arrived in Germany but it was not included in the two-part assemblage of such pieces he put together before he left.[22] He sent it to Coleridge, who responded to the lines "Uncertain heaven received | Into the bosom of the steady lake" with words that are almost as famous:

> I should have recognised [sc. them] any where: and had I met these lines running wild in the deserts of Arabia, I should have instantly screamed out 'Wordsworth!'... (*CL* 1:452–53)

Coleridge's response completely embodies the positive gift of affirmation so necessary for the flowering of Wordsworth's genius, and it may underlie the special place the lines at once occupied in Wordsworth's mind. Not only did he select this episode from among others of his childhood to publish separately, he placed it first among "Poems of the Imagination" when he came to arrange his 1815 *Poems*, devoting the better part of a paragraph in the preface to underline its foundational importance.[23]

The style and psychological implications of the poem have been subjected to some subtle and rewarding readings during the past fifty years that probe the significance of the boy's traumatic death. It is an event that connects with the poems on either side of it in the 1800 volume: something that Wordsworth's return to the changed landscape of his childhood brought home. Anne-Lise François suggests that the words "enter unawares" ("the visible scene | Would enter unawares into his mind") is recalled in the words of Coleridge's gloss added to the "Mariner" in 1817: "enter unannounced, as lords that are certainly expected, and yet there is a silent joy at their arrival."[24] Conscious or not, the echo bears on multiple aspects of the Wordsworth–Coleridge relationship: not least, Coleridge's peculiar sense of a death that cut him off from his childhood just before the age of ten and his belief in Wordsworth as one who could redeem the time in a way he himself might not be able to. Whatever negativity lurks in a Coleridgean reading of "Hart-leap Well" and "The Brothers" is as nothing to what "There Was a Boy" positively offers in the same regard. It almost explains Coleridge's acquiescent response to Wordsworth's treatment of what he had written.

5.4 FURTHER REFORMULATIONS

The core of the argument between Coleridge and Wordsworth (if that is what it is to be called) is contained in the "Ancient Mariner" and the poems written in response by Wordsworth during the following few years. What followed later still does not add up to a conclusion; it is better understood as a series of further rumblings, less a summation than in many cases a diversion. These further incomplete responses follow from confusions in what Wordsworth was able to achieve in the *Lyrical Ballads* of 1800. At that time, he was reaching forward to say things he hoped Coleridge would clarify for him, while Coleridge was of an uncertain state of mind and would remain so until after he moved to Highgate. Wordsworth took several more years to work out what he hoped to convey, publishing it in collections of shorter poems in 1807 and 1815. The ideal of resolution and independence symbolised in "The Leech Gatherer" became a certain Stoicism in "Ode to Duty," and an attitude to death in "Peele Castle" and "Laodamia," all the while he was working on his grander life-project that was part-published in *The Excursion* (1814). He attempted a statement of the consolidating position with reference to his old difference from Coleridge in two long-pondered poems: *The White Doe of Rylstone* (1815) in relation to "Christabel" and *Peter Bell* (1819) in a return to the "Mariner." Coleridge was meanwhile concerned to understand more of what the "Mariner" and "Christabel" had uncovered, and he chose to do this by means of writing in prose, thereby to underpin by logical means his sense of the supernatural. If the heroes of Wordsworth's poetry became more like Michael, Coleridge's remained like the faery child added to "Christabel" (*PW* 1:503–04), however much youth found itself overtaken by age. When he returned to the old argument with Wordsworth in *Biographia Literaria*, it was largely shadow play distracted by ill health and in terms oblique to what actually divided them. The Latin title disguises a book as wayward and almost as deliberately misleading as *Tristram Shandy* (as the correspondence between their subtitles suggest), and in such a spirit the argument broke up rather than concluded.

However, the argument in prose stands at the margins. Its deeper course runs through the poems. Wordsworth added an appendix to his 1800 preface to *Lyrical Ballads* in the 1802 edition. He also not only wrote a preface to his 1815 *Poems* but included an essay supplementary to the preface at the end of the same first volume. Coleridge's cause for upset in the first two editions of the *Ballads* has already been discussed above: Wordsworth's pronouncements on diction and meter in 1802 must have disturbed him further in a different way. He was roused by Wordsworth's 1807 collection to explore arrangements for a similar edition of his own—indeed, another round of revisions of the "Mariner" dates from this time and after[25]—and he was very quick to respond to the critical apparatus surrounding Wordsworth's new collection when it appeared in 1815. It follows that the introduction to his own collection, which became *Sibylline Leaves* in 1817, was complicated from the start by a desire to restate Wordsworth's pronouncements on Imagination and diction. He would have been better advised to return to the "Ancient Mariner," written at the time his views on the creative imagination were undergoing a rapid advance, by describing the philosophical difficulties he encountered, then and afterwards, and employing his discoveries—practical and theoretical—to contrast and describe Wordsworth's different approach to the same. As things stood, he had a better sense of what he meant by wholeness in 1815–1816, a better grasp of what he meant by Kant's Intellectual Intuition and was increasingly inclined to call Reason, but his commitment to this knowledge remained uncertain. In fact, the intellectual alternatives slid around so perilously that they endangered his emotional as well as spiritual life. His extended critique of the Wordsworthian Imagination is consequently, unsurprisingly, a mess; he scores easy points by knocking down Wordsworth's theory of poetic diction when he could and should have concentrated on matters of sound, which he held to be more central to an understanding of verse. If his book ever taught anybody anything, beyond the brilliant separate insights and formulations that appear on every page, it is through its evasions and distortions: making a reader wonder why it is as it is.

To repeat: Coleridge's lengthy involvement with Wordsworth over matters raised by the "Mariner"—the supernatural lying at their core—largely explains why he picked up with Wordsworth's discussion of Imagination in the 1815 preface in order to put the other side of their old argument. The *Biographia* discussion is an attempt to formulate a concept that had been on the table between them since Wordsworth first let him go his own way with the poem that brought the idea of Imagination to the fore in both their minds, and the concept had progressively attained different meanings thereafter. Thomas McFarland summed up the matter: "[I]magination as a philosophical connective exists alongside imagination as a poetic instrumentality."[26] The term was increasingly coming to serve the first function, connecting it with Reason in Coleridge's mind, but the re-engagement with Wordsworth confused the issue with thoughts of the earlier argument that was conducted in more restricted terms. *The White Doe of Rylstone* and *Peter Bell*, the two long-delayed, separately published poetical responses by Wordsworth are confused or partial but they underline the point. They show how far apart the friends had drifted, Wordsworth failing to answer Coleridge on his (Wordsworth's) terms as much as Coleridge failed when he tried to do the reverse (adopt Wordsworth's).

Wordsworth began writing *The White Doe* in June–October 1807, a year following Coleridge's return from Malta and Italy, and completed it in January 1808. Coleridge was closely involved in the later stages and in the negotiations for publication by Longman, although it received further revisions before it was finally published in 1815. It opens like the "Mariner," with goodly company in a churchyard, but has far more obvious ties with "Christabel": for instance, the young woman alone in the wood, the presiding spirit of her mother, even a "last leaf... upon a blasted tree" (lines 571–72) that recalls the more famous line in "Christabel" (line 49).[27] The larger elements of the story are nonetheless more important: the central emblematic animal recalls the deer of "Hart-leap Well," here surviving as an embodiment of natural piety distinct from those who physically struggle to preserve the old religion (superstition). It is as if, in a somewhat muddled way, Wordsworth would answer "Christabel" with a tale of the triumph of suffering in a way that flies free of the ugly forces that Coleridge suggests lie in wait to compromise human innocence. Although Jeffrey condemned the *White Doe* outright in the *Edinburgh* ("the very worst poem we ever saw"),[28] Wordsworth consistently held it in high regard:

He said he considered "The White Doe" as, in conception, the highest work he had ever produced. The mere physical action was all unsuccessful; but the true action of the poem was spiritual—the subduing of the will, and all inferior passions, to the perfect purifying and spiritualising of the intellectual nature; while the Doe, by connection with Emily [the female protagonist, of whom the Doe is the counterpart], is raised as it were from its mere animal nature into something mysterious and saint-like. (Woof ed. 1:539–48 at 539)

Coleridge thought highly of it in the same respect (see *BL* 2:154–56) although he had previously urged Wordsworth to correct "a disproportion of the Accidents to the spiritual Incidents" and to make Emily more active: she "neither speaks nor acts in all the first 3 fourths of the Poem" (*CL* 3:107–08). His words repeat what Wordsworth wrote to him a month before,[29] but in a manner closer to Wordsworth's previous (1800) list of faults in the "Mariner," as both of them were surely aware. The protracted seriocomic discussion between the two men is significant: as Kristine Dugas observes, "Because in some respects the poems shared intentions, they also shared peculiar problems in execution."[30] Wordsworth went back to Percy's *Reliques* for his story—a ballad named "The Rising of the North"—and the cancelled Advertisement shows he had Coleridge's metrical experiment in "Christabel" in mind when he settled on the meter.[31] Again, a comparison of the way the verse-paragraphs move in the two poems is not flattering to Wordsworth. What he put together remains a muddle and it can be summarised as a poem in which he responded to themes central to the "Mariner" and "Christabel" in a way that closely approximated to Coleridge's way. He deliberately avoided what was painful in the two Coleridge poems, and the "beatification" of Emily's mind and "the apotheosis of the companion of her solitude"[32] simply do not work out because they are not worked through. *The White Doe* stands as a particularly interesting failure, attempted as it was at a point when Wordsworth's grasp of spiritual matters had reached its maturity[33] and he measured this against his understanding of the still maturing Coleridge. The lines describing the solitary doe at the beginning of Canto I quoted in the *Biographia* describe a shared perception of permanent loss preserved in vision:

> Now doth a delicate shadow fall,
> Falls upon her like a breath
> From some lofty arch or wall,
> As she passes underneath (*BL* 2: 155)

The grasp of such matters Coleridge possessed at that time had still to be improved upon, but I feel that even then it was more subtle than Wordsworth's. And he would not perhaps have chosen the Bolton Abbey locale.

The White Doe can be understood as a late addendum to the *Lyrical Ballads*, but it was not the last instalment. That honour goes to *Peter Bell*—in its earliest form part of the package Wordsworth read to Hazlitt in May–June 1798—which suggests what the "Ancient Mariner" might have become if Coleridge had withdrawn from the collaboration leaving Wordsworth as the author to proceed alone. It continued a favourite poem in Wordsworth family circles—to be recited, copied, and improved—but when it was at last published in 1819 it was out of touch with its source, inviting as much parody of its author as comparison with the poem it originally sought to match. John Hamilton Reynolds's parody, which appeared a fortnight before the thing it parodied, was subtitled "A Lyrical Ballad," which to Coleridge's mind was "ALL FAIR" and gave him cause to "laugh heartily" (*CL* 4:938).

The ambition that drives *Peter Bell* is simpler than in the case of *The White Doe*. It is Wordsworth's fully worked answer to the "Ancient Mariner" in the same unique stanza form he invented for "The Idiot Boy" ($abccb_4$)[34] by way of a different treatment of the same themes. Thus, the Prologue places the supposed author in "a little Boat | Whose shape is like the crescent-moon"[35] which connects with the horned or crescent moon of the "Mariner," only for such aerial means of mental travel to be discarded in favour of one that is firmly grounded. The ensuing narrative in three parts matches Coleridge's protagonist with a "Methodistical" self-centred potter, making a donkey the counterpart of the slain albatross, and tells how:

> ...Peter Bell, who, till that night,
> Had been the wildest of his clan,
> Forsook his crimes, repressed his folly,
> And, after ten months' melancholy,
> Became a good and honest man.

It is a burlesque send-up—more comprehensive if more laboured than "The Idiot Boy"[36]—and Wordsworth spelled out his serious point in his dedication to Poet Laureate Southey:

> The Poem of Peter Bell, as the Prologue will shew, was composed under a belief that the Imagination not only does not require for its exercise the intervention of supernatural agency, but that, though such agency be excluded, the faculty may be called forth as imperiously, and for kindred results of pleasure, by incidents, within the compass of poetic probability, in the humblest departments of daily life.[37]

Such was the blunt conclusion to the dialogue that began more than twenty years before.

5.5 Legacy

So things stood and the two authors went their different ways. The verses on sundered friendship in "Christabel" have sometimes been taken as a comment on their relationship:

> Alas! they had been Friends in Youth;
> But whispering Tongues can poison Truth;
> . .. .
>
> They stood aloof, the scars remaining,
> Like Cliffs, which had been rent asunder;
> A dreary Sea now flows between,
> But neither Heat, nor Frost, nor Thunder
> Shall wholly do away, I ween,
> The Marks of that, which once hath been.
> (*PW* 1:496: lines 408–26)

Coleridge told Poole in 1813, with an unacknowledged borrowing from "The Brothers" on his mind, that they were "the best & sweetest Lines, I ever wrote" (*CL* 3:435), and they became immediately popular. Byron quoted them as an epigraph to his "Fare Thee Well" at the time of publication and they became a recurring anthology choice through the earlier nineteenth century. D.G. Rossetti pronounced them "one of the masterpieces of the language, but no doubt. .. written quite separately and then fitted into *Christabel*."[38] Whatever the case, the passage describes friendship that will not be forgotten, a division that ran deep but was never rivalry. Without Wordsworth, there would have been no "Ancient Mariner," and the writing of that poem for Coleridge was foundational. He would not have thought about the Imagination as he did without

Wordsworth's living presence and the challenge of both his example and counterexample. Similarly for Wordsworth: Coleridge's belief in his powers, along with the challenge presented by Coleridge's different grasp of the ideas they held in common, equally shaped his career. When Coleridge's life was almost at an end, in considered terms, he told William Rowan Hamilton that Coleridge and his sister Dorothy were the two beings to whom his intellect was most indebted.[39]

The period of mutual influence had its own history in turn: a surrounding context determined how the relationship was seen. When the "Ancient Mariner" reappeared in its new guise in 1817 it was welcomed as an already famous poem. The *Edinburgh* notice opened with the pronouncement:

> Every reader of modern poetry is acquainted of course with "The Ancient Mariner" of this author…which, when once read, can never afterwards be entirely forgotten.[40]

But there was little sense of a context in which it might be read and, to the extent that it was remembered as a *Lyrical Ballads* poem, the wider fame of the collection had been determined by Wordsworth in a way that left Coleridge's contribution in a no-place. It rested by the side of a different kind of poetry that formed the foundations of another poet's significant career, cherished as one of a few strangely magical poems Coleridge wrote before he gave up poetry, or poetry gave him up; part of an ending, not a beginning. In such a way, as time went on and Wordsworth's reputation strengthened and he became a respected Poet Laureate, his private view of Coleridge's lack of application combined with the published recollections of De Quincey, Cottle, and others to cement the picture of failure. Praise somersaulted into retrospective blame, a year of glory became the measure of unsuccess:

> Coleridge's twenty-sixth year was his "annus mirabilis," and… if he had not then suffered himself to be drawn aside from poetry he must have proved the chief poet of modern times.[41]

By this curious turn, Wordsworth's poetry—not Coleridge's—became the ideal of the latter's young disciples at Cambridge: serious souls like F.D. Maurice had little time for the "Mariner" and "Christabel," let alone "Kubla Khan," and John Sterling was the lone exception.[42] The turn was, however, not adventitious. Wordsworth, as his failed attempts to rewrite the Coleridgean supernatural demonstrate, found himself resisting something he described in private as "morbid." Coleridge, the while, privately regretted Wordsworth's "vulgar attachment to orthodoxy in the literal sense" (as well as, on the same occasion, Wordsworth's "disregard to the mechanism of his verse").[43] History was in Wordsworth's favour and, by the time of his death, his poetry had become the core of what Victorians had come to think of as the Romantic Movement: that is, inclusive of Byron. Keats and others; and this continued on for another hundred years and more, until protests were mounted against it as the Romantic Ideology. Coleridge's poetry lived all the while at a popular level and among poets, but his poetical reputation was adjunct to his greater fame as a savant and moral philosopher, which was perforce a mainly bookish reputation. Wordsworth's settled family life at Rydal Mount, in the region where he was born, left him open to autograph hunters and admirers. Coincident with the burgeoning popularity of the Lake District as a tourist destination, his physical presence among the scenery he wrote about made his work appear accessible, somehow also tangible. It made for a reputation to which Coleridge was attached as a junior partner or commentator for the cognoscenti.

I will not continue this story here: it is better told in Chap. 7 in relation to Coleridge's reputation at large. Suffice for the moment to say that interest shifted away from Wordsworth the laureate poet following his death, when new owners came to Rydal Mount, to his earlier years at Town End; that the *Lyrical Ballads* and the period in Somerset when they were composed were rediscovered; and that at the same time Coleridge's poems of the same period were, on different grounds, reapproached as something more than a diversion. During the twentieth century, the Wordsworth–Coleridge dialogue would be rehearsed over again, although sadly too often by critics who did not recognise that the two poets' ideas about poetry grew out of the different kinds of poetry they had written.

Notes

1. To William Sotheby, 13 July 1802: *CL* 2:812.
2. Fruman "Coleridge's Rejection of Nature and the Natural Man" 78 note 9; Whalley "Coleridge's Poetic Sensibility" 3.
3. See my reading in *Experimental Poetry*, 75–76. My comments apply to the 1828 text given in *PW* 1:232, but they apply equally to the earlier texts given in *PW* 2:322.

4. The quotations are from the beginning stanzas in *Poems in Two Volumes* (1807) 2: 27–29.
5. The two Jeffrey reviews are reprinted by Robert Woof (ed.) 153–59, 224–30. For the parody, see **420.X1**; *PW* 2:1052–53 and Arno "New Roots." The label "New School" was overtaken within a decade by "Lake School."
6. As the cottage on the fringe of Grasmere was known to the Wordsworths when they moved in during Dec. 1799. The present name, Dove Cottage, derives from the public house (The Dove and Olive Branch) the building served as up till 1793.
7. "Wordsworth's Conception of the 'Ancient Mariner'" in *Late Harvest* 96.
8. *Letters: Early Years* 264; and see also 263. Both letters are to Cottle.
9. Beer, with a greater emphasis on the confluence of ideas than the disparity of styles in the 1798 volume, describes how its arrangement was reshaped in 1800: see "The Unity of *Lyrical Ballads*."
10. The possibility that "Christabel" was on his mind when he carried Wordsworth manuscripts with him to Bristol in June 1800 is described by Reed *Chronology of the Middle Years* 65–66 note. The lines from the poem he read to the Wordsworths at Dove Cottage on 31 August are likely to have been from Part II.
11. *Letters: Early Years* 302. Cottle presumably began with the setting of Part I, which leaves open the question of whether Part II was in a finished state.
12. *Letters: Early Years* 309.
13. *Letters: Early Years* 310.
14. Blame for the drug dependency is prominent in Julien Temple's controversial *Pandaemonium* (London: Mariner Films, 2000). The words "pain" and "hatred" are in Cavell's *In Quest of the Ordinary* 41.
15. *Home at Grasmere* ed. Darlington 50 (MS. B, lines 238–39).
16. For instance, Averill *Wordsworth and the Poetry of Human Suffering* 214–22; Chandler "The Strange Design of a Lyrical Ballad"; and Hartman "False Themes and Gentle Minds" at 55–57 esp.
17. A rare word in Wordsworth and used by the Mother in his contribution to "The Three Graves" (**155**): see E. H. Coleridge (ed.) *Poetical Works* 1:272 (line 97).
18. "Coleridge's Sequel to *Thalaba* and Robert Southey's Prequel to *Christabel*" at 64–65 esp.
19. *Letters: Early Years* 290; see also *CL* 1:611, 616.
20. See "Reading 'Alice du Clós'" in Appendix B. Relevant to this theme here is that Coleridge's translation of Lessing's "Die Namen" (**236**) was published in the *Morning Post* 27 Aug 1799 (see *PW* 1:588–89, 2:774–76).
21. *Wordsworth: Language as Counter-Spirit* 51.
22. It does appear in Book V of the longer versions: see Norton Critical Edition 172–73, 492.

23. "Preface" to *Poems* (1815) 1:xxxi–xxxii. The passage describing the poem was omitted in 1845 and after: see *Prose Works of William Wordsworth* ed. Owen and Smyser 3:35n.
24. *Open Secrets* 159. François' reading of Wordsworth continues to p. 168 and, interspersed with her reading of his critics, is particularly recommended. See also her comment (p. 217 note) on the word, "remit," used in the 1815 Preface to describe the action of the Boy's mind.
25. For Coleridge's plans for an edition of his poems in 1807, plus revisions of the "Ancient Mariner" dating from the same time, see *PW* 1:365, 1244.
26. *Originality and Imagination* 148.
27. See *White Doe of Rylstone* ed. Kristine Dugas 48–50; references to "Christabel" are even more obvious in the superseded MS 62.
28. *Wordsworth: Critical Heritage* ed. Woof, 1:539–48 at 539.
29. *Letters of William and Dorothy Wordsworth: Middle Years* 1:221–22.
30. Introduction *White Doe* 39.
31. MS 61 f 36^v and transcript: *White Doe* ed. Dugas 200–01.
32. Fenwick "Notes and Illustrations of the Poems" in *Prose Works of William Wordsworth* ed. Grosart 3:123.
33. A large matter, I know, but I rely on Ulmer *The Christian Wordsworth, 1798–1805*.
34. Fussell 149–51 sketches the potentialities of the form and points to similarities with the earlier "mad-song" tradition in English poetry.
35. The verse quotations, here and below, form the beginning and end of the poem, which remain the same in manuscript and published versions. I quote from the Cornell edition by Jordan (1985) which provides references to the crescent moon in Dorothy Wordsworth's *Alfoxden Journal* during late March 1798: the moment when Coleridge finished his poem and Wordsworth's great surge of lyric energy began.
36. Not that it is always laboured: see Cooper *Late Harvest* 93–95 and 106–07 on how the Mariner's "glittering eye" is reflected in the "shining hazel eye" of the Ass and the Hermit's woodland chapel linked to the glade to which Peter is drawn. Besides such allusions to the "Mariner," cf. line 980 (ed. Jordan 135) "'My mother! oh my mother!'" to "The Three Graves," etc.
37. *Peter Bell* ed. Jordan 41. Jordan devotes a large part of his Introduction (20–27) to Wordsworth's struggle with the supernatural as he revised his manuscripts.
38. Byron *Complete Poetical Works* ed. McGann 3:380. For anthologies and selections, see those published by Corman and Blanc (1836), Thomas Allman (1837), William and Robert Chambers (1845), T. J. Allman ([1861],), Gall and Inglis (1862), etc. For Rossetti, see Caine *Recollections* 155.
39. *Letters of William and Dorothy Wordsworth: Later Years* 2:536.

40. *Edinburgh Magazine* (October 1817) in Jackson (ed.) 1:392.
41. Wordsworth in *Recollections of Aubrey De Vere* 42. I suspect Wordsworth also had Coleridge in mind when he once said to De Vere, "speaking of a departed man of genius, who had lived an unhappy life and deplorably abused his powers, to the lasting calamity of his country, 'A great poet must be a great man: and a great man must be a good man; and a good man ought to be a happy man'": "Recollections of Wordsworth" in *Prose Works of William Wordsworth* ed. Grosart 3:494. For Coleridge on a good man and a good great man, see "A Good Great Man" (**302**; *PW* 1:723–24) and refs.
42. See my *Experimental Poetics* 21–22 and 207 note 11.
43. For Wordsworth, see Henry Nelson Coleridge's report of his conversation in *TT* 1:546. For Coleridge, see *Crabb Robinson on Books* ed. Morley 1:288.

CHAPTER 6

Revision, Gloss, Choice

Poetry, like schoolboys, by too frequent & severe corrections, may be cowed into Dullness!—

S.T. Coleridge[1]

6.1 Variants, Versions, Phases

The text of the "Ancient Mariner" has been a cause of confusion for a long time. Soon after Coleridge's poetical reputation revived towards the close of the nineteenth century, at the time when James Dykes Campbell, Ernest Hartley Coleridge, and others were beginning to apply themselves to the business of establishing "reliable" texts, a character in a novel by George MacDonald, *There and Back* (1891), finds himself in a quandary. He begins to recite Coleridge's poem to a sympathetic young lady and is embarrassed because he has to choose between the several versions he has learned by heart. "Not many people know the poem as Coleridge first published it," he says, and describes how Coleridge altered it and made it "Much better." His commentary addresses many issues raised by later academic critics, not least concerning the relationship of the prose gloss, and it still makes a great deal of sense. For instance, his answer to the question, "Then why should you care any more for the first way of it?"

Just because it is different. A thing not so good may have a different goodness. A man may not be so good as another man, and yet have some good things in him the other has not. That implies that not every change he made was for the better. And where he has put a better phrase, or passage, the former may yet be good. So you see a new form may be much better, and yet the old form remain much too good to be parted with. In any case it is intensely interesting to see how and why he changed a thing or its shape, and to ponder wherein it is for the better or the worse. That is to take it like a study in natural history. In that we learn how an animal grows different to meet a difference in the supply of its needs; in the varying editions of a poem we see how it alters to meet a new requirement of the poet's mind. I don't mean the cases are parallel, but they correspond somehow. If I were a schoolmaster, I should make my pupils compare different forms of the same poem, and find out why the poet made the changes. That would do far more for them, I think, than comparing poets with each other. (123)

The "Ancient Mariner" becomes confusing when the different versions of the text are taken into account because what Coleridge first wrote quickly became a reference point for its author. He altered, added to, and subtracted from it, but every improvement opened the need to repair fresh inconsistencies that opened as a result. The poem provoked a continual involvement from which he was never delivered, not even perhaps by its final version. The situation is not unique in his writing: "The Eolian Harp" (**115**), written in 1795, was reconstructed to a comparable extent when it appeared alongside the "Mariner" in 1817, as well as in annotated copies of the same and in later *Poetical Works*. The final versions of all such poems are of interest not least because the pressure points on the original argument became more evident over time through the repairs that had to be made. The distracted character in MacDonald's novel settles on a later text because he, like his author, is anxiously concerned with the saving of a soul. If the poem had been his first priority, he might well have chosen the more vulnerable and exposed first version: it possesses a freshness, an unguarded openness that extenuates the technical faults from which the other versions, in their different ways, are also not free. When Coleridge began over again at the starting point to which the "Mariner" delivered him, in poems discussed at the close of Chap. 3 ("Christabel" **176**, the "Dark Ladiè" **182**, "Love" **253**), he increasingly came to exclude the supernatural element that was becoming, via the logic of Kant's transcendental deduction, the subject of his prose thoughts. If one had to name a total rewriting of the "Ancient Mariner," from the ground of the philosophical–theological position he finally arrived at, it would unavoidably be "Alice du Clós" (**655**); and this late poem, as earlier suggested, is Coleridge in unrelenting Calvinistic mode.

Jack Stillinger provided the most helpful introduction to the overall textual situation of the "Mariner" (60–73 and 158–84 specifically). He describes eighteen "versions" of the poem in chronological order, and then separately matches the changes in seventeen versions against the "final" 1834 version in a way that will be clearly understood. There are three caveats. First, the distinction between "versions" and "variants" in Anglo-American editorial terminology is loose; Stillinger takes "version" to mean any text that contains a variant, even one of several printed texts that contains a single handwritten emendation, and it might have been more helpful to reserve "version" for larger groupings into which the emended (and preparatory) texts fall, and the term "variant" for the smaller differences within such groups. For example, his Version 1 is *LB*, his Version 2 is the Trinity College Cambridge corrected copy of *LB*, his Version 3 is the part of the letter Coleridge sent Cottle (*CL* 1:598–602) that describe the changes to be made in a copy of *LB* in the printing of *LB 1800*, and his Versions 4–6 are *LB* 1800, 1802, and 1805. I think it would be more helpful to think of his Versions 2–6 as phases of single group associated with *LB 1800*: in effect, as variants preparing for and making up a substantive "Version 2." Second, Stillinger's list of "Variants" (in his sense) is incomplete: in fact, it doubles in length if one includes all the variants contained in the annotated copies listed in the Bollingen edition (*PW* 1: Annex C), some of which are very interesting. For instance, the correction made in Martha Fricker's copy of *LB* (*PW* 2:539; line 344.1.2–345) anticipates the correction Coleridge copied out for Cottle, which consequently appeared in *LB 1800*. He clearly felt uneasy at an early stage about the abrupt change of point-of-view here, and it continued to worry him as demonstrated by the patch provided by the gloss on "a blessed troup of angelic spirits" added in 1817. (More on this uneasy transition in the next section below.) My third caveat is connected with the first two. Stillinger says little or nothing about the peculiar circumstances behind and surrounding each of the printed versions. They need to be taken into account if the authority of these versions (and their corrections) is to be properly estimated, and again they are described in the Bollingen edition (*PW* 1: Annex B).

I would also recommend Martin Wallen's "Experimental Edition," where the listing of annotated copies is, like Stillinger's, incomplete and the discursive "Commentary" contains errors, but the typographic solution to the problem of presenting the three major versions of the poem in an immediately comprehensible way could not be more helpful. Each page is headed by a single stanza of the 1798 version; this is followed beneath by the *LB 1800* version of the same stanza or by a blank if the stanza has been omitted; and this followed by the same in the 1817 version, selected later variants of which are given in smaller type as footnotes. The solution matches my argument here and a reader can easily progress from the 1798 text given below in Appendix A to appreciate at one glance how the poem expanded and contracted, the minutiae of which is much amplified and sometimes corrected in the Bollingen edition.

Although the listing of texts in the Bollingen edition is, like Stillinger's, neutral and without favour, I willingly follow Wallen's example and suggest that a critical reader should understand the text developing through three substantively different phases or versions, each of which contains pre- and post-publication texts that may be considered variations of the same. I apologise to German, French, and Italian editors, from whose terminology I depart, but I think this will make sense to most readers of the present book. Phase or Version 1 has only one witness: the printed text of *Lyrical Ballads* 1798. There are references to a pre-existing version in 300 lines and 340 lines (*PW* 2:504–05), and the "finished" version comprises 658 lines. That is all that is certainly known, and the way the materials came together is guesswork based on the printed version: a process as precarious as speculation surrounding the composition of Spenser's *Faerie Queene*. For example, I speculated in Chap. 2 that Coleridge extended the poem when he reached Part V. It is equally possible that he added or at least developed the episode of the spectre-ship, with the two figures who dice for the Mariner's soul. In support, one might note that the transitions that connect the episode to the surrounding voyage were improved at the very first opportunity; and that the psychological depths touched upon are inherently more likely to date from a late stage of composition. In particular, the victory of Life-in-Death stands for the indecisive position (willlessness, languor) under which so many Coleridgean protagonists labour, from the "Sloth-jaundic'd all!" of such early poems as the lines on Fulwood Smerdon (**85**; *PW* 1:150) to the "dreary Mood" that opens "The Garden of Boccaccio" (**652**; *PW* I:1091). And, in light of this, it is specially relevant that the composition of the "Mariner" was followed immediately by "Christabel" (**176**) and "The Ballad of the Dark Ladié" (**182**), the one where a mother is prominent and the other in which a female figure is stricken by a malady of the soul. Coleridge appears to have brooded over the relationships within his family background throughout the 1790s and to be driving this towards some kind of conclusion at about the time he wrote the autobiographical letters to Poole (February 1797–February 1798). In short, Part III is as likely as any to represent a late stage of the original composition.

Phase 2 carries forward corrections that doubtlessly entered Coleridge's mind when he saw the first printed copies in 1798, but in a larger number of respects represents a fresh start, from a different (partly shared, slightly compromised) point of view. And Phase 3, although it has its beginnings in revisiting the poem in 1806–1807, is represented by the *Sibylline Leaves* version of 1817, in which one might say Coleridge to some extent recovered his poem from Wordsworth but was nevertheless, at that particular time, most uncertain of the ground on which he stood. He again made adjustments when he saw the 1817 version in print, but inconsistently; and he continued to fiddle with it perhaps until the month in which he died. The 1798, 1800, and 1817 versions represent a continuously evolving poem in its beginning, middle, and final phases.

At least one change made in 1800 can be reckoned a retrospective improvement to the first edition of *Lyrical Ballads*, but there is no point in speculating much further on what was in the first instance almost certainly composed orally: a voice in its author's head. As I explain further in Chap. 7, the two earlier versions (1798 and 1800–1805) were particularly important in establishing the popular reputation of the poem, which rested on a form of the text without the gloss or with the gloss following after, not accompanying the text—in widely circulating "out-of-copyright" or pirated editions. Such "non-transmissional" editions embody information about the manner in which the poem was read—its status among the reading public—which modern editions and bibliographies ignore at their peril. The three different versions of "Ancient Mariner" text also make clear that the still-standard practice of harnessing the differences to the last that appeared during the author's lifetime (as Stillinger does), or the alternative practice of harnessing the differences to the first (as the Collected Coleridge Variorum: *PW* 2:509–39 does), is hugely problematic. The provision of the earliest and latest text together or *en face* (e.g. *PW* 1:372–419) has been a convenience: it is not a solution (see 6.4 below under the heading "Gloss").

6.2 The 1800 Version

Wordsworth's unease over the way Coleridge developed their shared interest in guilt and the supernatural unwound during the spring and early summer of 1798 in an assertion of his own, different understanding of the same as described in Chap. 4. Coleridge apparently anticipated that Wordsworth would not fully understand: how else to explain the troubled reaction of the Wordsworthian figure of the Hermit in Part VII of the ballad, when the Mariner reaches home and still has not found peace? What began as an acknowledged sense of difference—"a sadder and a wiser man" matched against "a better and a wiser man"[2]—became a provocation that was exacerbated when most of the reviewers fixed on Coleridge's poem, which after all opened the volume in a way strikingly different from what followed, and criticised it for its Gothick element. No matter that the Gothick was exaggerated to an extent that it became a parody of the overblown fashion: even Southey missed the point when he complained specifically about the "Dutch attempt at German sublimity."[3] And the more Wordsworth's confidence grew in the new direction his writing was taking, in the new poems he wrote in Germany and on his return to a new home in the North, the more he resented the presence of the "Mariner" in a volume he increasingly felt the need to appropriate: this, even while he feared for the reception of his own new vein of poetry and was glad to shelter behind Coleridge's reputation while he could.

So much is clear, and so should be Coleridge's willingness to do all in his power to further Wordsworth's plans for success. It is impossible to determine whether he pruned the antique spellings of the original "Mariner" reluctantly to please his friend or because he willingly agreed they were a distraction. This most obvious change remained incomplete throughout his lifetime and is in reality superficial: striking on first acquaintance but almost completely forgotten by the time one advances into the poem. Other corrections are simple improvements: for instance, the more carefully contrived transition at the beginning of Part III that introduces the Spectre Ship; or the omission of four stanzas in Part V (1798 lines 362–77), which are partly repeated at the close of Part VII, and may represent roughly where the poem ended when it stood at 340 lines and before it expanded to include the Two Voices in the air. Other cuts—for instance, the five stanzas describing the Hand of Glory phenomenon in Part VI (1798 lines 481–502)—could have been made by Coleridge on his own initiative because they were unnecessarily macabre, excessive, and out of date only two years after they were introduced. At the same time, such tastefulness perhaps advanced at the expense of the poem. The macabre stanzas assist the shift from the voices above the ship sailed by dead men to the seraphs who emerge beside every corpse (lines 517–18). The foregrounding of pictorial horror allows a significant sleight of hand to take place in the shadows behind and, if they were removed to humour Wordsworth, one has to allow that the transition becomes markedly abrupt. The revision differs from a superficially similar one made in 1817, where a stanza in the Spectre Ship passage that mimicked the crude Gothickry of Matthew Lewis (1798 lines 181–85) is cut.[4] This later revision is part of a larger, more integrated pattern, and strong personal reasons as well as changing fashions may underlie it.

Similar points could be made by tracking all the changes that appear in obvious fashion in Wallen's edition, with further details and instances in the Bollingen. And it is important that not all the changes in the 1800 version were necessarily instigated by Wordsworth's prompting. To take two further examples, Coleridge previously inserted the stanza following line 180 of the 1798 text that he listed in his 1800 letter to Cottle in the copy of *Lyrical Ballads* 1798 now at Trinity College Cambridge: one of the rare copies of the Bristol first issue and so presumably an early second-thought made independently. This point is reinforced by the fact that the stanza carried forward was one of two inscribed in the Trinity copy, the second of which was subsequently abandoned. A similar situation existed with the stanza comprising lines 531–36 of the 1798 text: Coleridge redrafted the stanza in the Trinity copy and afterwards instructed Cottle to omit the stanza altogether. The places in the original poem where such interventions were made are always of particular interest because they indicate moments of uncertainty on Coleridge's part: often moments of transition in the narrative, or when dealing with the representation of some state of mind.

However, there are two changes in the 1800 text that are of a different order and do appear to result from Wordsworth's intervention. Their effect is complicating as much as anything else: perhaps the result of consternation that was still working its way out in his own writing. They both appear in the list Coleridge copied out for Cottle. He could have allowed the complications they raise because of the hope he invested in Wordsworth's grand ambitions.

The first alteration concerns the title, which became "The Ancient Mariner, A Poet's Reverie." Charles Lamb complained to Wordsworth about the addition: "[I]t is as bad as Bottom the Weaver's declaration that he is not a Lion but only the scenical representation of a Lion."[5] Just possibly Coleridge allowed it: after all, he and Wordsworth must have discussed their different conceptions of the supernatural, whence they arose and where they led, and "reverie" was not a word for Coleridge with such negative meanings as might be supposed. It connects with the theme of dreams in the poem and his ideas about "that willing suspension of disbelief for the moment, which constitutes poetic faith" (*BL* 2:6), as well as with the word "delirium" with which the beginnings of the poem are associated (see above Chap. 3). More greatly to be regretted, I think, is the loss of the word "Rime" from the title, which is not simply a synonym for "Ballad" or "Tale" but (meaning a white encrustation of ice) connects with "Frost at Midnight" and other Coleridge poems in which extreme temperatures stand for nature out of kilter: its "one life" destructively at odds with itself. Indeed, the loss of "Rime" is connected with the subordination of the "polar" theme, which is overridden again in the second alteration.

The Argument that stood at the head of the poem in 1798 begins: "How a Ship having passed the Line was driven by Storms to the cold Country towards the South Pole." It continues by describing the return journey through the tropics in the Pacific Ocean and onwards, and so by some unspecified route (presumably) around the top of North America to a home port in the British Isles. The Argument that replaced it in 1800 begins, "How a Ship, having first sailed to the Equator, was driven by Storms, to the cold Country towards the South Pole"; but then continues, "how the Ancient Mariner cruelly, and in contempt of the laws of hospitality, killed a Sea-bird; and how he was followed by many and strange Judgments: and in what manner he came back to his own Country." In short, the original argument that mapped the outline of a voyage in geographic terms is replaced by a moral story that tells of crime, punishment, and partial redemption. Coleridge's poem—a tale of a world beyond the boundaries of ordinary comprehension, of strange discovery, and of unexplained horror and wonder—thereby becomes something else: its theme much closer to Wordsworth's poems like "Goody Blake and Harry Gill" and "The Thorn," or "The Idiot Boy" and "The Mad Mother," that lead up to it in the re-arranged 1800 volume. Taken with Wordsworth's prose note that specifies the "great defects" of the poem and concludes the first volume, it looks like a stitch-up. Coleridge's poem is pushed into a corner and made to say something it was not initially written to say.

There is a copy of the same first 1800 volume, corrected in Coleridge's hand and later given by him (almost certainly) to Edward Irving in which the last part of the new Argument (from "and in what manner" to "Country") is cancelled and replaced by an extension that ignores talk of crime and instead emphasises "the Spirit, who loved the Sea-bird," and his "<guardian> Saint" and the "choir of Angels" who descended into the bodies of the dead sailors and accompanied the Mariner home (*PW* 2:536). It might date from soon after the date of publication, or 1807–1808, or later still. Whatever the case, it strengthens the thought that an argument about crime, punishment, and redemption was not originally at the forefront of Coleridge's mind—as it probably was for Wordsworth, who introduced the albatross in the first place. Say rather that, for Coleridge, it was a voyage into unknown waters where events followed in an inconsequential way and a promise of enlightenment was the goal. Coleridge had an interest in the imagery of the hunt, and its implications: it appears in "The Story of the Mad Ox" (**177**), reappears obliquely in the "sultry hind" of "First Advent of Love" (**574**), and is at the core of "Alice du Clós: A Ballad" (**655**). Whatever his interest might have been, it was noticed and incorporated into arguments against cruelty to animals by proponents like Frederick Thrupp (author of *The Ancient Mariner and the Modern Sportsman* 1881) and his kinsman Stephen Coleridge (1854–1936), strenuous opponent of animal vivisection. However, to cast the author of "Kubla Khan" (**178**) as a cruel hunter, as Wordsworth does in "Heart-leap Well," is a step too far. The animal theme was in the background of Wordsworth's mind for the poem they began together, but it was left far behind by what Coleridge wrote.

The following two editions of *Lyrical Ballads*, in 1802 and 1805 (Stillinger's Versions 5 and 6), likewise appeared under Wordsworth's name and may be considered under the present heading. They each omit "A Poet's Reverie" from the head of the poem (but not from the preceding half-title page) and, even more important, they omit the entire Argument. Both reversions can be interpreted as further grounds for doubting Coleridge's full approval of the changes made in 1800. The 1802 text took over a couple of corrections made in the copy of the annotated 1800 Irving copy; and, although a few more small changes appear in 1805 (one obviously a misprint), Coleridge was in Malta while this final variant of the 1800 version was in preparation

6.3   THE 1817 VERSION

As described in Chaps. 4 and 5, Wordsworth attempted to come to terms with his response to the "Ancient Mariner" in his own way in a number of poems across twenty years. Coleridge possessed an intellectual understanding of their differences from an earlier stage, whatever his difficulty in articulating the path he himself was on and in embracing its implications consistently. His view of what his poem did and did not achieve emerged from the rough treatment it suffered in successive editions of *Lyrical Ballads*, and the first signs of his recovering it for himself began to appear after his return from Malta in 1806–1807. It had more than once come to mind on the outward sea voyage (e.g. *CN* 2:2053 f 22) as well as during the lonely period he spent on the island and in Italy. Some preliminary revisions date from October 1806 (*CN* 2:2880; Stillinger's Version 7), and he entered into negotiations for the publication of a book of poems by Longman in early summer 1807 (*CL* 3:15). Possible allusions to the "Ancient Mariner" crop up in other poems he wrote about this time—for instance, in "Constancy to an Ideal Object" (**357**; *PW* 1:778) and "To William Wordsworth" (**401**; *PW* 1:819 fn)[6]—which may also be when he made the additions to the 1800 text of *Lyrical Ballads* given to Irving and already described. However, these stirrings are but premonitions of the major revision that came with *Sybilline Leaves* in 1817.

The latter volume was put together before (and its publication delayed by) the writing and publication of *Biographia Literaria*, which had begun long before as a preface (*BL* 1:liv–lv), which expanded to incorporate a response to the preface and supplementary essay in Wordsworth's 1815 *Poems*, and then became a long philosophical justification of their differences and other matter. The harried situation saw Coleridge led astray from the philosophical course he had long been embarked upon: something he quickly came to regret. In particular it led to the revision of many passages in poems that reverted to ideas he hoped he had overcome, and not a few details in the text of the "Mariner" that required to be altered before the new version was circulated—this after an already lengthy list of errata. Stillinger nominates the *Sybilline Leaves* text as his Version 8, and six annotated copies of the same as Versions 10 through 15. As it turns out, more than twice that number of annotated copies needs to be included, taking note of those in which the annotations are in the hands of different helpers. Stillinger's Variants 16 through 18 cover the three large collections—*Poetical Works* 1828, 1829, and 1834—and again he takes little notice of the circumstances in which each of them was assembled. These later texts incorporate only minor uncoordinated changes, some of which are of doubtful authenticity, and a few import errors. Although other poems in these collections were amended, a few copiously, the "Mariner" was not. One has to assume that Coleridge or others merely tinkered with the text so confusedly assembled in 1817, the author reckoning that the precarious balance reached there was as good as he could make it.

The way the 1817 text was composed and revised is set out by Stillinger (pp. 65–66) and in the Bollingen edition (*PW* 2:507–09); a visual impression of their location and extent can be gained by scanning Wallen. A good many changes represent simple improvements in the original text. For example, the original third stanza beginning "But still he holds the wedding-guest" (1798 lines 9–12), which was retained throughout all *Lyrical Ballads* texts, was cut and the information incorporated into the preceding gloss, presumably to speed up the entry into the Mariner's storytelling; the revision of the original stanza beginning "Listen, Stranger! Storm and Wind" at 1798 lines 45–48 completes a process already begun in 1800; similarly the next stanza beginning "Listen, Stranger! Mist and Snow" (1798 lines 49–52), with a further addition that anticipates a portentous moment in "Alice du Clós" when,

> with a baleful Smile
> The Vassal Knight reel'd off—
> Like a huge billow from a Bark
> Toil'd in the deep Sea-trough....

The two stanzas involving the "horned Moon" towards the end of Part III (1798 lines 199–207) again incorporate a process of revision begun in 1800; and new further thoughts, such as the two extra lines added onto line 92 assist in the same process of manipulating the pace (here, through repetition, to help build to the important statement made in the six-line stanza that follows).

There are fewer fresh interventions. The most obvious is the removal of a stanza from the spectre-bark passage: the 1798 lines beginning "*His* bones were black with many a crack" (lines 181–85) describing Death. And one wonders if Coleridge was prompted by the desire to remove more of the obviously Gothick parody that was stripped away in the 1800 text, by this time even further out of date. At the same time, it cannot be a coincidence that he dithered over the two stanzas following soon after: the one beginning "The naked Hulk alongside came" (lines 191–94) and the one after this beginning "A gust of wind sterte up behind" (lines 195–98). The first of these was printed in 1817 but struck out in several corrected copies, some accompanied by imprecations on the printer for his fault, if such it was (*PW* 2:537); the second was cancelled in the printed errata. All three stanzas involve the figure of Death and, while it is possible they were removed in order to reduce further the dimension of parody, Coleridge's indecision and excessive reaction to the "self-opinionated printer" suggest a raw nerve was struck when he saw the poem appearing under his own name. The two haunting figures had been associated with thoughts of his parents. His mother died at Ottery in November 1809 and he did not attend her funeral; perhaps he decided to dissociate his father from the murky thoughts he once entertained.

In short, a case can be made for the omissions and revisions in the verse stanzas of the poem as being continuous with the larger part of Coleridge's earlier thinking: they are clarifications, improvements, tidyings. Such a conclusion nevertheless omits the obvious, that his replacement of the previous Argument(s) by a long Latin epigraph drawn from Gilbert Burnet and his addition of an extensive prose gloss change everything. The gloss—comprising fifty-seven side comments as if by a second, unnamed seventeenth-century English author—became fifty-eight in the 1828 text. The two new features intervene in the way the verse stanzas are read and what the whole ensemble means. Perhaps they were not wholly unprepared for if one follows through the tussle contained in successive editions of *Lyrical Ballads*. After all, the epigraph makes emphatically clear what Wordsworth clearly resisted in Coleridge's speculations on the supernatural. It says at length what Coleridge added to the Argument in the Irving copy of the 1800 edition and omits what Wordsworth had substituted for the beginning of Coleridge's 1798 Argument. Following on, the new gloss provides a running commentary on the same theme, which again Wordsworth had attempted to bury in the substitute Argument on behalf of a theme of crime, punishment, and repentance, and in his own poems embodying a counterposition. If "The Idiot Boy" situated Coleridge's tentative ideal in a figure of lovable fun, the format of the 1817 "Ancient Mariner" repositioned the verses in an imposing (if mock-serious) frame.

The effect of the epigraph might be compared to the prose introductions Coleridge added to two of the three poems comprising the *Christabel* volume (1816). The preface to the title poem deflects attention from aspects Coleridge feared might be objected to (its "obscenity") onto technical matters of rhythm and meter in a way that has puzzled metrists ever since. The paragraphs headed "Of the Fragment of Kubla Khan" personalise the composition of that poem in a way that detaches the author from what he wrote. In a similar fashion, the context supplied by the new "Ancient Mariner" gestures at a historical fiction: a poem presented as if by a devout reader familiar with and taking seriously Josephus and Michael Psellus: a contemporary of Ralph Cudworth, say, with a better and less prolix prose style. The context in the notebooks in which the extract from Burnet was originally copied (*CN* 1:1000H) includes extracts from other Renaissance authors, including Henry More and Daniel Sennert, whose interests overlapped Coleridge's but whom he did not deeply respect (see, e.g. his dismissive note on More which I attached to the epigraph to Chap. 3). He omitted all the references to particular authors along with Burnet's suggestion that their ideas might be taken seriously. What remains is both an emollient and a tease: a preliminary statement that is certain, assured, and also obviously dated. The raw—and in important respects incomplete—poem Coleridge first published has been tidied and in minor respects improved, but it has also been given new "packaging" to determine how it should be received.

Coleridge added further layers of packaging that appear to promise greater clarity but do not always deliver. For example, he added a footnote to "furrow" (in 1798 line 100: cf. *PW* 2:513–14) to explain that he had personally observed how it appeared differently on board ship from on shore; and he added a footnote to "the ribb'd Sea-sand" (in 1798 line 219: cf. *PW* 2:519) thanking Wordsworth for the observation and recalling the circumstances when the poem was begun, thereby adding yet another perspective on the story. A multiplicity of points of view was an important feature of the poem from its beginning. An anonymous person, who turns out to be a wedding guest, tells of what he has been told; and the reader enters the mind of the teller of the story and becomes two-stages removed from what is happening, and yet paradoxically the more deeply involved. The new 1817 text inserts two further frames in Latin and English so as suggest the story in verse is to be read as an older (medieval) text presented by a later (learned) reader, which take one slightly sideways. But the footnotes describing the author aboard a ship and the Wordsworths as neighbours in rural Somerset take one back to an author telling the story from a more personalised point of view. Coleridge had trouble remembering where he stood within the action from the start, as the muddled quotation marks amply show through so many versions. He rescinded the change to "furrow" described above in *Poetical Works* 1828-1829-1834. The minor dispute over the word "drawn" in the gloss alongside the storm-blast of the rewritten stanza comprising 1798 lines 45–48 turns on this same uncertainty. J.D. Campbell and E.H. Coleridge followed by most modern editors emend the word to "driven" as the sense demands. Coleridge might nevertheless have left "drawn" so as to communicate the force of destiny that returns the ship homeward via the magnetic pole, and the resulting undecided position pinpoints the apparently contradictory but reconciliatory logic the poem demands. Coleridge noted a similar inconsistency in Spenser's *Faerie Queene*, where an action is described simultaneously from within and without (*CM* 1:54). And what Coleridge said of that poem applies equally to his own:

> it is neither in the domains of History or Geography, is ignorant of all artificial boundary—truly in the Land of Faery—i.e. in mental space—(*CN* 3:4501 f 136ᵛ).

6.4 Gloss

Coleridge's ability as poet to have his readers standing in several places at once was already present in the story-within-a-story structure of the first-published version of the "Ancient Mariner." Such duplication is key to a dilemma, demonstrating that Imagination can reach beyond what is understood towards a world wherein the impossible happens. His reluctance to leave the matter there pushed onwards towards a transcendental solution for what had been an alchemical sleight of hand: a way in which up till then, through Imagination, he might "[s]teal access through our senses to our minds" (*BL* 2:17). The means by which he achieved this end—making, over course of time, two subtly different kinds of poetry from two materially different poems with the same title (only differently spelt) in *Lyrical Ballads* 1798 and *Sibylline Leaves* 1817—nonetheless leave a critical reader or ordinary editor with a stark choice. How does anyone read "the poem," taking both versions into account? Or, more simply and specifically, how does one "read" the later version at all when it comprises verses in tandem with a running commentary in prose? The commentary is not exactly synchronised with the verse, and it sometimes tells you things not in the verse or seemingly at odds with it.

The contradictions have been made much of during the past fifty years,[7] but even before they are weighed they presuppose an impossibility: an aporia such as Derrida famously constructed in *Glas* (1974). Readers are faced by the task of reading two columns, invariably in different typefaces and type sizes, each with different content, simultaneously. Each page is inscrutable, unless one cares to believe Coleridge's merry boast that in his heyday he "used to read a volume, stereotype-wise by whole pages at a glance" (*CM* 4:336–37). I have remarked that, while collected editions of Coleridge's poems rolled off the press from the publishers Pickering and Moxon, retailing the 1834 version for forty years after Coleridge's death,[8] many more separate editions of the poem were being read in pirate versions pretending to derive from the out-of-print *Lyrical Ballads* that either placed the gloss separately following the verse or omitted it altogether.[9] This is obviously how the majority wanted to read the poem, whatever version they were given (even 1800 with 1817 or 1829 gloss!). Anticipating the expiration of family copyright by a few years, but apparently with Derwent Coleridge's assent, William Michael Rossetti's edition of Coleridge's *Poetical Works* (E. Moxon, Son 1871) was the first to add the 1798 text as an addendum or appendix to the 1834 text, which maintained its testamentary status as the last to be sanctioned by its author in his lifetime. The double-take pairing was quickly followed in a school edition by Andrew George (D.C. Heath 1897); other editions elected to promote the 1829 version to the more elevated position, following J.D. Campbell's influential example (Macmillan 1893); but the 1798–1834 pairing became *de rigueur* after E.H. Coleridge's Oxford edition in 1912. Two decades later, Stephen Potter (Nonesuch 1933) became the first to present the first and last texts in tandem on facing pages. Further choices in a similar format follow: for instance, 1798 facing 1817 (Bedford/St. Martin's 1999).

It strikes me that what has won approval as a practical—even elegant— editorial solution is a cop-out because it leaves unresolved a poem whose intentions are realised through its affect: that is, when it is "heard in the mind" of individual readers or auditors in the way the Authorised (or King James) Version says "the Lord spake unto Moses" (Leviticus 18:1), or to Paul in a vision (Acts 18:9). The process of reading a doubled or aporetic text is incomplete because what is being said is muffled: a forked tongue literally lacks authority; cannot claim to be an Imaginative statement because the sense of purpose is frustrated.[10] Most illustrated editions of the poem are subject to the same criticism because what they provide is supplementary (in Derrida's sense); that is, flagrantly invasive, offering a different interpretation of a text that is already aiming beyond interpretation. To return to now familiar examples, Mervyn Peake (Chatto and Windus 1943) and

Duncan Grant (Allen and Richard Lane 1945) interrupt the already interrupted version of the poem with their (different) reactions to the Second World War. To put the matter this way may seem harsh but it is a fact that one has finally to choose between Coleridge and the illustrator. David Jones (Douglas Cleverdon 1929) may justly be claimed to have produced the most sophisticated and elegant designs. He obviously engaged with the poem very deeply but the overall result is a Pentecostal jumble quite foreign to any version that Coleridge projected.[11] His text imports odd fragments of Coleridge manuscript and additional text of his own: for example on the final page (p. 37) the engraved inscription from the Offertory of the Tridentine Mass beginning *Accendat in Nobis*. This is as far from the mark as Hunt Emerson's comic-book version (Knockabout Books 1989) and Nick Hayes's graphic novel (Jonathan Cape 2011), and much more profoundly misleading. Better say the majority of illustrated editions are a world apart and value them for being so. More illuminative for those interested in Coleridge's poem, in whatever version, are the results produced by select book designers, working with different typefaces on different papers within different text areas. The range of results achieved is as wide as the better-known illustrated editions and can serve the cause of the poetry better.

My argument assumes that Coleridge's poem is and remains a poem about the supernatural dimension of what he came to call Imagination, and embodied his feelings about this which were unfixed in 1798 and less fixed than many believe during the troubled years while the 1817 version came together. His thoughts clarified thereafter in prose reflections that turned on Reason and the higher Understanding, but from this time on he left the "Ancient Mariner" more or less as it stood. The two versions meanwhile remain a choice every reader must determine: between first and last, 1798 and 1817–1834. I assume the difference between the revised 1817 texts and those coming later is negligible; and assume also that the changes made in the 1800 through 1817 texts do not solely improve pacing, smooth transitions, and the like, but at the same time serve as an amelioration, a subtle shift towards the compromise the radical addition of epigraph and gloss require; although I admit the latter assumption requires further demonstration. Either way, all the texts contain an element inserted into the story by Wordsworth that remained, despite Coleridge's efforts, beyond his control: the albatross, which became the soubriquet of the Mariner from the moment his tale became popular and upon which "serious" interpretations have forever fixated. He failed to cope with a reading-public to which his more professional friend was more astutely attuned, and not much more than that can be said.

One could argue that Coleridge was aware of how his first readers received the poem. He was certainly candid in conversation four years before he died:

> The fault of the Ancient Mariner consists in making the moral sentiment too apparent and bringing it in too much as a principle or cause in a work of such pure Imagination. (*TT* 1:149)

He reversed Wordsworth's attempt in 1800 to say otherwise, but must have realised during the course of the following decade and more that Wordsworth's reading would prevail. What therefore more plausible than that the devout reader who added the gloss is being mocked, at least in part? In short, that the gloss, with all its contradictions and solemnity, is a mild riposte to those who would try to make sense out of what his verse shows to lie beyond sense, albatross, and all? Karl Kroeber put the matter with characteristic directness:

> What the gloss especially dramatizes for us is both the human compulsion to interpret, to seek a pattern of meaning within a puzzling sequence of events, and the dangerous misapprehensions resulting from such interpreting. (84)

One supposes Charles Lamb would have read the gloss as in part ironic, appreciated the element of drollery, while Mrs. Barbauld demonstrably did not (*TT* 1:272–73). It resembles the addition of "Christabel" Part II in so far as it supplies a prose rationale for a world of mystery, which— deliberately? impishly? at the least with Coleridge's full knowledge, surely?—does not properly fit. "Obscure keys may open simple locks, but simple keys obscure locks never."[12]

The difficulty of the 1798 spellings has been exaggerated and the fine-tuning of some transitions in 1800 and after may be debatable, but many will hold that to dispense with the gloss is to lose the most celebrated prose sentence in English Romanticism. Surely this has to be taken seriously:

> In his loneliness and fixedness, he yearneth towards the journeying Moon, and the stars that still sojourn, yet still move onward; and every where the blue sky belongs to them, and is their appointed rest, and their native country, and their own natural homes, which they enter unannounced, as lords that are certainly expected, and yet there is a silent joy at their arrival.[13]

It is indeed an exhibition performance: the rhythm accumulates a force that carries the imagery and vaguely scriptural overtones upward and onward over a crest of feeling, where it is delivered with a sensation of release. Readers are made to feel on the pulse a yearning for a homecoming that is wholly anticipated in Imagination even if not actually reached. The proviso is important, the mood hangs on future promise, and wistfulness is part of the mood. To an extent, one might say that what is not achieved is part of what is gained: a sense of total perfection that can only exist in hope. The gloss also carries overtones of political meaning from earlier poems by Coleridge, where dreams of release from slavery are fuelled by memories of their native country (see below Chap. 8). And so, if there is a hint of pastiche in the highly worked style, this is also appropriate, as an act of recognition. One should not exaggerate: it does not undercut and there is no mockery here; the touch of realism is entirely appropriate and it can be paralleled in similar epiphanic moments in Coleridge's writing. The gloss is indeed Coleridge's last word on the poem but its ambiguities only magnify those inherent, not contained, in the original version.

6.5 Choice

The necessity of choice must still be faced: how it is possible to read the "Ancient Mariner" properly without committing oneself wholly to one text? Printing the poem with different versions in tandem on facing pages is only a convenience; and the sole advantage of having a second text to hand is that comparison might sharpen awareness of the text one is focused upon. Otherwise, one is stymied like the character in George MacDonald's novel who knew every version of the poem by heart. Meanings can co-exist and overlap in the mind but they cannot be uttered, made outer, without bringing judgement to bear. The need for choice is connected to a theme close to Coleridge the moralist, and just as his ideal poet manages his verses with a light rein (*BL* 2:16), so Will, to some extent or other (*LS* 65–66), must be part of every human act.

> As we know what Life is by *Being*, so we know what Will is by *Acting* (*AR* 269).

Involuntary action is at the mercy of a mechanistic universe: the idea of selfhood dissolves into pantheism; a world of "It is" as opposed to "I am." In short, the position set out in his later prose writing follows from the agenda that emerged over time from writing his earlier poem.

This is not a book about Coleridge's philosophy, and I rehearse the above to make a point about the reading of a poetical text. The present chapter has been concerned with editorial matters as much as literary values, and two further considerations concerning the Variorum part of the Bollingen *Poetical Works* (viz. vol. 2) are relevant here. The first concerns a common misapprehension concerning the synoptic display. The second concerns its relation of the Reading Text (vol. 1).

The "Ancient Mariner" is a good example of the way Coleridge made poems "ingenuously" as a process of discovery, thinking of them more in terms of their process than with an eye on how the finished product might be received. It left him beginning more poems than he finished, as many critics like to observe, but what remained unfinished in one way was in another way better said. For this reason among others, the Bollingen Variorum chooses not to anchor variant readings to the final version (as in E.H. Coleridge's Oxford edition and as Stillinger presupposes). Instead it shows them depending from the earliest version and growing therefrom. In effect, it provides a genetic text developing from its origins in a not wholly predetermined way; and possibilities that arose *en route* and were not pursued are evident in a manner that a final text-display disguises. The model was provided by twentieth-century editions of German Romantic poets—for instance, the great Hölderlin edition of Freidrich Beissner (1943–1985)— with a few modifications and modest improvements. Hans Gabler's "Critical and Synoptic Edition" of *Ulysses* appeared in 1984, adapting a synoptic display to prose, but it is important that it worked towards an Anglo-American (Greg-Bowers) ideal of a final text based on a "continuous manuscript" amalgam that was already, at that time, being challenged by other Joyceans like Daniel Ferrer, Michael Groden, and Claude Jacquet.[14]

The Variorum has sometimes been understood as a print model of what might exist even more satisfactorily in digitised form, where a zero-gravity "matrix of surds"[15] floats weightlessly, its options summoned at a keystroke. For example, a recent report of the Modern Language Association (MLA)'s Committee on Scholarly Editions praises the Bollingen *Poetical Works* as one that enables readers to "toggle back and forth" between texts, as if this was the ultimate purpose of reading (using) it. It must be said plainly that such an activity applies only to a restricted kind of reading. It is true that, when editors work to appraise material, to dissect the bodies of poems and probe their interconnections and reassemble them for intelligible display in the most suitable of available contexts (formats), they must indeed operate like surgeons: their eyes fixed on the job at hand in an insulated limbo, every detail treated as of equal potential significance.

But it is equally true that texts only become alive when literary values come into play, that is, when texts move out of such a removed, impersonal situation. Multiple versions can exist alongside one another in neutral space, their relation comprehended in a passive sort of way, but text loses one kind of complexity to gain another when it moves from a condition of simultaneous possibility into the world of accountability and influence. Texts cross a gap from multiple intention to restricted realisation, in which meaning is simultaneously restricted and fulfilled.

The MLA report cites Jerome McGann in support of the position it takes, that digital-age readers can use the Bollingen Variorum to encounter Coleridge's poems "in a permanent state of multiple vision,"[16] but I think it misunderstands us both. Speaking for myself, the Variorum, for all its many practical advantages, can leave its enthusiasts suspended like Borges's protagonist, "Funes, the Memorious," who is constitutionally unable to forget. Everything lives in his mind, as it was received, without interpretation. "He was the solitary and lucid spectator of a multiform world which was instantaneously and almost intolerably exact" (114). A world of ferocious splendour imprisons him within a world of unrealised potentiality, of dead knowledge, of inaction.

In the foundation period of German editorial theory, F.A. Wolf analysed the Homeric poems as layered composites and argued that the original form of the text "could [n]ever be laid out save in our minds" (47). This is indeed how we understand the many sorts of synoptic edition: multiple layers of document are suspended on the page or screen in a way that can be apprehended, a puppet-theatre of unrealised possibility. What Blake termed "the What" requires a slower, more deliberate response when it is translated into a human situation.

> "O let me be awake, my God!
> "Or let me sleep alway!" (lines 475–76)

Slowness is particularly important when working with digital tools that work faster than we naturally think or feel. Sten Nadolny's novel, *The Discovery of Slowness*, first published as *Die Entdeckung der Langsamkeit* in 1983, describes the life of John Franklin who failed to discover the Northwest Passage that the Mariner and his readers miraculously travel. Digital reading goes faster with clicks, but it can fetishise process as crudely as the old "intentional fallacy" ever did. The most rewarding reading of the "Ancient Mariner" proceeds by a considered appropriation of a single text, in touch with the surrounding public space.

NOTES

1. Gutch Notebook, [23 Mar.–6 Apr. 1795]: *CN* 1:35.
2. At the close of two drafts of "The Ruined Cottage" ("*The Ruined Cottage*" *and "The Pedlar"* ed. Butler 256–59), which Wordsworth completed about the same time as Coleridge finished the "Mariner."
3. *Critical Review* (Oct 1798) extracted in Jackson (ed.) 1:53. Compare Lamb's complaint against this particular phrase to Southey himself in *Letters* ed. Marrs 1:142.
4. Lewis's lines—from his ballad "Alonzo the Brave, and Fair Imogine" in his novel *The Monk*, which Coleridge reviewed—are given in my *Experimental Poetics* 102. The larger pattern of revision is described in the next section below.
5. *Letters* ed. Marrs 1:266.
6. The phrase "becalmed Bark" is also repeated in an earlier line of "To William Wordsworth" (line 30) in a description of France trembling on the edge of revolution, which is curious.
7. They are usefully listed by Dyck at 596–600 esp.
8. Wallen 109 is incorrect to say the single-volume 1852 edition from Moxon is an exception and follows the 1828 text. I suspect he only collated the texts as far as line 74: compare lines 213, 260, and 511.
9. For editions that placed the gloss following the text, separately, see e.g. those published in London by Charles Tilt 1836 and Charles Daly 1837, and in Philadelphia by Herman Hooker 1842. The gloss was omitted in later versions of the text included in anthologies in particular; and both practices remained common well into the 1870s.
10. Some comments by Janzen are helpful here: see his "Samuel Taylor Coleridge on Resonance in the Nature of Things."
11. A sympathetic reading of the illustrations by Larkin, followed by Halsey, was published in *The Coleridge Bulletin*. Beare and Koostra 72 detail the extraordinary liberties Jones took with the text.
12. Beckett *Watt* ed. Ackerley 106.
13. The gloss that accompanies 1798 lines 255–58 in the *Sybilline Leaves* version. The text of the same printed in *Poetical Works* 1828, 1829, and 1834 removes some commas.
14. See, for instance, Attridge and Ferrer (eds.) *Post-structuralist Joyce* and Groden's later conversation with Ferrer in *Romanic Review* (1995).
15. Beckett *Murphy* ed. Mays 72.
16. Clive Hart's words apropos the reader of *Finnegans Wake* cited in *PW* 1:clvi and cited by McGann *New Republic of Letters* 115. The larger point McGann makes about "social context" (113–124) is one I tried to make with reference to reading my edition in a literary (human) way in "Wobbling Pivot."

CHAPTER 7

A Reputation by Default

> Publication – is the Auction
> Of the Mind of Man –
>
> Emily Dickinson[1]

7.1 Terms of Acceptance

This chapter picks up with the argument about Wordsworth in Chaps. 4 and 5. The relation between the "Ancient Mariner" (together with attendant poems like "Christabel" **176** and the "Dark Ladiè" **182**) and certain poems by Wordsworth is of particular interest, partly for reasons of comparison and partly to explain the pressure on Coleridge to rethink, clarify, and amend. Another way of saying this is that Wordsworth—the more ambitious poet who worked to establish himself in the public mind and succeeded in doing so—helped create the context by which the "Mariner" was and still is read. So much is commonplace:

> Wordsworth did more than anyone else to establish the vocation of literature in relation to which Coleridge's, and our own culture's, idea of the literary critic took shape. (Arac 3)

The task is to enlarge the focus in these terms, and explain how the poem arrived at its position in history by a circuitous route.

Wordsworth's success is one background. The other, in tandem, is Coleridge's unsuccess and the mismatch fits perfectly—like Laurel and Hardy, or Vladimir's bad breath and Estragon's smelly feet. Before news of Coleridge's plagiarism or drug addiction became a scandal, he had already been castigated as a reprobate and a turncoat; this by old friends and hostile critics alike, Thelwall and Hazlitt alongside the writers of the conservative *Anti-Jacobin*. His emergent fellow-Lakers, Southey and Wordsworth, the reputation of the second rapidly overtaking the first and living longer, meanwhile stood as counterexamples of family values and moral probity. Very few asserted Coleridge to be the greater man, and Lamb startled Crabb Robinson in 1811 by saying he preferred the "Mariner" to anything Wordsworth had written.[2] D.M. Moir, the erstwhile "Delta," enunciated long-established opinion when, forty years later, he described Coleridge as Wordsworth's equal—"and probably, at one time, superior in genius"—only to reverse the compliment by asserting that Coleridge "started in the race like a Flying Childers, and yet, infirm of purpose, drew up ere the race was half run" (82). The relationship was not based on competition, and one can argue that Coleridge achieved what he set out to do more completely than Wordsworth, but so things appeared then and, only with less moral opprobrium, so they may appear now.

Of course, the misrepresentation is partly Coleridge's fault—in some ways, he worked more easily as a sheltering failure than as a public success—but the unfortunate consequences forever skewed the shape of biographies and selections of his poems. They work their way out in the history of the reception of his best-known poem, each generation inheriting, modifying, and even reacting against the preconceptions of its predecessor instead of trying to begin over again directly with the poem. The once-fashionable cry, "There is no such thing as the thing itself: we are all prisoners of history," is simply an excuse not to make the attempt.[3]

7.2 Provisional Welcome (1800–1850)

The *Edinburgh* review of *Sybilline Leaves* opened with praise of the "Mariner" as a poem "which, when once read, can never afterwards be entirely forgotten" (see Chap. 5). In fact, the review continues in the next sentence to report that the poem is "a very good caricature of the genius of its author," displaying "all the strength and all the weakness, all the extravagancies and eccentricities" of the author. In short, not much had changed since the reviews of the first *Lyrical Ballads*: the poem impressed itself strongly on the minds of readers but they did not know what to make of it and the reports were confused. Thus, the *Critical Review* in 1805 described it as "frantic"; Thomas Noon Talfourd in 1815 (percipiently) as "spell poetry"; the *Monthly Magazine* in 1818 as Coleridge's only work of genius; the *Monthly Review* in 1819 as a forgotten experiment; and Leigh Hunt in 1819 as "that voyage. .. to the brink of all unutterable things."[4] "Christabel," when it appeared in 1816, provoked much more discussion for and against among the chattering classes, while the earlier poem "Love" (aka "Genevieve" **253**) won more uncontested widespread approval.

> Many, who had allowed no merit to my other poems, whether printed or manuscript, and who have frankly told me as much, uniformly made an exception in favour [sc. of both "Christabel" and "Love"]. (*BL* 2:238)

The "Mariner's" fame was part-notoriety—it was too varied to be easily summarised and not long enough to be considered a major statement—and so, without much official approval or understanding, it slipped easily into the public repertoire. Perhaps the moment was ripe for ballads to find readers among those who did not ordinarily enjoy new poetry.[5] Whatever its early accidental success among naval men, it offered adventure and marvels to those who remained at home, while at the same time Wordsworth's sonnets and blank-verse poems were beginning to appeal to more stoic, island virtues.

The three editions of *Poetical Works* published during Coleridge's lifetime positioned the "Mariner" at the opening of Volume 2, following a volume made up of a section headed Juvenile Poems and the remaining titles of *Sybilline Leaves*; and so the same arrangement of poems continued in both multi- and single-volume collections for as long as the family retained copyright up to 1870. Henry Nelson Coleridge—the nephew/son-in-law who had a hand in the 1834 volume—had literary interests; his essays on the poetry in *The Etonian* (1821) and the *Quarterly Review* (1834) are of considerable value; but both he and his wife, Sara Coleridge/Coleridge's daughter, were altogether more occupied with defending Coleridge's general reputation and what one could call his prose interests in the editorial work they undertook. They left the poems and plays largely to look after themselves, as did Derwent Coleridge who took over after the death of Sara; although he did take the opportunity, in the last edition published under his care, to enlarge greatly on what he thought of his father's poetry—an indulgence it seems his sister long forbade.

If the family tidied away Coleridge's poetry (in England, at any rate) in an unhelpful arrangement with relatively expensive publishers, freelance publishers were smarter. The Copyright Act of 1814 set a term of either twenty-eight years or the natural life of the author so that, while the *Christabel* volume and *Sybilline Leaves* were off limits, earlier selections that contained his poems were not. The first anthologists to include verse by Coleridge all passed over the "Mariner" in favour of generally more didactic subject matter,[6] but in 1836, two years after Coleridge's death, Charles Tilt brought out a volume in his Miniature Classical Library for 1/6d under the title *The Ancient Mariner and Other Poems*; and the same selection under the same title continued in print—afterwards from other publishers—up to 1858. Thomas Cox published an edition of the same poems bulked up with the *Wallenstein* translations also in 1836, Charles Daly the same in 1837, Thomas Allman in 1837, and John Chidley in 1838: the four last under the title, *The Poetical and Dramatic Works*. These again were often republished, and it is interesting to note Daly's extensive negative comments on "Christabel" in his Introduction, quoting it at length the while, presumably to persuade purchasers they were missing nothing of worth. American publishers appear to have preferred to follow the family arrangement of poems (they were not constrained by the same copyright laws); and the many Philadelphia reprintings of the 1829 Galignani/Paris piracy after 1831, that bundled Coleridge with Keats and Shelley, followed *Poetical Works* 1829 with a few additions (see *PW* 1:cxxiv–xxv). However, Herman Hooker's pretty little selection (Philadelphia 1842 and much reprinted) opened with the "Mariner"; and the price of the pirate English publications meanwhile reduced so that they also circulated ever more widely. Sherwood, Gilbert, and Piper published an *Ancient Mariner and Other Poems* in their Pocket English Classics series in 1843 for 6d, H.G. Clarke in their Cabinet Series for 1/–, William and Robert Chambers in their *Miscellany of Useful and Entertaining Tracts* No. 59 in 1845[7]; and so the story goes.

All the evidence suggests the fame of the "Ancient Mariner" spread rapidly during the half-century following its first publication: this among a fast-growing audience who were drawn to the poem because of its hearsay reputation, which they in turn spread further. They wanted handy, often pocket-sized editions, sometimes in better bindings for gifts. One might reasonably suppose they made up a readership that spread far beyond the circles of those interested in Coleridge's prose writings.

Others were meanwhile reading in other ways. One has only to remember the comments that Leigh Hunt dropped, in a variety of contexts, on Coleridge's handling of sound in verse; or De Quincey's distinction between three sorts of readers of the "Ancient Mariner"; or Fenton Hort's unequalled discussion of the poem in relation to all of Coleridge's writing as it was then known.[8] Alongside these recorded voices were untold others coming to the poem for the first time and perhaps often not wanting to progress much further. Coleridge's poem was beginning to acquire a totemic resonance it has never lost. It was becoming one of those few English poems everyone has heard about even if they have not read it.

The essential point is the muddle and the celebrity combined. For example, Nathan Drake, who cited Coleridge's verse as "an example of modern excellence in lyric" in 1798, continued to express his enthusiasm in 1820 by nominating the "Mariner" "one of the most tremendous tales of supernatural horror in existence."[9] The restriction was that, for the most part, such enthusiasm was most often expressed in like general terms: "singular," "whimsical," "wild and powerful," "intensity," "awful phantasmagoria" are some of the words and phrases used. Doubts were raised about the lack of moral purpose in the poem, as one might expect in the year when Tennyson succeeded Wordsworth as Laureate.[10] All this while doubts continued to be expressed about the propriety of "Christabel" and "Kubla Khan" (**178**), and while "Love" remained the Coleridge poem most favoured by anthologists. The small selections that appeared in the now-overflowing stream of *Beauties* and *Poetical Forget-Me-Nots* vary in their choices, suggesting there was no consensus about what Coleridge had to offer as a poet. General readers looked to enjoy "The Quarrel between Sir Leoline and Sir Roland de Vaux" (**176** lines 408–26) and "Dialogue Concerning a Good Great Man" (**302**), and, if not, then more poems that were lightly toned, anodyne. The younger generation of Romantic poets (Byron, Keats, Shelley) had earlier found more to engage their serious interest in other poems by Coleridge ("Christabel" in particular), although this is not to say they did not enjoy the "Mariner" in the same spirit as everybody else. For example, Dyce reports that the Byron circle "used to rave" about it and "were constantly quoting it":

> whenever they were guilty of any unfortunate piece of awkwardness,—such as breaking a wine-glass, or spilling a cup of coffee,—they would exclaim, in allusion to their favourite poem, 'Dear me, I have shot an albatross!' (177)

The relative paucity of early parodies of the "Mariner" compared to the number and variety elicited by "Christabel" is however significant: more celebrated the ballad might be, but what to do with it was not so obvious.

7.3 Illustrated and Examined, Honoured and Altered (1850–1910)

What brought the "Mariner" into the mainstream and made it respectable was almost fortuitous. Early stirrings (other than Wordsworth's) to show that the poem had a serious moral purpose can be set aside. The Cambridge Union debate of 1829 in which it figured in an argument about cruelty to animals was only half-serious: that was the point of centring the debate on an albatross and not on fox-hunting. It might as well have been a unicorn: the widespread circulation of the poem rested on uncritical popular appeal. A modern historian, assessing the public debate provoked by the loss of Sir John Franklin's fourth Arctic expedition in 1845, and struck by the number of times the "Mariner" was alluded to or quoted, supposed "it must have been memorized by every English schoolchild after 1798."[11] The subsequent change of status was brought about by an indirect cause: its illustrators. They were attracted to the quickly changing, varied, and dramatic scenes of the poem and able to ignore the considerations arising from Coleridge's aural imagination sketched in Chap. 2. New printing technology had enlarged and improved the means of reproduction, its quality as well as costs, so that publishers were eager to receive and commission illustrated book projects. The first such was the one by David Scott, published in 1837, which Coleridge was shown and on which he commented: as described in Chap. 2, the twenty-five etchings are relatively crude and had a small circulation in comparison with what came later. The publishers, Sampson Low, brought out a trade illustrated edition with twenty-six woodcuts by three artists (Edward Wehnert, Edward Duncan, and Myles Birket Foster) in 1857; the Art Union of London brought out a more elaborate edition of twenty lithograph plates by Sir Joseph Noel Paton in 1863 and, most famously of all, Gustave Doré's large woodblock plates based upon his own pen and wash drawings appeared in 1876, after he had already produced fine and trade editions of many authors (including Milton and Tennyson, but not Wordsworth). The moral element and Christian symbolism is strongly emphasised in the first two of these publications, and if it is less prominent in the third, the sheer scale and dedication of Doré's enterprise—its solemnity and detail—reconstruct the poem as a Victorian icon equivalent to the Albert Memorial. The three publications in their different ways—each of them many times reprinted on both sides of the Atlantic—were not the only illustrated versions to appear. For instance, they were preceded by another publication by Sampson Low in 1854—*A Book of Celebrated Poems, Containing Forty-Three of the Most Popular Poems in the English Language Unabridged*—that presented the "Mariner" (without gloss) accompanied by seven drawings by Kenny Meadows (who also engraved them). By the 1870s, when the forty-two-year period of copyright determined by the 1842 Act ended, and a wave of new editions of collected *Poetical Works* mushroomed, many of them were also illustrated in one way or another; often recycling versions of the originals already cited. By such means, the poem became, so to speak, incorporated.

The Birket Foster and Doré productions were at first expensive, but they worked their influence on another trend that pushed the "Mariner" toward the centre: educational publishing. Joseph Payne, first professor of education at the College of Preceptors in London, had included Coleridge poems in textbooks for children in 1839 and 1845; but Thomas Shorter, secretary of the Working Man's College, after including a few Coleridge pieces in a selection "for School and Home" in 1861, appears to have been the first to include the full text of the "Mariner" (minus gloss) in a much larger school selection published later that same year and many times reprinted. From this later time onward, the poem also began to appear more often in anthologies aimed specifically at children: for instance, and again both times without gloss, in Coventry Patmore's *Children's Garland* (Macmillan 1862) and in *Playtime with the Poets* selected by "a Lady" (Longmans Green 1863). Such titles heralded a storm to follow. Chambers published the poem in a twenty-eight-page "English Classics for Use in Schools" series in 1872; Collins followed with something similar in 1873; James R. Osgood of Boston, Mass., issued the poem as their Vest-Pocket Series No. 14, price 50 cents, in 1876 (this last with five woodcuts which are reliant on Paton's). Other series boasting named editors were the next refinement—the Longman, Green edition of 1878 annotated by E.T. Stevens and D. Morris may be the first—and from then onward a trickle became a river and then a torrent. I must possess twenty—perhaps thirty—separate small editions on my shelves, some edited by university teachers who afterwards became famous, others illustrated by artists who receive only a footnote in history books, cumulatively a testament to an extraordinarily rapid shift of taste and fashion at this time. Coleridge came to be perceived as the author of a single poem that was long but not too long, attractive to children but with "difficulties" to explain and be comprehended, with a moral that could be pointed to and argued for, that could support pictures to make a book for lessons into a book for birthdays, and so the "Ancient Mariner" suddenly appeared to possess everything. When Lowell's "Vision of Sir Launfal" and Tennyson's "Enoch Arden" were the alternative texts for the entrance examinations for university, or as gifts, it was the clear winner.

I should mention one further factor that assisted the "Ancient Mariner's" rapid ascent: a shift of taste that took place in the course of the century, largely separate from the factors so far described, and affected by those particularly sensitive to new currents in poetry. First, although the popularity enjoyed by the poem "Love" owed a good deal to Victorian preconceptions about women, Coleridge's treatment of the subject and comments upon it appealed particularly to members of the Pre-Raphaelite Brotherhood, whose paintings and ideas gained increasing acceptance. D.G. Rossetti, their leader,[12] considered Coleridge at his greatest as a love-poet, but so in a different way did Henry Nelson Coleridge in *The Etonian*: Rossetti's ideas were mixed up with an interpretation of "Christabel" and a heightened sense of love that destroys as well as saves, the ultimate statement of which is Theodore Watts-Dunton's novel *Aylwin* (1898).[13] Contemporary with this shift of fashion, Pater published his thoughts on Coleridge, first in the *Westminster Review* in 1867, then as his introduction to his selection of Coleridge's poems in 1880, and he brought the two pieces of writing together in *Appreciations* (1889). It was an aesthetic view of Coleridge, consonant with movements of art and poetry in France that defined the *fin de siècle* in England and indeed America. By such means—or call them circumstances—a quality of feeling evolved in which the "Mariner" was seen afresh. "Christabel" was the preferred poem— Swinburne placed it first in his 1869 selection—and it is no accident that the theory of meter it was supposed to embody gained in favour and was much discussed at the time. The ballad was also a beneficiary. Besides the illustrated editions and the school editions, the dozen or twenty years following 1890 saw the production of a number of tastefully produced anthologies, selections, complete editions, and illustrated editions. Andrew Lang's *Selections* with illustrations by Patten Wilson (Longmans, Green 1898) and Ernest Hartley Coleridge's *Poems* with illustrations by Gerald Metcalf (John Lane/The Bodley Head 1907) certainly deserve special mention alongside the earlier illustrated editions I have singled out. Others are masterpieces of book production and include some of the most intelligent commentary—by Richard Garnett, Alice Meynell and Arthur Symons among others—that the poems as a body of work have ever received, a golden moment when the "Mariner" always asked to be read on its own terms. Although the myth of Coleridge as failed poet prevailed, his poem emerged unscathed as, in Pater's words:

> Coleridge's one great complete work, the one really finished thing, in a life of many beginnings.[14]

A lot changed in the later half of the nineteenth century. The poem that the ten-year-old Macaulay came upon in a copy of *Lyrical Ballads* on Hannah More's bookshelves in 1810, and devoured "with what delight and horror,"[15] survived an ascendant Victorian reputation as an unsound, even dangerous oddity, and became a favourite to be read in the nursery and taught in the classroom: an adventure story that told a moral lesson. More sophisticated poetasters—nay, sophisticated literary sensibilities like Ernest Rhys and W.B. Yeats—were at the same time translating Coleridge's supernatural into something Celtic, more purely faery and altogether less moral. Baudelaire's "L'Albatros" threw a new perspective on the animal hanging from the Mariner's neck, and Rimbaud's "Bateau ivre" and Conrad's *Lord Jim* in their different ways destabilised notions of the voyage as redemption. When Andrew Lang included just three Coleridge poems in his iconic *Blue Poetry Book*—selections from the "Mariner" and "Christabel" and all of "Kubla Khan" (not "Love")[16]—he established the core of any discussion of Coleridge's poetry for the next hundred years. He could affirm in his Introduction:

> The three most famous poems of Coleridge may be above a child's full comprehension, but they lead him into a world not realised, "an unsubstantial fairy place," bright in a morning mist, like our memories of childhood. (10).

History was to modify his hopes somewhat.

7.4 Researched, Cherished, Changing Places (1890–1934)

Scholarly research began to catch up with Coleridge as his poetical reputation revived. Editors began to take notice of different versions and retrieve uncollected texts (Richard Herne Shepherd in 1880, Thomas Ashe in

1885), and bibliographers began to set to work (W.F. Prideaux revising R.H. Shepherd in 1900, and J.L. Haney moving forward afresh in 1903). Ernest Hartley Coleridge (EHC) produced editions of the letters and a selection from the notebooks (both 1895); also a facsimile edition of "Christabel" (1907), small and large selections of the poems (1905, 1907), and his two-volume edition of *Poetical Works* (1912) that was immediately recognised as authoritative. The new standard in editing Coleridge texts was anticipated by James Dykes Campbell (JDC), who produced a single-volume *Poetical Works* (Macmillan 1893) that continued in print to 1938. The two editors came from different literary backgrounds (EHC personally acquainted with Hopkins and Swinburne, JDC with Robert Browning and with a scholarly interest in Thomas Lovell Beddoes) and the difference left its mark on the way they presented their shared concern. Despite his advantages, JDC lacked the family connection that made EHC's work the more complete.

In all these advances, Coleridge studies followed in the wake of Wordsworth, whose fame was far greater,[17] and whose *Poetical Works* had been published, in eight volumes edited in chronological order by William Knight, between 1882 and 1886 (with a *Life* following in three further volumes in 1889). Wordsworth had drawn readers to the landscape he wrote about to a remarkable extent. After he died and the new occupants of Rydal Mount settled in, visitors turned towards Dove Cottage as a place of pilgrimage so that subtly, as a result, different poems achieved prominence (Yoshikawa 99–124). The shift of taste was enormously accelerated by Matthew Arnold's selection of the *Poems* in 1879, which by its strong emphasis on Wordsworth's shorter poems encouraged public taste to move further away from the laureate poet, directing it instead towards poems written in the decade 1798–1808. The changing attitudes towards Wordsworth's earlier years and writing bear on Coleridge in that the poets' year as neighbours in Somerset was better remembered; attempts to save the Nether Stowey cottage followed the rescue of Dove Cottage for the nation[18]; and the *Lyrical Ballads* venture was resurrected as an historical moment. Edward Dowden published his type-facsimile of the 1798 text in 1890 (reprinted in larger runs in 1891 and 1898), which was followed in turn by annotated editions for school use in 1898 (ed. Thomas Hutchinson), 1903 (ed. George Sampson), and 1911 (ed. H. Littledale).

In some respects, the pairing of the two poets continued as it always had been for Coleridge: the one who failed to fulfil his promise. In other respects, his reputation as author of three magical poems was never higher.

The "Mariner" was in process of losing some of its sense of danger, which transferred as the twentieth century dawned to the emergent "Kubla Khan" where it was more narrowly contained. The evidence of his poems as they were printed and bound at this time suggests a new audience that wanted suede bindings and tastefully decorated covers; and specialist publishers of the "Mariner"—like Siegle Hill and Lamley—delivered the goods. The style fitted into houses built by Charles Voysey and furnished at the recently founded Liberty's on Regent Street; Roger Fry, along with Duncan Grant and Vanessa Bell, founded Omega Workshops in July 1913 as an enterprise that would carry forward the design standards of Manet and Cézanne into the decorative and fine arts. However, I am afraid the caustic way Wyndham Lewis and Ezra Pound read the cultural situation in *Blast* and "Hugh Selwyn Mauberley" is probably just, and the First World War only compounded a sentimental hold on the good things that were being threatened and lost. From this point of view, Britain's economic and political decline was matched by a turning-inwards of its cultural life. Edward Thomas toured the Quantocks on his bicycle and lost his life dreaming of Adlestrop,[19] Geoffrey Grigson read Coleridge through Samuel Palmer's eyes, and Coleridge the poet was inserted into a neo-romantic landscape of which Culbone Church, etched in its wooded combe, is a representative emblem.[20] The poems were taken to heart, much cherished, and lost in the bosom of the family. The situation in America is obviously different, but it was an American who applied the phrase Conversation Poems to Coleridge's blank-verse meditations[21] and thereby encouraged a way of misreading those finely tuned, highly experimental poems to suit the climate of the coming times. The reception of Coleridge's poem in Europe was different again—a line traced backward through Baudelaire and Poe enabled some notable translations that recaptured the adventurousness of the original[22]—but the English way, back through the lost generation that bequeathed Ronald Firbank, the Woolves, and Arthur Whaley, has not been so lucky. The assimilation of Coleridge the poet into the Southey-Rogers-Scott equivalents of subsequent times overlooks the fact that, unlike Wordsworth, he wrote outside and against his own time to the end. The "Mariner" was incorporated into the British national tradition separately from his thinking in prose, and has survived only because it contains the diverse range of appeal described above.

To return to the main narrative. As the fruits of Coleridge being researched and cherished began to make themselves known in the early decades of the twentieth century, the number of basic educational textbooks slowed down considerably. Their scope enlarged to include a broader sample of Coleridge's poems, often with a longer introduction. Most of them showed an awareness lacking fifty years before of the difference between the first and later versions of the "Mariner" text, often printing two versions. Otherwise they represent no advance on earlier annotated selections like those of Tuley Francis Huntington (New York 1899) and Andrew George (Boston, Mass. 1902): the first of these, after many reprintings, was reissued in a revision by H.Y. Moffett and illustrations by A. Gladys Peck in 1929 and continued to be reprinted up to 1938.[23] The burden of them all continued to be that the gap between the three inexplicably great poems and the remainder was huge but might be ameliorated slightly in ways suggested by the different choices of surround: choices if not of poems then morsels of criticism. The "Ancient Mariner" continued to receive special treatment by artists, as if it existed apart from all else, of which Willy Pogany's treatment (1910) is the most extravagant and David Jones's (1929) is the best known. Meanwhile, old quarrels on the wider front were renewed, as in René Wellek's attack on Coleridge's plagiarism in *Immanuel Kant in England* (1931); and new ground was uncovered, as in Alice Snyder's researches into Coleridge's later unpublished prose and in John Muirhead's *Coleridge as Philosopher* (1930). So history advanced towards the centenary of Coleridge's death in 1934, which proved to be a well-advertised familial affair. Meanwhile two further events that determined the approach to Coleridge through the decades following are yet to be described.

7.5 Two Landmarks and Some Twisted Wires

First, John Livingston Lowes's *Road to Xanadu* (1927, rev. 1930) enjoyed an instant success outside the world of Coleridge scholarship and at the same time had a distorting effect on the narrow world within. While what it said was not entirely new,[24] it was published by a commercial company (Houghton Mifflin, with Constable in Britain) who made sure it was reviewed in a plethora of national newspapers and periodical magazines as well as in academic journals. It was written in a personable style that made research appear a process of exciting excavation and discovery: an accumulation of apparently random details that came together, miraculously, in a way that matched poems that had already achieved singular eminence as mysteries. Lowes's serendipity beggared belief; it seemed a perfect match; it was a prolonged glimpse into the scholar's and the poet's mind; the book was an instant classic, went into many editions and is still in print.

However, while it will indeed remain a classic—"the Great Pyramid of John Livingston Lowes"[25]—one might wonder if its very success did not exert a baleful influence. It set the "Ancient Mariner" and "Kubla Khan" apart, not just from "Christabel" but from the surround of poems from which all three developed and throw light on. It is a study of sources that are certainly behind the text but the "Mariner" as a ballad stands strikingly free of allusions (with which sources are often confused): nothing in the story depends for its full appreciation on knowing where it came from. A lot of thinking also stands behind the poem: not alluded to but no less relevant (for instance, Coleridge's reading in Hartley and Neoplatonism) but that is ignored. What happens when the poem is read as a poem—the continuous shifting of points of view, the felt connections, the modifications of style—are of little account in Lowes's story. *The Road to Xanadu* certainly lifted Coleridge's name out of purlieus of learning into a unique place in higher education, but it skewed the understanding of his poetry. Its methodology encouraged an attention to attendant circumstances: produced a bevy of specialist articles on further sources and aspects. The majority of succeeding book-length studies of Coleridge's verse are also of this sort. The best is John Beer's *Coleridge the Visionary* (1959, and many times reprinted): what amounts to a second volume in the same vein. I hope this will be understood as the highest compliment; nevertheless the Great Pyramid lies heavy upon ground where green shoots should have grown.

The second landmark person was I.A. Richards, whose *Principles of Literary Criticism* (1925) promised a modern fresh start, commonsensical and deliberately "lacking in the condiments which have come to be expected in writings upon literature" (3). He cites Meynell's comments on the "Mariner" as of a kind to be shunned, recommends the *Biographia* definition of Imagination on condition its theological implications are ignored, and labels Coleridge's separate critical comments as erratic but provocative (76–77, 191, 224). The approach was applied to the reading of a number of poems in his next book, *Practical Criticism* (1929), the title borrowed from the *Biographia* (*BL* 2:19), while *Coleridge on Imagination* (1934) engages more fully with the subject of its title, in its turn taking issue with Lowes's argument that Fancy and Imagination are not two powers but one (31–35). Kathleen Coburn said afterwards on behalf of her generation, in her essay on "I.A.R. and S.T.C.":

> [H]is was the first really critical use of *Biographia Literaria* to make us take it seriously in the context of our own time. (242)

Richards's three books together succeeded in establishing a programme for reading in North America whose influence quickly spread wider than the parallel movement in England (the *Scrutiny* group) during the 1930s.[26] Protocols for the close reading of texts per se, separate from their background and larger implications, were quickly established and the New Criticism was born. Coleridge was somehow at the centre, but more as patron saint, and consulted only to be fitted to the new dispensation. Richards's respect for Coleridge continued, and grew in a different direction from the uses made of his earlier interpretation. His friendship with Coburn led him to admit the crudity of his earlier views, he edited *The Portable Coleridge* (Viking 1950), which included some seventy-three poems, and he published a lecture ten years later on behalf of Coleridge's later poems.[27] His feeling for poetry was intense—I remember him quoting Swinburne, Coleridge's earlier champion, by the yard on the one occasion we met—but the influence of his earlier books proved stronger than his later ones, which I feel were more apologetic than persuasive. Vain attempts to recover an audience for Coleridge's later poems had been made before and were to be made by others after.[28]

The reputation of the "Mariner" advanced through the nineteenth century, as I have described, with a logic of its own untouched by Coleridge's writing in prose. While the *Biographia* caused a momentary stir at the moment of first publication, the second edition with its lengthy introduction and defensive notes by Henry Nelson and Sara Coleridge in 1847 passed relatively unnoticed. Coleridge's reputation as a theologian was the point of discussion at the time and a second edition of *Inquiring Spirit* in 1849 attracted far more attention. Collections of miscellaneous, Shakespeare and other criticism appeared in the last two decades of the century, and the nudge given by the upcoming *Lyrical Ballads* centenary encouraged the indefatigable Andrew George to publish relevant selected chapters of the *Biographia* under the title *Coleridge's Principles of Criticism* in 1897.[29] However, John Shawcross's new edition from the Clarendon Press in 1907 decisively established Coleridge the critic on a new footing.[30] Its principal feature was the addition of Coleridge's otherwise hard-to-find Neoplatonic musings on aesthetics at the close of Volume 2, but very few readers took much notice of them.[31] They concentrated instead on the discussions of Imagination in Chaps. 13 and 14, and again on Wordsworth's poetry in the chapters following. In this way, they prepared the ground for the sort of makeover Richards had in store and at the same time bolstered Coleridge's role as supporting critic to poet Wordsworth. The effect was a double whammy: Coleridge's thoughts about poetry became separated from his practice as a poet at the same moment that he slid more firmly into the role of privileged explicator of his brother-poet's meaning.

Thomas Raysor's highly regarded and useful collections of *Coleridge's Shakespearean Criticism* and *Miscellaneous Criticism* appeared in 1930 and 1936, respectively. And here I quote from a letter that I found tucked into a second-hand copy of the former, which I purchased from an American bookseller, in which Raysor replies to a fellow scholar who had written with comments and congratulations on the collection:

> I was delighted to have you go beyond these historical details to raise frankly the question of values. I have often been disturbed by the semi-religious references made to Coleridge's Shakespearean criticism and to *Biographia Literaria*, and I have been puzzled by the indifference of critics to all of Coleridge's poetry except the three great poems of black magic which appear in the anthologies for secondary schools.[32]

Raysor's reflections bear with special authority on the present discussion and they continued to apply through his working lifetime and beyond. In a similar vein one might complain that the continuous interest in Coleridge's life story, nourished by E.L. Griggs's two-volume *Uncollected Letters* (1932) and embodied in the succeeding biographies by Edmund Chambers and Lawrence Hanson (both 1938), reflects the same indifference. The new materials being uncovered were used to reignite and maintain a predetermined story: not to reconstruct it.

During the next fifty years, the majority of commentators used Coleridge's comments on the One Life of Nature to explicate Wordsworth without taking into account that Coleridge was himself moving away from such ideas during the time he advised Wordsworth on his epic project; they discussed Coleridge's Mystery Poems in a manner that lost sight of their mystery. Educators ignored the danger that classroom discussion was becoming restricted by classroom procedures in a way unknown before; that their growing emphasis on language, images, and symbolism might encourage deafness to the music of words. The blindness that accompanied the many insights gained by the New Criticism between the Coleridge anniversaries of 1934 and 1972 are well enough known to leave the matter here. They can be summed up by saying that a great many minor things about the "Ancient Mariner" became known and better understood, while some fundamentally important things were mislaid, or overlaid, or even lost.

7.6 Apotheosis and Aftermath (1934–1972)

The public perception of Coleridge enlarged in the decades between 1940 and 1960 to elevate him into something like a cult figure: a name to conjure with like Einstein or Picasso or Freud that passed like a relay baton between several succeeding and competing generations of critics. Stanley Edgar Hyman's popular survey of the critical scene, *The Armed Vision* (1948) took its title from the *Biographia* (*BL* 1:118) and found reason to discuss Coleridge's influence more than any other predecessor. At the same time, while the reputation of Coleridge's critical prose inflated as a thing apart from his own poetry, it was reaffirmed as an adjunct to Wordsworth's. The major architect of this construction was M.H. Abrams, who was in the beginning stages of the Bollingen project named as editor of the *Biographia*, a task later assumed by his old Harvard teacher W.J. Bate in conjunction with James Engell. In two magisterial monographs and a series of influential essays, alongside his editorship of *The Norton Anthology of English Literature*, Abrams set up Wordsworth and Coleridge as the complementary poet–critic pair at the core of English Romanticism and, by implication, at the foundation moment of Modern Literature. The strong Transcendentalist strain in the American tradition bequeathed a particular understanding of what Coleridge meant by Imagination that was modified by a prior immersion in Wordsworth's poetry. Abrams was cogent and hugely informed, and well able to read his interpretation into the prevailing sense of Coleridge's poetry—not least the so-called Conversation Poems. I suggest (in Chap. 8) that his reading lacks Coleridge's "bodied sense" of Reason (Janzen's term) but it gained near universal assent in its time. So Coleridge ruled at Wordsworth's side for several decades, but the inevitable reaction followed and is now also part of history. Deconstruction turned the New Criticism on its head, New Historicism in America and a more frankly materialist criticism in Britain combined with Feminism in both territories to open up formalist readings to wider cultural concerns (Post Colonialism, Media Studies, etc.). The "Romantic Ideology" was identified as a spectre hanging over twentieth-century views of the past, although it was never made sufficiently clear that it was an early Victorian, retrospective construction,[33] and that Wordsworth and Coleridge were not exactly in step as poets or critics.

So the 1934 and 1972 anniversaries turned out to mark rising and falling moments in Coleridge's reputation and influence as a literary critic, as well as his status as something of a celebrity. There were celebrations and exhibitions again in 1972, but the two publications that caused the most stir were Norman Fruman's *Damaged Archangel* and William Empson's and David Pirie's selection of Coleridge's poems. Neither of them said anything new to the cognoscenti, but Fruman's rehash of the old charges of plagiarism and Empson's sclerotic indignation that the "Mariner" was being pushed as a Christian poem made good journalistic copy. The real scandal meanwhile continued unnoticed: the nineteenth-century paradigm of a poet with three poems to his name, otherwise destroyed by metaphysics and drugs, prevailed through Coleridge's rise and fall as a critical eminence. The aftermath encouraged some slim pickings among the political implications of his earlier poems; for instance, noting the background of the Bristol slave trade in the "Mariner," but this brings the understanding of the workings of the poem no further forward than any of Lowes's sources. The depressing truth is, that if one looks at the succession of selections from Coleridge for educational use that appeared during the middle and later century, they vary little, either from each other or from their predecessors when the "Mariner" was discovered as an educational text. The general introductions are shaped by the biographical formula bequeathed by Hazlitt and the alignment with Wordsworth; critical prose joined verse early on, with increasing snippets from letters, table-talk, and notebooks. Following mid-century, and the biographical interest in Sara Hutchinson, "Dejection: An Ode" (**293**) became a necessary component; and a token interest in Coleridge's "later poems" is evident to a varying extent although little guidance was given as to how they might relate to earlier poems. Differences arise: some presentations are strikingly dull; some for the first time print different versions of the "Mariner" on facing pages; it is always interesting to see where the three Mystery poems are placed in a non-chronological arrangement; on a few occasions, the editorial comment becomes genuinely engaged (the Dell edition by G. Robert Stange 1959 and the Signet edition by Harold Bloom 1972 are rare examples). Otherwise, the list makes an assemblage of routine jobs. There is clearly a perennial market for Coleridge poems as gift books and for classroom use; the products are made over into "new improved versions" every decade, or contrived to offer a "unique selling-point," and the differences are marginal. You make your choice as if you were buying a birthday card.

I hope this will not be misunderstood. A lot of very well-informed professional research has been devoted to understanding a complicated subject and helping serious students. Previously unknown or forgotten facts have been discovered, presented clearly, and debated with passion. Literary discussion was more detailed and exact ("professional") by the end of the twentieth century than at the beginning. I am only claiming that when you line up fifty selections of Coleridge poetry from the past hundred years they differ less than fifty automobiles from the same period: small changes in design and arrangement, yes, but not able to travel any faster to the desired destination in current circumstances—which itself, in the interim, is often forgotten. This sounds extreme but I can think of no English writer who has been stuck in such a rut for so long. Donne and other Metaphysical Poets were rediscovered in the twentieth century: Coleridge, who achieved equal fame during the same period, did so within parameters that were fashioned before 1850. The encircling, stifling myth is what I complain of: it clearly has a life of its own. See for instance Derek Mahon's comment in an interview with Nicholas Wroe: "Heaney is a Wordsworth man and I'm a Coleridge man. I love the poetry, and the trajectory of his life has always fascinated me."[34] That trajectory, which Coleridge's biographers have mimicked with glorious beginnings and less successful endings, has been superimposed on what he wrote, as the archetypal Romantic myth. "Christabel" has emerged from the shadows where Lowes's exclusion left it to become a favourite among vampire lovers, "Kubla Khan" is particularly cherished by sci-fi (science-fiction) enthusiasts, but, when the author of the "Ancient Mariner" joins them, all three become lesser things. Following literally in Coleridge's footsteps is no way to go when so much of his life was in the mind. Watchet is quite unlike most reader's mental picture of the little port the Mariner left behind; Ilfracombe, with its chapel-lighthouse atop a hill adjacent to the harbour is far closer (see cover and Chap. 1), but Wordsworth and Coleridge cannot be proven to have walked so far. The poem in question asks its readers to perform an imaginative act, to disarm their mundane search for explanation. It means nothing unless one allows oneself to be spellbound and works from there.[35]

7.7 Begin Again Better

No chapter should end on such a downbeat note:

> Where no Hope is, Life's a Warning
> That only serves to make us grieve.
>
> ("Album Verses" **593**; *PW* 1:1014)

And I have passed over a project that occupied the larger part of the last century and might yet deliver Coleridge when its lessons are fully absorbed. I mean of course Kathleen Coburn's work on the Notebooks that put them, and eventually the larger part of Coleridge's extant manuscripts, into the public domain, together with the Bollingen project that eventually funded the publication of all Coleridge's writings excepting his letters.[36] She gave her own account of the story, *In Pursuit of Coleridge* (1977), and I need only make a few additional observations before turning to the change one would hope the Collected Coleridge might bring about.

Coburn's inspiration grew directly out of the state of Coleridge studies as they were developing while she was a student. As I said, I doubt if *The Road to Xanadu* helped anybody to read the "Ancient Mariner" as it primarily asks to be read but it very directly inspired her to leave no stone unturned as a researcher into Coleridge's background: it stands directly behind the extraordinary lengths she (and George Whalley) went in their pursuit of Coleridge's reading. Her response to I.A. Richards was as much personal as academic, from the moment "the guideless climber" leapt onto a table to lecture at Oxford.[37] My impression was that she particularly admired his physical and intellectual fearlessness, his dedication to finding practical solutions, the sparkling vitality of his mind and person: in the same way as she also admired a few others, like Owen Barfield, whom she knew less well, "Richards gave us a new vision of the role of Coleridge." Otherwise, beside her innate sense of fairness and of an injustice to be redressed, she remembered family members like Sara Coleridge who did so much, at such cost, and left so much to be done. She also spoke fondly of the inspirational lectures of Pelham Edgar on the Romantic poets at Victoria College and dedicated her Alexander Lectures to his memory.[38] Perhaps enough to say that she knew she was lucky to be a Canadian, and was being treated as such by the Ottery Coleridges; it helped her afterwards as well in her dealings with Herbert Read and others in gaining Bollingen support. A charmless lad from Derbyshire or Oklahoma might not have fared so well. She was not a natural organiser, but the way she facilitated the many things that happened around her was miraculous.

The Bollingen collected edition was planned in the late 1950s and began to appear in 1969 with Barbara Rooke's edition of *The Friend*. This was warmly received in a wide range of journals but, like the two editions published in Coleridge's lifetime, never yet made the impression it should. I charted the uneven progress of the edition at large in an essay published some years ago,[39] and three further observations are relevant.

First, the later published volumes made a much less immediate impression than the earlier ones. This clearly results from changing intellectual fashions, and given where Coleridge stood at the start there are no grounds for complaint. Second, the cumulative impression of the edition has become more properly important as it has been absorbed. The lecture "On the Prometheus of Aeschylus" (together with much else in *Shorter Works and Fragments*), the re-edited *Aids to Reflection* and *Opus Maximum* constitute a body of work that put an end to the legend that Coleridge's years at Highgate were spent in idle talk, his imaginative and intellectual powers in decline. The edition contains, from end to end, the record of an extraordinarily sustained, endlessly provocative journey. Third, the idiosyncrasies of the edition will become more apparent as readers become more familiar with it by use, which I sincerely intend as a tribute to Coburn's style of command and partly a reflection on the complicated background history of publication.

What of the *Poetical Works* volumes, in particular? Their considerable bulk and corresponding expense has undoubtedly limited their usefulness. The publishers at one stage intended to publish an affordable, single-volume paperback of the poems alone (as they did of the *Biographia* in 1984), but they decided not to proceed in the evolving circumstances of the new millennium. My guess—or hope—is that the *Poetical Works* will none the less combine with the remainder of the set and thereby constitute a body of work in which poetry and literary-critical interests are mutually part of the larger whole. Put another way, that poetry—and the "Ancient Mariner" in particular—will be integrated into the larger body of work containing philosophy and theology as well as politics and criticism. The overwhelming evidence of the liveliness and originality of Coleridge's mind in his late prose-writing is the greatest encouragement to recognise that the poems he was writing at the same time contain similar qualities. His writing demonstrates that he was always on a different track from Wordsworth, although the sense of intense affinity at the beginning of their friendship might obscure the fact; just as his disinclination to protest openly against Wordsworth's repeated recasting of his supernatural "by daylight," described in Chaps. 4 and 5, has clouded the critical, almost parodic dimension of "Christabel" Part II and the "Mariner's" 1817 prose-surround. One might compare the overall effect of the complete Bollingen Coleridge to the Cornell Wordsworth that proceeded under the general guidance of Stephen Parrish, to discover a new early Wordsworth that later revisions overwrote. The recovery of Coleridge's late prose in particular encourages a fresh look at what he wrote, alongside his verse, and it will be seen that his end follows from his beginning and casts a backward light.

NOTES

1. *Poems: Reading Edition* no.788.
2. *Henry Crabb Robinson on Books and Their Writers* ed. Morley 1:17; see also Lamb *Letters* ed. Marrs 1:143 on how the "'Marinere' plays more tricks with the mind" than "Tintern Abbey."
3. I mapped the evolution of Coleridge's poetical reputation at large in *Experimental Poetics* 15–40. The present chapter focuses specifically on the peculiar history of the "Ancient Mariner" and pays more attention to matters like Coleridge's reputation in relation to Wordsworth's. In the few places where the discussion overlaps, I have not duplicated references.
4. Anon *Critical Review* 3rd ser. 5 (1805: 229); Talfourd *Pamphleteer* 5 (1816: 458–61); Anon *Monthly Magazine* 46 (1818: 407–09); *Monthly Review* 88 (1819: 24–38); Hunt *Indicator* 1 (1819: 75–76).
5. As persuasively suggested by Bennett in her Introduction to *British War Poetry in the Age of Romanticism* 46–67. Cf. the popularity of Kipling's ballads during both World Wars.
6. For example, S[tephen?] J[ones?] *Poetical Beauties* (London: I. Wallis, 1798), C. Earnshaw *The Wreath* (Huddersfield: T. Smart [1801?], and John Evans *The Parnassian Garland* ([London:] Albion Press, 1807)—all of whom, of course, were in breach of copyright.
7. A sympathetic mainly biographical note on p. 17 of the Chambers *Tracts*, following the *Ancient Mariner* and praising that poem in particular (by quoting liberally from the *Quarterly Review* 1834), laments that Coleridge's poems are excluded from ordinary readers by their price.
8. For Hunt, see the numerous entries in Haven, Haven and Adams *Bibliography* and Crawford *Bibliography*. For De Quincey (originally published in 1847), see *Collected Writings* ed. Masson 13:195–96. And for Hort, see "Coleridge" in *Cambridge Essays*.
9. *Literary Hours* (1798: 456); *Winter Nights* (1820) 1:125.
10. See e.g. James Elishama Smith, ed. "Wildness and Extravagance" (1850).
11. Maurice Hodgson "The Literature of the Franklin Search" 9–10.
12. His pen-and-ink drawing entitled *Genevieve* (1848) is now at the Fitzwilliam Museum, Cambridge.
13. Catherine Maxwell has a good discussion of *Aylwin* in her *Second Sight* 166–96.
14. "Coleridge" in his *Appreciations* (1889: 101).

15. Macaulay *Journals* (14 Sept. 1852) 3:287. He does not specify which edition of *LB*, but it appears likely to have been the first: see Derwent Coleridge "Introductory Essay" xl–xli. More and Coleridge met in person only once, in 1814.
16. Illustrated by W.J. Ford and Lancelot Speed; published by Longmans, Green, 1891; and reprinted many times.
17. Palgrave's *Golden Treasury* (1861) included forty-one poems by Wordsworth, more than any other poet, and only two by Coleridge ("Love" and "Youth and Age"). "Kubla Khan" and the "Ancient Mariner" were included in Palgrave's *Golden Treasury of English Song* (1875), and "Kubla Khan" was added to the *Golden Treasury* in the 1891–1896 editions. Hamo Thorneycroft's bust of Coleridge joined the life-size statue of Wordsworth in Westminster Abbey (installed 1854) in 1885.
18. In 1908 and 1890 respectively; see Miall on the Stowey campaign.
19. I need hardly add that I share W.B. Yeats's view *contra* Wilfred Owen that poetry is not in the pity. The high reputation and still-enlarging influence of Thomas rests on the same kind of non-literary judgement that in Coleridge's case worked to his disadvantage.
20. The period taste is surveyed only too kindly by Alexandra Harris *Romantic Moderns*.
21. See Harper "Coleridge's Conversation Poems." Interestingly, the Utilitarian reviewer John Bowring was one of the few earlier critics to read these blank-verse poems in this way: see him on "Fears in Solitude" in *Westminster Review* Jan. 1830 in Jackson (ed.) 1:525–56 at 532–35 in particular. Stopford Brooke's *Golden Book of Coleridge* (J.M. Dent 1905; reprinted in Everyman's Library 1906 and many times thereafter) was the first important selection to give the Meditative Poems special prominence.
22. See the comments on French, Spanish, Italian, and Portuguese translations in Shaffer and Zuccato.
23. And I add for the record that the second of these, George's *Select Poems*, was reissued in England in a different binding in 1903, selling at 2/6d, but was quickly withdrawn because it infringed the copyright of J.D. Campbell's widow, W. Hale White acting on her behalf.
24. For instance, although Lowes xi took care to record that much of what he wrote "had already found place in courses at Harvard and Radcliffe as early as 1919," Ivor James previously discussed the influence of one of his most important exhibits, Thomas James's *Strange and Dangerous Voyage*, in his widely noticed *The Source of "The Ancient Mariner"* (1890); which in turn only developed a local awareness which circulated in Bristol circles during the 1860s and 1870s (see J.F. Nicholls *Bristol Biographies* 76–77). Again, William Hale White recorded and continued J.D. Campbell's early prosely-

tising on behalf of Thomas James as a source up until the time of his death in 1913: see *Last Pages from a Journal* 53.
25. McFarland "Foreword: John Livingston Lowes and Coleridge's Poems" xvi. I also note that my 2014 Princeton Legacy Library reprint misspells the author's name on the top cover: a sign that Lowes's fame is crumbling or that university presses are not what they used to be?
26. I quickly add that Richards's most adept pupil in England, William Empson, was equally indebted to Laura Riding and Robert Graves's *Survey of Modernist Poetry* (1927). How different the direction of English studies might have been if that eccentric but penetrating book had enjoyed the same success as *Practical Criticism.*
27. For the modification of his views, see the introductory material to the third, Midland Book edition of *Coleridge on Imagination* (Bloomington 1960). For the lecture, see *Coleridge's Minor Poems* (Missoula 1960).
28. Before by John Rickards Mozley in *Quarterly Review* (1868). Afterwards by George Whalley in *Transactions of the Royal Society of Canada* (1964).
29. Published by D.C. Heath, Boston, Mass. The same selection of Coleridge was published alongside Wordsworth's Prefaces ed. George Sampson (Cambridge University Press) in 1920. Compare the tandem poetry selections, like Guy Boas's *Wordsworth and Coleridge* (Thomas Nelson and Sons, 1925), where the "Mariner" is paired with *Peter Bell* under the heading "Poems of Retribution."
30. A few biographical remarks on Shawcross (1871–1966) are included in his son's autobiography, *Life Sentence* 11–13, 24, 269–70. He was a visiting professor of English at Giessen (Hesse) in 1902, where his son whom he named Hartley was born, and, much later, for a period, a lecturer at Liverpool. His translation of *Faust* into English rhyming-verse appeared in 1934 and 1959.
31. Ezra Pound was one: see John Espey "The Inheritance of Τό Καλόν."
32. One-page typed letter, signed and dated 28 Mar. 1931, on University of Nebraska headed paper. The recipient is not named ("Dear Sir") but I wonder from other references in the letter if it was Ernest Bernbaum, professor at the University of Illinois and author of *Anthology of Romanticism and Guide Through the Romantic Movement* (1929). Bernbaum later wrote the chapter on Wordsworth, and Raysor the chapter on Coleridge's poetry (with Wellek adding a separate chapter on Coleridge's philosophy and ideas), in *The English Romantic Poets: A Review of Research* (New York: Modern Language Association of America, 1950; 2nd ed. revised. 1956) of which Raysor was the general editor.
33. As shown in impressive detail by Whalley "England: Romantic-Romanticism." The irony is, I'm afraid, that Whalley's own critical commentaries on Coleridge as poet are afflicted by the ideology he historicises.

34. In "A Sense of Place" (2006). See also his poem "Biographia Literaria" in *Life on Earth* (2008: 13–14).
35. Karl Kroeber makes some excellent recommendations to this effect in his "Mariner's Rime to Freud's Uncanny."
36. I might add that, if it had not been for Earl Griggs's tragic early death in a traffic accident, there might have been a seventh, supplementary volume of *Collected Letters*. Certainly enough material had accumulated to fill such a volume by the 1990s but by that time Coleridge's fortunes were on the wane and it was not deemed financially viable.
37. For Richards's self-description, see "The Lure of High Mountaineering" (1927); for the table and the quotation at the end of the next sentence, see Coburn "I.A.R. and S.T.C." 236 and 244, respectively.
38. *Experience into Thought* (1979). In his early days at Vic (as associate professor of French), Edgar published an edition of *The Ancient Mariner and Other Poems* (New York: D. Appleton, 1900; republished several times in different series). Northrop Frye, Coburn's fellow student, dedicated his book on William Blake, *Fearful Symmetry* (1947), to Edgar.
39. "The Life in Death of Editorial Exchange" (2003).

CHAPTER 8

Today and To Do

She said

What I like more than anything
Is to visit other islands...

George Oppen[1]

8.1 THE DOUBLE-BIND OF BEING INGENUOUS

As the preceding chapter described, the place of the "Ancient Mariner" in the minds of readers changed a good deal during two hundred years: from inexplicable delight or disturbed refusal, to a poem for children, to a poem for educators and artists, to a canonical text to be analysed and disputed, all the while becoming common property, its title and odd phrases part of general conversation between persons who had never read it. It was fantastic, frightening, exciting, taken very seriously or not seriously at all, even boring, depending on who you were, and where and when.

The basic condition of such diversity was established at an early stage. Coleridge's name was well known at the time the poem was published: in some circles, notorious. He and Southey had been parodied in the weekly *Anti-Jacobin* and appeared with asses' heads in James Gillray's satirical print, *New Morality*, despite the poems Coleridge wrote recanting his earlier radicalism in spring–summer 1798, namely, "France: An Ode" (**174**), "Fears in Solitude" (**175**), and "The Story of the Mad Ox" (**177**).

The following few years continued to be an awkward time as the political scene developed and Bonaparte's intentions were confirmed, with the result that, by the time "Christabel" (**176**) and the first *Lay Sermon* were published in 1816, former radical friends like Hazlitt renewed the earlier, sparkier assault with venom. As Owen Barfield put the matter:

> It was unfortunate for Coleridge that his bitterest enemy had that Shavian knack of asserting matters of opinion as matters of fact with an ebullient gaiety, clothed in competent, picturesque and vigorous language, that carries its own deceptive conviction. We feel it *must* all be so, just as he says—until we start looking into the matter for ourselves. (78)

It was an assault that was renewed again—and doing so renewed Hazlitt's and Thelwall's critical fortunes—in the last decades of the twentieth century, a period when, during a similar period of political realignment, conservative forces in Britain and the USA pursued unpopular, nay retrogressive policies in the name of free-market capitalism.

However, as I said, whatever the failings of academic misappropriation, the new large editions of Coleridge's writing prove that he did not lose his way as had been held. The enormous amount of material retrieved in the published letters, notebooks, and Collected Coleridge testify to a life project of great ambition and originality. If at first the early-published volumes in the latter project (the 1795 *Lectures, Watchman* and *Essays on His Own Times*) were at hand to bolster Hazlitt's charge, the later-published ones answer it by overwhelming evidence. There was no retreat into obfuscation: a grand idea was evolving in many directions, and just as important for my present argument, continuous with what came before, in verse no less than in prose.

So much, I hope, is confirmed by *Coleridge's Experimental Poetics*: that the preface to his 1796 *Poems* makes a case for a poetry of feeling (as distinct from Wordsworth's "orphic song": *PW* 1:816 and cf. *CM* 1:218), whatever about the public poems like "Religious Musings" (**101**) which the 1796 collection also contained. Coleridge became interested in the possibility of poetic—particularly metrical—experiment before Wordsworth became his neighbour at Alfoxden, and he was only too glad to nominate Wordsworth as the coming figure of the age who would "hereafter be admitted as the first & greatest philosophical Poet" (*CL* 2:1034)[2]: not only because this was the truth but because, curiously, it gave him more space of his own. He wrote less verse with publication in mind after his three great poems, while the Wedgwood annuity enabled him to apply himself seriously to his prose magnum opus. The circumstances likewise created a condition in which his later poems gained an equivalent autonomy. Their style develops out of the extension of the "Mariner" experiment in "Christabel" and has many registers: rarefied love poetry, political satire, private meditation, personal compliments, and squibs. In this, Hunt was correct to say of "the new school of poetry" of which Wordsworth was counted "the most prominent ornament," that Coleridge was the "inner priest of the temple," "the real oracle of the time."[3]

The "Ancient Mariner" is a poem that never found a settled place because its author did not quite know what he was doing when he wrote it; and for that very reason, perhaps, it retains its edge, its readers' self-identification as the one "that must hear me" (line 622). What it at the same time achieved was to open vistas that were too important to found a career upon; that pressed to be understood, not exploited for sale. His lifelong project was henceforward conducted in prose while verse remained the medium in which he put feelings to the test, sought to achieve balanced resolution in an objective, pleasure-giving form. Later poems regret the decay of body, but in a mental–moral sense Coleridge never aged; the project remained the same. In "Alice du Clós" (**655**) he returned, a sadder and a wiser man, and wrote a poem worthy to stand alongside the "Mariner."

All this appears to me self-evident but unrecognised because Coleridge failed to create the public by whom he would be appreciated. What lay behind the enmity of old friends who felt betrayed, like Hazlitt, was not only his political change of mind but the affront of one who appeared to adopt a superior position, a "refusing" attitude towards the majority. He resisted the public that was ready to hand because he had no interest in becoming a popular poet, and he failed to make a new public for his poetry as he did to a limited extent for his religious ideas. The different language the two lecturers used in their lectures and their prose writing says it all: one larding his lengthening paragraphs with recondite references, the other directly appealing to immediate feelings. One could say that Hazlitt, the younger man, with fewer advantages and slighted by what he took as condescension, brooded over Coleridge's rejection of the revolution gone wrong and took it personally; but the misinterpretation goes deeper than that. It had to, in order to take root so quickly and last so long, and it leads to the further double-edged consequence contained in the familiar story of decline into obscurity.

Some of the most interesting and sympathetic comments on Coleridge in comparison to Wordsworth have been made by other writers. I have cited Trickett's novel, *The Elders*, in Chap. 1, and scattered remarks by Laura (Riding) Jackson that remained unpublished during her lifetime make a similar point, if less elegantly.[4] She contrasts Coleridge's poetical ingenuousness with Wordsworth's professionalism, by which she intends the candidness, openness, innocence-in-the-ways-of-the-world of the one compared to the sense of laying-claim-to-ownership of the other. She describes Coleridge as

> not merely philosophically but religiously a more serious man than Wordsworth. And he was serious in his conception of the nature of poetry with an angelic philosophic seriousness. His poetic ideal was itself so elevated that he had not an ounce of professional poetic elevation in him. Wordsworth had a weighty talent in this. It was his intensely professionalistic view of poetry and of himself as poet that allowed of his making the matter-of-fact prescriptions for good poetic practice, in connection with the *Lyrical Ballads*, that later haunted Coleridge, distressingly, when he looked back on this—and on his past association with Wordsworth generally.

There is much good sense in this if one allows that Coleridge's nervousness about engaging with the reading public, combined with his oft-repeated warnings against an authorship that can only succeed by giving its paymaster more of what it wants, complicates the issue. There is indeed a reserved position on certain theological matters and such reserve comes across as evasiveness, breeding suspicion among those addressed. Coleridge was in part the casualty of his own innocence: the *ingenu* appeared to be hiding something, which by writing for himself I suppose he was. In Trickett's novel, the Coleridge character is in every way the more exciting candidate for the position he does not get because he fails to instil trust.

8.2 Rerun an Other Way

There is on the other hand an "other" tradition of poetry that has successfully avoided catering to the reading public in the past and consciously manages to do so today. In the careful phrasing of Chap. 15 of the *Biographia*, Coleridge explains the ideal standards of poetry by saying as much about the larger number of poems that fall short of the ideal:

> Imagery (even taken from nature, much more when transplanted from books, as travels, voyages, and works of natural history); affecting incidents; just thoughts; interesting personal or domestic feelings; and with these the art of their combination or intertexture in the form of a poem; may all by incessant effort be acquired as a trade, by a man of talents and much reading, who, as I once observed, has mistaken an intense desire of poetic reputation for a natural poetic genius; the love of the arbitrary end for a possession of the peculiar means. (*BL* 2:20)

From this it follows that the subject matter is often best chosen from "subjects very remote from the private interests and circumstances of the writer himself."

> At least I have found, that where the subject is taken immediately from the author's personal sensations and experiences, the excellence of a particular poem is but an equivocal mark, and often a fallacious pledge, of genuine poetic power. (*BL* 2:20)

Such statements are important because they are flatly at odds with the easy, widespread assumption that Coleridge is the theorist of "the Romantic lyric I." In fact, they are consonant with his practice in the "Mariner," the essence of which is to take the mysterious for granted as in the traditional ballads; to involve everyone directly in what is happening ("It is an ancyent Marinere"), as if the teller of the tale watched it unfold and with the consequence that his auditors, alongside him, are immediately involved in the act. The author ideally participates in the emotions described but remains separate, even "alienated" or "aloof" (*BL* 2:22), so that the reader is never entirely lost in the imagery or incidents.

> As little can a mind thus roused and awakened be brooded on by mean and indistinct emotion, as the low, lazy mist can creep upon the surface of a lake, while a strong gale is driving it onward in waves and billows. (*BL* 2:22)

The list of prescriptions develops the argument with respect to imagery: "[I]mages however beautiful, though faithfully copied from nature, and as accurately represented in words, do not of themselves characterize the poet" (*BL* 2:23). And the list ends with an all-inclusive ideal—"No man was ever yet a great poet, without being at the same time a profound philosopher"—by which Coleridge means "creative power" and "intellectual energy" wrestling "as in a war embrace," "possessed by the spirit, not possessing it" (*BL* 2:25–27). The too-often-dismissed early poems of Shakespeare contain signs of the myriad-minded largeness of mind that made his mature plays so awe-inspiring. Coleridge asks his reader to respond in the same way he did instinctively when, as an undergraduate, he was struck by such signs of genius in Wordsworth's *Descriptive Sketches* (*BL* 1:77–78).

To repeat, although Coleridge presents his ideal standard with reference to Shakespeare and Milton, his eye is on the everyday verse of his age, which he emphasises even more strongly in Chap. 16 through comparisons with painting and sixteenth-century madrigals. The fashion of his own time is tricked out "in the soiled and over-worn finery of the meretricious muse" (*BL* 2:30) and he concentrates particularly on language to prepare for the argument with Wordsworth over poetic diction that follows after. Coleridge had particular reason to be sore about his relation to the reading public and their spokespersons, the periodical reviewers, but his argument turns on a situation that developed rapidly during his time and continues today. There is indeed a gap between the ideal reader and popular taste, as there is between those who write for themselves with versions of Coleridge's ideals in mind and those who write to achieve fame and fortune or just a living. The publications of "other" writers circulate as part of a gift economy, exchanged between likeminded persons or circulating from small press publishers who separately discover small clienteles with a shared taste. Blake discovered such an audience for his illustrated books while he made a living as a professional engraver; William Barnes wrote for himself and was published by local printers until he too was discovered by a wider circle. So it also went with Basil Bunting and so I suggest it might have gone with Coleridge if he had lived at a later time. As it was, his poetical fame turned out to rest on a tiny fraction of his published *Poetical Works* and was assisted by a sense of celebrity often only dimly understood. One might say he was writing for himself all the time from 1798 onwards, and publishing under a reputation foisted on him by circumstance. Even Wordsworth, on the evidence of the developing *Lyrical Ballads*, failed to see what his friend was trying to do.

I therefore suggest there are lessons to be learned from a comparison of Coleridge's situation as an "ingenuous" or "other" poet with that of J.H. Prynne at a later time. Prynne has been labelled as a coterie "Cambridge" poet in pretty much the same way Wordsworth and Coleridge were dismissed as members of a "Lake School," straining to distinguish themselves by being different and incomprehensible except to devotees. After Prynne's first volume, *Force of Circumstance* (1962), which one might categorise as nicely contemporary in the manner of, say, Charles Tomlinson's early volumes, he abandoned the path to which it pointed and embarked on a different kind of poetry influenced by Charles Olson and poets to be found in the *New American Poetry* anthology edited by Donald Allen. Subsequent poems appeared in chapbooks and pamphlets published by small non-commercial publishers and increasingly in limited runs published by Prynne himself. As far as I know, no effort was made to publicise them but they found and impressed a small and receptive audience. I read them at the time they appeared and quickly came to believe they fitted the high standards set by Coleridge in a way no other contemporary English poet did. Several collective editions have since appeared and during the past few years the broadsheets have been more respectful, although all the time emphasising that the writing is "difficult" or "not for everyone." It is certainly not for everyone who finds their ideal satisfied by "professionals" like Simon Armitage or Mark Strand. Prynne does not perform his poems like Billy Collins, doesn't work instinctively to please like Seamus Heaney or to be cherished like Elizabeth Bishop. Nor did Coleridge in poems like "Constancy to an Ideal Object" (**357**) or "The Last Words of Berengarius" (**625**). If the "Mariner" pleases on many levels, that is of course a blessing but these levels sometimes interfere with one another. The revisions of the "Mariner," and particularly the addition of the gloss, can be interpreted as Coleridge tripping over himself to please (or somewhat differently to clarify) when sometimes he might have been better advised to leave alone.

The strongest reason I can give for citing Prynne's poetry in relation to Coleridge's is that reading Prynne, and other contemporaries of the same ilk, taught me how to read Coleridge. The obvious differences in style and subject matter are in this respect, I emphasise, incidental: the similar breadth of interests that underpins all of Coleridge's specific indications of poetic power are far more important. Take for example Prynne's "Write-Out," which appeared in a small volume titled *Bands Around the Throat* (1987). It is an odd-looking poem made up of two narrow columns of print with four horizontal lines of print running across them; two of these longer horizontals are positioned at top and bottom of the columns, and the other two divide the columns between into three sections. At first glance, only the last horizontal line appears to make sense—"Sporadically by bus into the heart of the country"—and it possesses a completely different character from the rest of the words on the page. It is only too obviously easy, relaxing, promising, quite separate from the mere nuggets of sense that make up the phrases in columns, and the connected but tortured language of the previous horizontal connectors–dividers. The intrigued reader looks again at two texts at cross-purposes with each other, separately difficult to fathom and together just as "unreadable" as the "Mariner" alongside its gloss. The vertical columns contain punctuation but the meaning as line follows line is just over the edge of discontinuous. Words and phrases connect syntactically in the run-over but not semantically; they contain elements of personal phrasing and communicate a confused sense of urgency but are for the most part nonsense. By contrast, the horizontal lines crossing over, between and beneath them are grammatically continuous but incomplete statements; the first three comprise monotonous, a-rhythmic, business-talk platitudes disguising ugly actions and the fourth is the saccharine line quoted above. At this point, one might remember Coleridge's specific complaint that his contemporaries slip easily from an improper use of words into errors concerning the things they refer to. He quotes a host of authorities in support of a central truth: "language is the armoury of the human mind" (*BL* 2:30–31). So many words in Prynne's poem possess double or twisted meanings, wrenched away from their roots. The only word most people need to look up is "tantulum," a precious metal used because of its non-corrosive properties to bind suppurating wounds, for instance after trepanning; if you look it up online, you will find references to its more recent use in electrolytic capacitors and in connection with wars in central Africa (a "resource curse"). This poet thereby becomes the prophet of future events when the direction of his poem is fully grasped.

The original booklet in which the poem was published has green covers with horizontal (tantulum?) strips running continually across them Very many—perhaps all—the poems within it make reference to musical "bands," mostly contemporary, and other music equally self-regarding. "Ein Heldenleben" ("A Hero's Life"), for example, alludes to Richard Strauss's grandiose tone poem. In the case of "Write-Out," which follows immediately after, the reference is to Paul and Linda McCartney's banal but highly popular hit song of 1971 entitled "Heart of the Country." Prynne's preference has been to write serial poems—collections from the start to be read as a whole—and, although this volume reverts to an earlier practice in which separate poems are titled, it conforms to the manner of organisation initiated by Jack Spicer and Robert Duncan. The copyright page states that a hundred copies were "[p]ut into production on 1st June 1987," that is, in the run-up to the General Election of 11 June, which turned out to be the third consecutive election victory for Mrs. Thatcher, thought by many, following a decade of industrial, social, and political strife, to be one of Britain's least glorious moments. The poem thus encapsulates a moment of swallowing doom that the majority on both sides evade (deafen themselves to?) by retreating to a fool's paradise. "Sporadically," from the Greek word for sowing, was originally used in English in connection with the spread of disease; "bus" is not only short for omnibus (in Latin "for all") but a shortened form of "business." The title "Write-Out" not only conjures up White-Out, Wash-Out, and Opt-Out: Write can be heard as Right as opposed to Left in politics, in a country divided over issues that neither side properly articulates.

It seems to me that Prynne has discovered in his poem a strikingly apt form to communicate a situation with powerful succinctness. It is a broadside that does not rhyme and may be a puzzle to read aloud, but the parts close in around you and by so doing produce a frisson of pleasure: above all, "a human and intellectual life is transferred to them from the poet's own spirit" (*BL* 2:23). To the extent that the poem turns on the difficult word, *tantalum*, (the left hand vertical column to the mining? the right hand one to its consumption?), the moral refers to the crime and punishment of Tantalus in Greek mythology. Did he reveal the secret of the gods, or serve up his son Pelops to be eaten by them, or simply hide Zeus's magic golden dog? It does not matter: his punishment was to be caught between an impossible choice, movement either way self-checking. That makes as clever a response as any one of Coleridge's political poems, and one equally measured. It is also a good illustration of what Coleridge meant by destructive contraries as distinct from creative opposites.

Prynne, following his first, never-collected volume, wrote a kind of poetry that resists consumption and does not seek publicity, which, after a long interval of being derided for being perversely elitist, is luckily discovering its wider audience. Coleridge—more preoccupied with the need to earn money where he could and with a quite different, wholly absorbing philosophical project at the forefront of his mind—never went so far to show altogether what he was doing as a poet but was damned none the less. The "Ancient Mariner" has been used in all sorts of ways to bring satisfaction and pleasure, but with notably few exceptions these advance under the supposition that, after writing it, he committed poetical suicide.

It is true that Prynne most often gains his effects by lexical (and here typographical), not musical means. "Write-Out" is typical in this respect, although the too easily musical last line is the "key" to the poem and links it to the surrounding volume. However, as in the work of Prynne's early mentor, Olson, the visual placement of words controls the way they are experienced. They can be balanced at measured intervals across the page— or in other poems in all sorts of other ways—to register the pace at which they are apprehended, their relative weight, and so on. Indeed, one might hold that the escape from traditional measures enables, at the present time when Classical metrics are not part of the furniture of many readers' minds, greater scope to allow grammar to control pitch and tone; to "place" what enters their mental ears. Above all, both poets unite the contemporary and the hieratic.

For example, Prynne's allusion to tantalum/Tantalus is no more obscure than Coleridge's word "lavrock" in the "Mariner," or his allusion to "gentle mind" in "First Advent of Love" (**574**). In Prynne's case the allusion is obvious, stands out, requires attention, whereas in "First Advent" Coleridge takes more for granted and runs the risk of being misunderstood. "Gentle mind" alludes to the genre and values of Renaissance pastoral, confirming the fragmentary echoes of Sidney's *Arcadia* that some readers might pick up, and specifically to Guinizelli's celebrated phrase "Al cor gentil" ("the gentle heart").[5] Many pass too quickly over Coleridge's poem, taking for granted that it is a mannered exercise—a conventional landscape with attendant feelings—whereas it asks to be read as a concentrated, finely balanced emblem of what the Greeks meant by kalokagathia, beauty and goodness, tinged by a typically Coleridgean awareness of the latent instability of the Classical ideal: the pathos of its limited secular foundation. The subtle method of the verse he wrote after summer 1798 is too often missed, its superficial meaning too hastily assumed, although the signal here is no more obscure than the copyright statement on Prynne's original booklet. In both cases you are prompted to get the point, and then you understand the source of energy both authors tap into that turns their complicated poems into poetry. Their mental span expands beyond the particular and benefits from a kind of "*surview*" (*BL* 2:58) or largeness of vision, an Idea or Method that speaks from beyond the author. The more comprehensive such a *forma informans*—with Shakespeare and Milton among those setting the highest standard—the more poetical will the poem be.

There is an obvious puzzle element in "Write-Out" and, if there is puzzlement in the "Ancient Mariner," it is quite unselfconscious and more deeply problematic. Prynne's poem is about the lack of real choice; Coleridge's is about the very basis of choice and self-direction. The political allusions in "Write-Out" may be paralleled in the "Ancient Mariner" by an awareness of the Bristol slave trade and the state of mind of those who labour in the tropics which is at the edge of Coleridge's poem, but not as an overt protest.[6] The moving forces are polar opposites—extremes of hot and cold, light and dark, positive and negative—that are destructive when they become contraries. Slavery may be the resultant manifestation, the Mariner may be forever shackled to his experience, but a metaphysical–psychological dilemma is the controlling paradigm. The sentiments concerning a release from slavery that appear in the 1817 prose gloss from Part IV of the "Mariner," quoted at the close of Chap. 6, echo those of Coleridge's prize-winning ode on the slave trade (**48**), written when he was a first-year undergraduate. When he quoted stanzas from the ode in a note to his contribution to Southey's *Joan of Arc* (**110**; *PW* 1:222) and again in "The Destiny of Nations" (**139**; *PW* 1:297), they still retained a direct political thrust. The faint echo in the gloss, however, expresses wistful hope for a return to a "native country" and "natural home" from a place in the mind where the intervening history is not an issue. The later context makes the impulse more a sentiment than a political intervention.

8.3 The Labels Are Important

One quality I would not claim for Prynne is the supernatural, at least as the word applies to Coleridge. It is an important dimension of the latter's poetry that received little recognition during the long history of its reception. Enthusiasts like Andrew Lang and W.B. Yeats incorporated the concept into their Celtic Revival interests towards the end of the nineteenth century, George MacDonald being perhaps Coleridge's most serious student in this respect,[7] but the faery otherwise verged towards the fey and the occult. The occult dimension, when mingled with erotic fantasies entertained by what remained of the Pre-Raphaelite Brotherhood, naturally attached more to "Christabel" than the "Mariner"; but Harry Clarke's illustrations for the latter, heavily influenced by Aubrey Beardsley, reflect this uncannily "horrid" dimension. However, a little more needs to be said about the supernatural than the miscellaneous remarks made so far. It is a word that frequently occurs interchangeably with the sublime and the numinous in present-day discussion, while in common parlance its meaning can be close to "paranormal," and clarifying the differences will help to refine its meaning for Coleridge. At the same time, the relative lack of interest—or interest shown—in Coleridge's thinking about Imagination,

Reason, and the like in relation to the "Mariner" is unfortunate. The classroom protocols that began to emerge with I.A. Richards's bracing, practical, no-nonsense approach to literary texts advanced to a point where an important dimension of the "Mariner's" power was conveniently parcelled up and forgotten. The transcendental was more acceptable in classrooms than the transcendent, although I clearly remember the time when I proposed a dissertation on Coleridge and was warned the English Faculty would take a dim view if there was too much Philosophy in it.

Richards's—and Tate's and Ransom's, and so many other instructors'—young students were encouraged to do a practical criticism of the poem, going backwards and forwards in order to understand "how it works"; but in the end all they were doing was understanding the poem and ignoring the poetry. Then the revolution came, close reading was overturned, and students began to be taught cultural criticism, "cultural" meaning variously historical, material, or political. By understanding how a poem works, however, I mean the "lower-order" operation in Coleridge's Order of Mental Powers diagram (*CM* 5:798), several times referred to above. It mediates between Sense and Understanding: sorting, arranging, trying to clarify, and set thoughts in order "in the light, and joyousness of day."[8] Understanding the *poetry* in a poem, as Coleridge emphasises in Chap. 14 of the *Biographia*—the literary-critical rerun of the not-entirely-satisfactory philosophical definition of Imagination in Chap. 13—is entirely different from the operation that became ascendant during the twentieth century. It eschews replacing one set of lower-order procedures by another of the same lower kind: rather a progress that should have happened all along, which Richards and others suppressed on the same Benthamite grounds that later reformers referred to when reforming Richards. As I said in Chap. 1, the Coleridgean argument involves a transition from matters that are "simple, sensuous, and passionate" (sounds echoing sounds, images, a material happening) to an event that supersedes sense (is at the edge of sound, cannot be seen, happens in ways that exceed explanation). Coleridge enlarges upon the stanzas by Sir John Davies to communicate the transition from object to Idea; it is encapsulated in the line "Steal access through our senses to our minds" (*BL* 2:17).

I add that the topic in hand is quite separate from what is sometimes discussed under the heading "voice": how a reader can understand that, say, Philip Larkin or Robert Frost has a distinctive way of talking, a style that resonates with a particular character, or (as in the case of Yeats) with a personality deliberately distanced from the real-life person. If one has to talk of

Coleridge's voice in poetry, it was not that of the man who spoke with a Devonshire accent. It had differently, as poetry, even if not physically voiced, a touch of something that transcended his selfhood, something of which he was conscious and which he valued beyond all else. And to write poems that crossed that barrier, however fitfully, was his justification as a poet.

An increasingly secular twentieth century recognised the quality I am talking about on its own terms when it rediscovered the eighteenth-century sublime. The concept has consequently been much belaboured. There are discussions of its origins in Longinus's *Peri hypsous*, the transformation of a rhetorical category into a material cause, the evolving dialogue involving Burke, Kant, and others, down to versions of sublime in the writings of Nietzsche and Freud.[9] However, although Coleridge's father made a translation of Longinus (now lost)[10] and Coleridge the son was led to tour newly fashionable North Wales with a fellow undergraduate, he seems not to have been much impressed with the experience until he listened to Wordsworth and later travelled to the North. Up to then, raised among the gentle valleys of East Devon and afterwards living in central London, Bristol and Stowey, any material sublime in his writing—for instance, the "Ice mast-high came floating by" in the "Mariner"—came from reading, or visiting Cheddar Gorge and the like. As far as he derived ideas on the subject from Kant, Herder, and others, they were tempered by a sense of the sublime as a less terrific elevation of spirit, something closer to German *Das Erhabene* (more simply "Raised up, Uplifted"); and thereby he can be said to have turned Wordsworth into a more faithful disciple of Kant than he was himself.[11]

His shift from describing the poem as an object to poetry in terms of the poet is again not a failure to follow through a materialist argument: rather, the change of position is exactly the point, a turn beyond the same. It rests on his life-changing decision to move from Unitarian to Trinitarian Christianity, from a philosophy of "It is" to one of "I am." One can argue that his earlier political pronouncements in "The Destiny of Nations" (**139**) and "Religious Musings" attempt the political sublime deconstructed as apocalypse, but it was an argument he quickly left behind. *Biographia* Chap. 14 adds poetics to philosophy and communicates the transition to transcendent at-one-ment by means of a prose style where opposites merge and accumulate a momentum that enables it to convey more than the sum of its parts (*BL* 2:15–17). The following quotation from Davies then describes the sublime in the alchemical sense in which base metals are turned to gold by the Philosopher's Stone, "Bodies to spirit by sublimation strange":

> As fire converts to fire the things it burns,
> As we our food into our nature change.

This may look like a poetical solution to a poetical problem and it is certainly more successful in its way than the awkward philosophical statement at the close of the previous volume, which had to wait several more years before Coleridge was able to improve on it. However, it was not just poetical fancy. The concept of sublimation was in the air at the time Coleridge wrote, being the chemical means that led to the discovery of iodine.[12] Bernard Courtois isolated the new substance just before Coleridge copied out Davies's verses in 1811 (*CN* 3:4112 ff 14^v-15). Although the achievement was not in the public domain, Coleridge quite possibly learned of it through Humphry Davy, who received a sample from André-Marie Ampère on which he worked before identifying it as a new element to the Royal Society in December 1813–January 1814.

If the fashionable sublime is a misleading point of reference for Coleridge's supernatural, what then of the concept of the numinous? Rudolf Otto, who shaped the modern meaning of the word, has had a mixed reception from professional philosophers and theologians, although that in some circles might be held to his credit. By extending the meaning from the literal presence of divine will to a general sense of the spiritually transcendent, and further again as equivalent to the non-rational in psychology, it has proved particularly suited to modern discussion. It frees the concept of the supernatural from *fin-de-siècle* associations of Ouija boards and Madame Blavatsky or New Age Gothic; and at the same time, loosened from its etymological moorings, it is a more easily handled counter among those who hold their gods no longer to be real. Its only disadvantage—which is fundamental and obvious in respect of any discussion of Coleridge—is that of course Coleridge did take the numinous for real. Words like Idea, Reason, Imagination, and Poetry are used in a sense that assumes they reach towards a specific real unutterable truth. In short, although the concept of the numinous is useful in comparing Coleridge's sense of the supernatural with that of, say, Wallace Stevens, there is a yawning gulf between the original and the present developed senses of the word. For Coleridge it designates something very close and ever present: another world both above and below the one in which he exists, both elevated and subliminal, from which intimations of both joy and dread emanate. For Stevens, it is a world that the Imagination might conjure up but always at a distance and always lost. He asks, "What, then, is the nature of poetry in a time of disbelief?" And the only answer he can find is that:

> . . . Poetry
>
> Exceeding music must take the place
> Of empty heaven and its hymns,
>
> Ourselves in poetry must take their place.[13]

As I say, while the word numinous might offer itself as a useful counter with which to engage with contemporary mores, it is a dangerous one. The phrase M.H. Abrams made popular, "Natural Supernaturalism," fudges the essential part of the meaning Coleridge assumed, and is no better substitute or gloss than the materialist concept of the sublime.

What then to do? How to engage with Coleridge's supernatural in a way that goes beyond pointing to processes like sublimation, that describes how the word embodies an idea that "feeds upon infinity,"[14] but not in Wordsworth's way and which always takes the sense of numinous to involve a real and particular (Christian) God? As I have repeatedly said, the essence of poetry is more difficult to describe than the components of a poem: it involves a value judgement involving poems that are not poetry, or are poetry only in the loose sense of the term.

> Each individual must bear witness of it to his own mind, even as he describes life and light: and with the silence of light it describes itself, and dwells in *us* only as far as we dwell in *it*. (*LS* 70)

There is not much a pragmatist can do with such an argument when it appears to go round in a circle, other than to say, so be it: Coleridge has disappeared into a soaring vision of his own making, like Richard of St. Victor, into a state of mind beyond human dialogue. If that is where practical criticism parked the majority point of view, as it seems agreed that it has done,[15] all is not lost. Robert Frost describes how we can make do and still retain an inkling of what is at the heart of it all:

> We dance round in a ring and suppose,
> But the Secret sits in the middle and knows.[16]

I propose that several earlier suggestions about Coleridge's practice as a poet can be brought together to clarify further the "secret" truth that occupied his mind.

The two-part movement of Wordsworth's *Prelude*, in which the sense of expectation and disappointment describing his crossing of the Alps is matched and resolved in the closing harmonious vision atop Snowdon has come to be conventionally understood as a conscious mirroring of the double action of the sublime, as it was understood in his time; and, as I describe in Chap. 3, the same pattern is also characteristic of poems written by Coleridge before, after, and including the "Ancient Mariner." Whatever the question of influence, the relation between such epiphanic or transcendent moments in Coleridge's poems is much less clear than in Wordsworth. The narrative in the "Mariner" advances only to stall and then revive, emotions gather to a point when they go into reverse, the sequence of scenes is literally discontinuous and rests on a fluctuating emotional logic within the simple voyage pattern. This feature is consonant with Coleridge's preference for a motile supernatural that shifts without cause between positive and negative registers above and below the level of consciousness. The point opens onto further observations regarding Coleridge's supernatural. Anthony Harding has compared the meaning of the word Reason in Coleridge with that of Emerson, for whom it is more often "my Reason." What it means for Coleridge, and its relation to Imagination, has already been described in Chaps. 1 and 3. For Emerson, it means an exhilarating sense of God-like power, "much more an apotheosis of self than a true transcending of self."[17] Harding connects this with distinctive features of American Transcendentalism like the compulsion to feel original, all of which are linked to American views of English Romanticism and the reaction against it that followed. Again, while Wordsworth's epiphanies are so often either "something evermore about to be"[18] or full-blown moments of power, Coleridge's few essays in the latter mode (like the close of "Hymn before Sun-rise" **301**) are not his most glorious: they ring hollow as if he was not fully behind them. Instead, and more characteristically, in such moments when the light of Reason shows itself, it is as sunlight diffused through dappled shade or sounds overheard or blending. Jonathan Arac writes of the Sun and Moon imagery in the "Mariner" and how Coleridge distances himself from the blinding, stunning power of the former, preferring the displaced, more intimate light of the latter.[19]

To sum up, the philosophy behind Coleridge's poetry is not a hinterland that can be ignored: it is an adjunct that underlies and determines the features that appear to sense in his poems. His Imagination does not terminate in a cloud of unknowing or inner silence: even the most

Neoplatonic of his love poems like "Phantom" (**347**) are addressed to a notional other, Asra. Of course he acknowledged and celebrated the fact that:

> Whene'er the Self, that stands twixt God and Thee,
> Defecates to a pure Transparency
> That intercepts no light and adds no stain—
> There Reason is; and then begins *her* reign!
>   ("Where is Reason?" **575**; *PW* 1:995)

But poetry is not "defecation"—that is, wholly clarified of all things material—and Coleridge was generally suspicious of the mystic *contemplatio*. Even while he was sympathetic to humbler exponents like George Fox, he entertained reservations about St. Teresa. He pursued Understanding to its limits, as his assiduous dedication to Kant's categories in the *Logic* and his "scientific" assessment of discrepancies in the Gospel story prove. In a similar fashion, the philosophical enterprise that began at the time the "Mariner" was being written ended with a trinity of persons, not a blank Idea. Indeed, it is most important that the supernatural was not a blank for him at any time: it was always filled with Nature, or Persons, or a combination of both.

8.4   All the Dead Voices

Coleridge's writing in verse and prose is connected in ways that are often ignored. However, the two modes of meditation answered different needs at different times. Specifically in the present instance, while philosophical conclusions articulated in the later 1820s clarify the direction of his thought during 1797–1798, they should not be too firmly imposed upon the earlier time. The "Ancient Mariner" was written during a moment of life-changing transition in several respects. It contains threads that would continue to be important parts of the texture of Coleridge's thought to the end—most obviously what one could call the visionary or idealist parts—but it also contains remnants of other ties—call them sceptical or empiricist—that were difficult to reconcile. The making of the poem in which these forces hang in unresolved contemplation is the nature of its achievement and, for this reason, one has to allow that the modern, looser understanding of numinous may fit the poem as it stood in its original version better than the different thing Coleridge would have liked it to be in his later years.

If the special quality of the poem rests upon a degree of intellectual and moral confusion at the crossroads, it is important that this is contained in the poem itself. Contained is not the right word, projected would be better:

> Saying and saying, the way things say
> On the level of that which is not yet knowledge.[20]

Coleridge began his ballad to earn money, albeit while cocking a snook at the literary taste of his readers, and the process of writing became a means of pondering matters that only a poem could address. In the present context, it is especially important to remember that the "Mariner" became in the writing a test of the validity of feelings dimly understood, and that the application of concepts in a similar state of chassis was of secondary concern. As I argued in *Coleridge's Experimental Poetics*, the submerged tradition of other poets is a better guide than the majority of critics, who tend to address each other rather than what is in front of them. A key phrase in the *Biographia* like "we can only *know* by an act of *becoming*" (*BL* 2:244) makes better sense read alongside the writing of Robert Duncan and David Antin than it does in the context of much academic criticism. In my earlier book (p.111), I suggested that the "Ancient Mariner" should be compared to Beckett's *Godot*, another work which accidentally—and because it was accidentally—included all manner of things the author found his previous writing had pushed to one side, and that turned out to be the turning point in his career and, to his sometimes regret, the most popular thing he ever wrote. *Godot* proposed nothing more than what Beckett tried to say in earlier verse and prose fiction, was merely another way of saying it, but the objectified form of drama opened a gap into which flooded qualities the other writing pushed aside. One could say the same for Coleridge's extended ballad: about the formal requirements that facilitated the unexpected opportunity for a richer humanity to express itself. The ironic consequence for both writers is they are each best known for works that they casually undertook and that each thereafter wrestled to revise in ways that confuse posterity.

A contemporary author whose work serves to reinforce and extend the point about writing that pursues a meaning beyond the words—poetry beyond the poem—is Susan Howe. Her poems and other writing has, like Prynne's, been known to a small and growing number of readers for a long time. It circulated in small magazines—American, not English—and in chapbook form in limited runs for several decades among interested readers until it was taken on by a New York publishing house (New Directions), a publisher with a history connected with the avant-garde. She began as a visual artist, and turned to writing almost accidentally with a first collection entitled *Hinge Picture* (1974), alluding to the balanced arrangement of facing pages. Like Prynne, she was early on influenced by Olson and others such. Although she came in later years to teach at a university and win notable prizes, she would not, I think, count her career as that of a professional poet. As Prynne has been branded a "Cambridge Poet," so she has been linked in passing to various American movements (feminist poetry, L=A=N=G=U=A=G=E poetry, SUNY at Buffalo) but likewise mainly to satisfy journalistic convenience. I repeat that her ambitions are primarily to write her own poetry as she wants it to be; she is simply glad if she finds it chiming with her readers' concerns. Ingenuous but not elitist, other but not oppositional, the work naturally occurring the way oysters produce pearls.

What her writing adds to the argument about Coleridge is that it connects with the present sense of the supernatural. Wallace Stevens is a writer who has been specially important to her in a way that has puzzled admirers already educated into the knowledge of who-was-in and who-was-out. Stevens was not a professional poet but he has somehow been incorporated into the conventional pantheon and the core educational syllabus. Howe's interest is different: not in the grand guru who put the New Critics' version of Coleridge's Imagination into circulation—the Wallace Stevens celebrated by Frank Kermode, Denis Donoghue, and others—but private Stevens who explored echoes of a world beyond the day-world he inhabited while he worked in insurance: the Stevens who heard the dead voices of Irish neighbours in the part of rural Pennsylvania where his ancestors settled and who addressed poems to an unseen Thomas MacGreevy in Ireland. Whereas Hillis Miller read Stevens as the poet of an absent God, Howe reads him—as did James Boulger[21]—as a poet of the numinous (although I doubt very much that she has read James Boulger). The address to MacGreevy is, Boulger says, a "reversal of direction... from rationalism and Steven's usual postures to a suppressed petition for the epiphany of the absent gods of the East," that is, MacGreevy's Europe from which Stevens also ultimately derived. Howe is interested in these voices at the edge of words for various personal reasons: she grew up in a Massachusetts landscape filled with her ancestors' history, and in particular the lost voices of women who left only fragmentary traces; her mother's background in Ireland was different, but it shared the same haunting quality. Such voices open onto a world that is known but that can be touched only in surviving fragments; a world larger and older than everything surrounding, yet no less ever present. Her body of work correspondingly rests on the way words can reach towards *Pythagorean Silence*, the title of a collection published in 1982, the task of their embracing such a concept being by definition impossible. I believe her most recent work approaches most nearly to success, although of necessity it might appear the most obscure. I recommend anyone coming to it for the first time to search out her readings in collaboration with the composer David Grubbs.[22]

What has this to do with the "Ancient Mariner"? The numinous, in the proper sense in which it is most relevant to Coleridge (connected with a living God), is likely to be misunderstood in a predominantly secular context, and it must anyway be applied with particular care to a poem written when Coleridge was still in large part (an English) Unitarian. The sense in which its current usage unfolds in Howe's writing, on the other hand, is an extraordinary restatement by another poet of what inhabits and vivifies the Coleridge poem: the same kind of supernatural. This is eerie, haunted, gladsome, but most of all Imaginary in the Coleridgean sense all through his writing career, leading to imaginary gardens with real ghosts in them. The means Howe has developed to communicate such meaning are lines of print-fragment of which only the top- or bottom-half of words are fully legible, part-words and part-meanings often overlaying one another. What you read is what you get (and, if you doubt yourself, listen to the readings).

Tom Tit Tot, a collaboration with Howe's daughter, the artist R.H. Quaytman, is at the moment of writing only available in a limited and expensive edition. The justification of such a restrictive format is that letterpress printing and fine paper converts reading into a more directly physical experience, raising separate letters above the surface of the page, allowing them to interact separately from the space that encloses them (or, more accurately, sometimes only part encloses those that bleed off the page margins). The production is altogether a *tour-de-force* of book art: a physical object cooperating with the other means of signification to produce a magnifying, sharpening effect. Words and phrases float in a state of mind above their usual allotted places, but where they float, and consequently how, has been determined very carefully. The mystery of it is the poetry. The fact of it is the poem. The fields of energy that run across and interconnect elements of the "Ancient Mariner" are here abstracted—Ian Hamilton Finlay's "Acrobat" and other earlier pieces have meantime intervened—but the two poets separated by two centuries find equivalent ways of touching on deep truths. This deep accord is far more important than superficial differences of the means employed. Indeed, the deep-down originality of either set of means binds them closer than many more superficially obvious connections that could be made.

Like Prynne, and indeed like Coleridge, Howe has often found herself writing outside the comfort zone of many readers, impelled by a project that must compel considerable respect. High-minded it might be: it is certainly not for reasons that are self-regarding. As a Parthian shaft, I note that fragments of the Bollingen *Poetical Works* have entered the page area of *Tom Tit Tot* (as well as fragments from the Cornell Yeats). They find a place in the swirl of coruscating thoughts and memories, and the promises which the words evoke. If Wordsworth could find poetry in a stunted thorn, it should please readers of Coleridge that poetry can also be found in the daunting Bollingen Variorum display of variants.

> To be dead is not enough for them.
> It is not sufficient.
>
> They make a noise like feathers.
> Like leaves.
> Like ashes.
> Like leaves.[23]

Notes

1. "Ballad" in *New Collected Poems* ed. Davidson 207–08 at 208.
2. This to Richard Sharp in 1804. Coleridge returned to the same thoughts ten or more years later, when his thoughts were turning towards the *Biographia* (*CL* 4:574, *BL* 2:156, and see also *TT* 1:309).
3. *Foliage* (1818: 10–11). Hunt, at this early stage very much under the influence of Hazlitt, continues: "and who ought to have been the greatest visible person in it, instead of a hopeless and dreary sophist."
4. *Failure of Poetry* 38–39, 92–93, 114–16. The passage quoted appears on p.116. Cf. also *CM* 1:258 and 2:822 for Coleridge on the word "ingenuous."
5. My reading of "First Advent of Love," and the source of its allusions, is documented in "Contemplation in Coleridge's Poetry."
6. As David Simpson argues when, after beginning promisingly with an avowed intention to read the poem as a "variation upon the genre of voyage narratives," he finds it deals with matters of trade, colonisation, labour, and so on: "How Marxism Reads 'The Rime of the Ancient Mariner.'"

7. See Dearborn *Baptized Imagination* 29–34, etc.
8. The description of Part II of "Christabel," probably written by John Morgan under the influence of STC: see Griggs "An Early Defense of *Christabel*" 180.
9. *The Sublime* ed. Costelloe provides a good conspectus and further references. See also Cohn and Miles "The Sublime: In Alchemy, Aesthetics and Psychoanalysis."
10. *Coleridge's Father* 255, 267, etc.; and see index there under "Rhetoric" and "Robert Lowth." Coleridge's own opinion of *Peri hypsous* could be surprisingly low (*CM* 1:8), although see *Friend* 2:257, *CM* 2:355 and 1068–70 for comments that suggests he at this moment had in mind contemporary misappropriations of Longinus (by Burke, Herder et al.).
11. See Modiano *Coleridge and the Concept of Nature* 101–19, 129 esp.
12. I owe this point to Professor David Knight of Durham University.
13. "Two or Three Ideas" in *Collected Poetry and Prose* 846; "The Man with the Blue Guitar" in *ibid.* 136–37.
14. *Prelude* (1805) XIII 70; Norton Critical Edition 460.
15. See e.g. Ruoff "Romantic Lyric and the Problem of Belief" and Abrams (ed.) *Literature and Belief*; also cf. Jennings *Every Changing Shape* 142–43 for a doomed attempt to connect the mid-twentieth century view of Coleridge on Imagination to the Catholic mystical tradition. Coleridge's reading of St Teresa (*CM* 5: 818–23 and refs.) makes clear both his deep sympathy with and ultimate reservations concerning her "enthusiasm." He had Crashaw's lines on Teresa in mind "whilst writing the second part of Christabel" (Allsop 1:196), the significance of which is often mistaken: the second part appraises the witchery by the light of day.
16. "The Secret Sits" in *Collected Poems, Prose, and Plays* 329.
17. "Coleridge and Transcendentalism" at 243–46 specifically.
18. *Prelude* (1805) VI 542: Norton Critical Edition 216.
19. *Critical Genealogies* 86–88. Arac goes on to discuss this preference in Coleridge's poem "To William Wordsworth" (**401**) and his moderating influence on Wordsworth's revised statement of Imagination in the Snowdon episode (pp.89–90).
20. Stevens "The Region November" in *Collected Poetry and Prose* 472–73 at 473.
21. "The Numinous in Poetry" 159–61. For Hillis Miller, one of the critics against whom Boulger's larger argument is directed, see the chapter on Stevens in *Poets of Reality* 217–84.
22. CD titles published by Blue Chopsticks are listed in the bibliography. Also, several performances are available free online.
23. Beckett *Waiting for Godot* ed. Bryden 58 (alternate speakers' names and stage directions omitted). The present section heading begins the same passage, intervening lines omitted.

Appendix A

THE RIME OF THE ANCYENT MARINERE,
IN SEVEN PARTS.[1]

ARGUMENT.

How a Ship having passed the Line was driven by Storms to the cold Country towards the South Pole; and how from thence she made her course to the tropical Latitude of the Great Pacific Ocean; and of the strange things that befell; and in what manner the Ancyent Marinere came back to his own Country.

I.

It is an ancyent Marinere,
   And he stoppeth one of three:
"By thy long grey beard and thy glittering eye
   "Now wherefore stoppest me?

"The Bridegroom's doors are open'd wide   5
   "And I am next of kin;
"The Guests are met, the Feast is set,—
   "May'st hear the merry din.

But still he holds the wedding-guest—
    There was a Ship, quoth he—   10
"Nay, if thou'st got a laughsome tale,
    "Marinere! come with me."

He holds him with his skinny hand,
    Quoth he, there was a Ship—
"Now get thee hence, thou grey-beard Loon!   15
    "Or my Staff shall make thee skip.

He holds him with his glittering eye—
    The wedding guest stood still
And listens like a three year's child;
    The Marinere hath his will.   20

The wedding-guest sate on a stone,
    He cannot chuse but hear:
And thus spake on that ancyent man,
    The bright-eyed Marinere.

The Ship was cheer'd, the Harbour clear'd—   25
    Merrily did we drop
Below the Kirk, below the Hill,
    Below the Light-house top.

The Sun came up upon the left,
    Out of the Sea came he: 30
And he shone bright, and on the right
    Went down into the Sea.

Higher and higher every day,
    Till over the mast at noon—
The wedding-guest here beat his breast,   35
    For he heard the loud bassoon.

The Bride hath pac'd into the Hall,
    Red as a rose is she;
Nodding their heads before her goes
    The merry Minstralsy.   40

The wedding-guest he beat his breast,
    Yet he cannot chuse but hear:
And thus spake on that ancyent Man,
    The bright-eyed Marinere.

Listen, Stranger! Storm and Wind,   45
    A Wind and Tempest strong!
For days and weeks it play'd us freaks—
    Like Chaff we drove along.

Listen, Stranger! Mist and Snow,
    And it grew wond'rous cauld: 50
And Ice mast-high came floating by
    As green as Emerauld.

And thro' the drifts the snowy clifts
    Did send a dismal sheen;
Ne shapes of men ne beasts we ken—   55
    The Ice was all between.

The Ice was here, the Ice was there,
    The Ice was all around:
It crack'd and growl'd, and roar'd and howl'd—
    Like noises of a swound.   60

At length did cross an Albatross,
    Thorough the Fog it came;
And an it were a Christian Soul,
    We hail'd it in God's name.

The Marineres gave it biscuit-worms,   65
    And round and round it flew:
The Ice did split with a Thunder-fit;
    The Helmsman steer'd us thro'.

And a good south wind sprung up behind,
    The Albatross did follow;   70
And every day for food or play
    Came to the Marinere's hollo!

In mist or cloud on mast or shroud
    It perch'd for vespers nine,
Whiles all the night thro' fog smoke-white   75
    Glimmer'd the white moon-shine.

"God save thee, ancyent Marinere!
    "From the fiends that plague thee thus—
"Why look'st thou so?"—with my cross bow
    I shot the Albatross.   80

II.

The Sun came up upon the right
    Out of the Sea came he;
And broad as a weft upon the left
    Went down into the Sea.

And the good south wind still blew behind,   85
    But no sweet Bird did follow
Ne any day for food or play
    Came to the Marinere's hollo!

And I had done an hellish thing
    And it would work 'em woe;   90
For all averr'd, I had kill'd the Bird
    That made the Breeze to blow.

Ne dim ne red, like God's own head,
    The glorious Sun uprist:
Then all averr'd, I had kill'd the Bird   95
    That brought the fog and mist.
'Twas right, said they, such birds to slay
    That bring the fog and mist.

The breezes blew, the white foam flew,
    The furrow follow'd free: 100
We were the first that ever burst
    Into that silent Sea.

Down dropt the breeze, the Sails dropt down,
   'Twas sad as sad could be
And we did speak only to break   105
   The silence of the Sea.

All in a hot and copper sky
   The bloody sun at noon,
Right up above the mast did stand,
   No bigger than the moon.   110

Day after day, day after day,
   We stuck, ne breath ne motion,
As idle as a painted Ship
   Upon a painted Ocean.

Water, water, every where,   115
   And all the boards did shrink;
Water, water, every where,
   Ne any drop to drink.

The very deeps did rot: O Christ!
   That ever this should be!   120
Yea, slimy things did crawl with legs
   Upon the slimy Sea.

About, about, in reel and rout
   The Death-fires danc'd at night;
The water, like a witch's oils,   125
   Burnt green and blue and white.

And some in dreams assured were
   Of the Spirit that plagued us so:
Nine fathom deep he had follow'd us
   From the Land of Mist and Snow.   130

And every tongue thro' utter drouth
   Was wither'd at the root;
We could not speak no more than if
   We had been choked with soot.

Ah wel-a-day! what evil looks 135
    Had I from old and young;
Instead of the Cross the Albatross
    About my neck was hung.

III.

I saw a something in the Sky
    No bigger than my fist; 140
At first it seem'd a little speck
    And then it seem'd a mist:
It mov'd and mov'd, and took at last
    A certain shape, I wist.

A speck, a mist, a shape, I wist! 145
    And still it ner'd and ner'd;
And, an it dodg'd a water-sprite,
    It plung'd and tack'd and veer'd.

With throat unslack'd, with black lips bak'd
    Ne could we laugh, ne wail: 150
Then while thro' drouth all dumb they stood
I bit my arm and suck'd the blood
    And cry'd, A sail! A sail!

With throat unslack'd, with black lips bak'd
    Agape they hear'd me call: 155
Gramercy! they for joy did grin
And all at once their breath drew in
    As they were drinking all.

She doth not tack from side to side—
    Hither to work us weal 160
Withouten wind, withouten tide
    She steddies with upright keel.

The western wave was all a flame,
    The day was well nigh done!
Almost upon the western wave 165
    Rested the broad bright Sun;

When that strange shape drove suddenly
   Betwixt us and the Sun.

And strait the Sun was fleck'd with bars
   (Heaven's mother send us grace)   170
As if thro' a dungeon grate he peer'd
   With broad and burning face.

Alas! (thought I, and my heart beat loud)
   How fast she neres and neres!
Are those *her* Sails that glance in the Sun   175
   Like restless gossameres?

Are these *her* naked ribs, which fleck'd
   The sun that did behind them peer?
And are these two all, all the crew,
   That woman and her fleshless Pheere?   180

His bones were black with many a crack,
   All black and bare, I ween;
Jet-black and bare, save where with rust
Of mouldy damps and charnel crust
   They're patch'd with purple and green.   185

Her lips are red, *her* looks are free,
   Her locks are yellow as gold:
Her skin as is white as leprosy,
And she is far liker Death than he;
   Her flesh makes the still air cold.   190

The naked Hulk alongside came
   And the Twain were playing dice;
"The Game is done! I've won, I've won!"
   Quoth she, and whistled thrice.

A gust of wind sterte up behind   195
   And whistled thro' his bones;
Thro' the holes of his eyes and the hole of his mouth
   Half-whistles and half-groans.

With never a whisper in the Sea
    Off darts the Spectre-ship;   200
While clombe above the Eastern bar
The horned Moon, with one bright Star
    Almost atween the tips.

One after one by the horned Moon
    (Listen, O Stranger! to me)   205
Each turn'd his face with a ghastly pang
    And curs'd me with his ee.

Four times fifty living men,
    With never a sigh or groan,
With heavy thump, a lifeless lump   210
    They dropp'd down one by one.

Their souls did from their bodies fly,—
    They fled to bliss or woe;
And every soul it pass'd me by,
    Like the whiz of my Cross-bow.   215

IV.

"I fear thee, ancyent Marinere!
    "I fear thy skinny hand;
"And thou art long and lank and brown
    "As is the ribb'd Sea-sand.

"I fear thee and thy glittering eye   220
    "And thy skinny hand so brown—
Fear not, fear not, thou wedding guest!
    This body dropt not down.

Alone, alone, all all alone
    Alone on the wide wide Sea;   225
And Christ would take no pity on
    My soul in agony.

The many men so beautiful,
    And they all dead did lie!
And a million million slimy things   230
    Liv'd on—and so did I.

I look'd upon the rotting Sea,
    And drew my eyes away;
I look'd upon the eldritch deck
    And there the dead men lay.   235

I look'd to Heaven, and try'd to pray;
    But or ever a prayer had gusht,
A wicked whisper came and made
    My heart as dry as dust.

I clos'd my lids and kept them close,   240
    Till the balls like pulses beat;
For the sky and the sea, and the sea and the sky
Lay like a load on my weary eye,
    And the dead were at my feet.

The cold sweat melted from their limbs,   245
    Ne rot, ne reek did they;
The look with which they look'd on me,
    Had never pass'd away.

An orphan's curse would drag to Hell
    A spirit from on high: 250
But O! more horrible than that
    Is the curse in a dead man's eye!
Seven days, seven nights I saw that curse,
    And yet I could not die.

The moving Moon went up the sky   255
    And no where did abide:
Softly she was going up
    And a star or two beside—

Her beams bemock'd the sultry main
    Like morning frosts yspread;   260
But where the ship's huge shadow lay,
The charmed water burnt alway
    A still and awful red.

Beyond the shadow of the ship
    I watch'd the water-snakes: 265
They mov'd in tracks of shining white;
And when they rear'd, the elfish light
    Fell off in hoary flakes.

Within the shadow of the ship
    I watch'd their rich attire: 270
Blue, glossy green, and velvet black
They coil'd and swam; and every track
    Was a flash of golden fire.

O happy living things! no tongue
    Their beauty might declare: 275
A spring of love gusht from my heart,
    And I bless'd them unaware!
Sure my kind saint took pity on me,
    And I bless'd them unaware.

The self-same moment I could pray;   280
    And from my neck so free
The Albatross fell off, and sank
    Like lead into the sea.

V.

O sleep, it is a gentle thing
    Belov'd from pole to pole!   285
To Mary-queen the praise be yeven
She sent the gentle sleep from heaven
    That slid into my soul.

The silly buckets on the deck
    That had so long remain'd,   290
I dreamt that they were fill'd with dew
    And when I awoke it rain'd.

My lips were wet, my throat was cold,
    My garments all were dank;
Sure I had drunken in my dreams   295
    And still my body drank.

I mov'd and could not feel my limbs,
    I was so light, almost
I thought that I had died in sleep,
    And was a blessed Ghost.   300

The roaring wind! it roar'd far off,
    It did not come anear;
But with its sound it shook the sails
    That were so thin and sere.

The upper air bursts into life,   305
    And a hundred fire-flags sheen
To and fro are hurried about;
And to and fro, and in and out
    The stars dance on between.

The coming wind doth roar more loud;   310
    The sails do sigh like sedge:
The rain pours down from one black cloud
    And the Moon is at its edge.

Hark! hark! the thick black cloud is cleft,
    And the Moon is at its side: 315
Like waters shot from some high crag,
The lightning falls with never a jag
    A river steep and wide.

The strong wind reach'd the ship: it roar'd
    And dropp'd down, like a stone!   320
Beneath the lightning and the moon
    The dead men gave a groan.

They groan'd, they stirr'd, they all uprose,
    Ne spake, ne mov'd their eyes:
It had been strange, even in a dream
    To have seen those dead men rise.   325

The helmsman steer'd, the ship mov'd on;
    Yet never a breeze up-blew;
The Marineres all 'gan work the ropes
    Where they were wont to do: 330
They rais'd their limbs like lifeless tools—
    We were a ghastly crew.

The body of my brother's son
    Stood by me knee to knee:
The body and I pull'd at one rope,   335
    But he said nought to me—
And I quak'd to think of my own voice
    How frightful it would be!

The day-light dawn'd—they dropp'd their arms,
    And cluster'd round the mast: 340
Sweet sounds rose slowly thro' their mouths
    And from their bodies pass'd.

Around, around, flew each sweet sound,
    Then darted to the sun:
Slowly the sounds came back again   345
    Now mix'd, now one by one.

Sometimes a dropping from the sky
    I heard the Lavrock sing;
Sometimes all little birds that are
How they seem'd to fill the sea and air   350
    With their sweet jargoning,

And now 'twas like all instruments,
   Now like a lonely flute;
And now it is an angel's song
   That makes the heavens be mute.   355

It ceas'd: yet still the sails made on
   A pleasant noise till noon,
A noise like of a hidden brook
   In the leafy month of June,
That to the sleeping woods all night   360
   Singeth a quiet tune.

Listen, O listen, thou Wedding-guest!
   "Marinere! thou hast thy will:
"For that, which comes out of thine eye, doth make
   "My body and soul to be still."

Never sadder tale was told   365
   To a man of woman born:
Sadder and wiser thou wedding-guest!
   Thou'lt rise to morrow morn.

Never sadder tale was heard   370
   By a man of woman born:
The Marineres all return'd to work
   As silent as beforne.

The Marineres all 'gan pull the ropes,
   But look at me they n'old: 375
Thought I, I am as thin as air—
   They cannot me behold.

Till noon we silently sail'd on
   Yet never a breeze did breathe:
Slowly and smoothly went the ship   380
   Mov'd onward from beneath.

Under the keel nine fathom deep
   From the land of mist and snow
The spirit slid: and it was He

That made the Ship to go. 385
The sails at noon left off their tune
   And the Ship stood still also.

The sun right up above the mast
   Had fix'd her to the ocean:
But in a minute she 'gan stir 390
   With a short uneasy motion—
Backwards and forwards half her length
   With a short uneasy motion.

Then, like a pawing horse let go,
   She made a sudden bound: 395
It flung the blood into my head,
   And I fell into a swound.

How long in that same fit I lay,
   I have not to declare;
But ere my living life return'd, 400
I heard and in my soul discern'd
   Two voices in the air,

"Is it he? quoth one, "Is this the man?
   "By him who died on cross,
"With his cruel bow he lay'd full low 405
   "The harmless Albatross.

"The spirit who 'bideth by himself
   "In the land of mist and snow,
"He lov'd the bird that lov'd the man
   "Who shot him with his bow." 410

The other was a softer voice
   As soft as honey-dew:
Quoth he the man hath penance done,
   And penance more will do.

VI.

FIRST VOICE.
"But tell me, tell me! speak again, 415
   "Thy soft response renewing—
"What makes that ship drive on so fast?
   "What is the Ocean doing?

      SECOND VOICE.
"Still as a Slave before his Lord,
   "The Ocean hath no blast: 420
"His great bright eye most silently
   "Up to the moon is cast—

"If he may know which way to go,
   "For she guides him smooth or grim.
"See, brother, see! how graciously 425
   "She looketh down on him.

      FIRST VOICE.
"But why drives on that ship so fast
   "Withouten wave or wind?
      SECOND VOICE.
"The air is cut away before,
   "And closes from behind. 430

"Fly, brother, fly! more high, more high,
   "Or we shall be belated.
"For slow and slow that ship will go,
   "When the Marinere's trance is abated.

I woke, and we were sailing on 435
   As in a gentle weather:
'Twas night, calm night, the moon was high;
   The dead men stood together.

All stood together on the deck,
   For a charnel-dungeon fitter: 440
All fix'd on me their stony eyes
   That in the moon did glitter.

The pang, the curse with which they died,
    Had never pass'd away:
I could not draw my een from theirs   445
    Ne turn them up to pray.

And in its time the spell was snapt,
    And I could move my een:
I look'd far-forth, but little saw
    Of what might else be seen.   450

Like one, that on a lonely road
    Doth walk in fear and dread,
And having once turn'd round, walks on
    And turns no more his head:
Because he knows, a frightful fiend   455
    Doth close behind him tread.

But soon there breath'd a wind on me,
    Ne sound ne motion made:
Its path was not upon the sea
    In ripple or in shade.   460

It rais'd my hair, it fann'd my cheek,
    Like a meadow-gale of spring—
It mingled strangely with my fears,
    Yet it felt like a welcoming.

Swiftly, swiftly flew the ship,   465
    Yet she sail'd softly too:
Sweetly, sweetly, blew the breeze—
    On me alone it blew.

O dream of joy! is this indeed
    The light-house top I see?   470
Is this the Hill? Is this the Kirk?
    Is this mine own countrée?

We drifted o'er the Harbour-bar,
    And I with sobs did pray—

"O let me be awake, my God! 475
    "Or let me sleep alway!"

The harbour-bay was clear as glass,
    So smoothly it was strewn!
And on the bay the moon light lay,
    And the shadow of the moon. 480

The moonlight bay was white all o'er,
    Till rising from the same,
Full many shapes, that shadows were,
    Like as of torches came.

A little distance from the prow 485
    Those dark-red shadows were;
But soon I saw that my own flesh
    Was red as in a glare.

I turn'd my head in fear and dread,
    And by the holy rood, 490
The bodies had advanc'd, and now
    Before the mast they stood.

They lifted up their stiff right arms,
    They held them strait and tight;
And each right-arm burnt like a torch, 495
    A torch that's borne upright.
Their stony eye-balls glitter'd on
    In the red and smoky light.

I pray'd and turn'd my head away
    Forth looking as before. 500
There was no breeze upon the bay,
    No wave against the shore.

The rock shone bright, the kirk no less
    That stands above the rock:
The moonlight steep'd in silentness 505
    The steady weathercock.

And the bay was white with silent light,
   Till rising from the same
Full many shapes, that shadows were,
   In crimson colours came. 510

A little distance from the prow
   Those crimson shadows were:
I turn'd my eyes upon the deck—
   O Christ! what saw I there?

Each corse lay flat, lifeless and flat; 515
   And by the Holy rood
A man all light, a seraph-man,
   On every corse there stood.

This seraph-band, each wav'd his hand:
   It was a heavenly sight: 520
They stood as signals to the land,
   Each one a lovely light:

This seraph-band, each waved his hand,
   No voice did they impart—
No voice; but O! the silence sank, 525
   Like music on my heart.

Eftsones I heard the dash of oars,
   I heard the pilot's cheer:
My head was turn'd perforce away
   And I saw a boat appear. 530

Then vanish'd all the lovely lights;
   The bodies rose anew:
With silent pace, each to his place,
   Came back the ghastly crew.
The wind, that shade nor motion made, 535
   On me alone it blew.

The pilot, and the pilot's boy
   I heard them coming fast:
Dear Lord in Heaven! it was a joy
   The dead men could not blast. 540

I saw a third—I heard his voice:
    It is the Hermit good!
He singeth loud his godly hymns
    That he makes in the wood.
He'll shrieve my soul, he'll wash away   545
    The Albatross's blood.

VII.

This Hermit good lives in that wood
    Which slopes down to the Sea.
How loudly his sweet voice he rears!
He loves to talk with Marineres   550
    That come from a far Contrée.

He kneels at morn and noon and eve—
    He hath a cushion plump:
It is the moss, that wholly hides
    The rotted old Oak-stump.   555

The Skiff-boat ne'rd: I heard them talk,
    "Why, this is strange, I trow!
"Where are those lights so many and fair
    "That signal made but now?

"Strange, by my faith! the Hermit said—   560
    "And they answer'd not our cheer.
"The planks look warp'd, and see those sails
    "How thin they are and sere!
"I never saw aught like to them
    "Unless perchance it were   565

"The skeletons of leaves that lag
    "My forest brook along:
"When the Ivy-tod is heavy with snow,
"And the Owlet whoops to the wolf below
    "That eats the she-wolf's young.   570

"Dear Lord! it has a fiendish look—
    (The Pilot made reply)

"I am afear'd.—"Push on, push on!
    "Said the Hermit cheerily.

The Boat came closer to the Ship,   575
    But I ne spake ne stirr'd!
The Boat came close beneath the Ship,
    And strait a sound was heard!

Under the water it rumbled on,
    Still louder and more dread: 580
It reach'd the Ship, it split the bay;
    The Ship went down like lead.

Stunn'd by that loud and dreadful sound,
    Which sky and ocean smote:
Like one that hath been seven days drown'd   585
    My body lay afloat:
But, swift as dreams, myself I found
    Within the Pilot's boat.

Upon the whirl, where sank the Ship,
    The boat spun round and round: 590
And all was still, save that the hill
    Was telling of the sound.

I mov'd my lips: the Pilot shriek'd
    And fell down in a fit.
The Holy Hermit rais'd his eyes   595
    And pray'd where he did sit.

I took the oars: the Pilot's boy,
    Who now doth crazy go,
Laugh'd loud and long, and all the while
    His eyes went to and fro,   600
"Ha! ha!" quoth he—"full plain I see,
    "The devil knows how to row."

And now all in mine own Countrée
    I stood on the firm land!

The Hermit stepp'd forth from the boat,   605
    And scarcely he could stand.

"O shrieve me, shrieve me, holy Man!
    The Hermit cross'd his brow—
"Say quick," quoth he, "I bid thee say
    "What manner of man art thou?   610

Forthwith this frame of mine was wrench'd
    With a woeful agony,
Which forc'd me to begin my tale
    And then it left me free.

Since then at an uncertain hour   615
    Now oftimes and now fewer,
That anguish comes and makes me tell
    My ghastly aventure.

I pass, like night, from land to land;
    I have strange power of speech;   620
The moment that his face I see
I know the man that must hear me;
    To him my tale I teach.

What loud uproar bursts from that door!
    The Wedding-guests are there;   625
But in the Garden-bower the Bride
    And Bride-maids singing are:
And hark the little Vesper-bell
    Which biddeth me to prayer.

O Wedding-guest! this soul hath been   630
    Alone on a wide wide sea:
So lonely 'twas, that God himself
    Scarce seemed there to be.

O sweeter than the Marriage-feast,
    'Tis sweeter far to me   635
To walk together to the Kirk
    With a goodly company.

> To walk together to the Kirk
>   And all together pray,
> While each to his great father bends,   640
> Old men, and babes, and loving friends,
>   And Youths, and Maidens gay.
>
> Farewell, farewell! but this I tell
>   To thee, thou wedding-guest!
> He prayeth well who loveth well   645
>   Both man and bird and beast.
>
> He prayeth best who loveth best,
>   All things both great and small:
> For the dear God, who loveth us,
>   He made and loveth all.   650
>
> The Marinere, whose eye is bright,
>   Whose beard with age is hoar,
> Is gone; and now the wedding-guest
>   Turn'd from the bridegroom's door.
>
> He went, like one that hath been stunn'd   655
>   And is of sense forlorn:
> A sadder and a wiser man
>   He rose the morrow morn.

NOTE

1. The title is given on a separate title page in 1798 and repeated thus (but not given here) at the head of the poem. The argument is given on a second separate title page. Each of the seven parts begins on a new page. I have added line numbers. See also *PW* 1:365–419, 2:504–39 (poem **161** in series).

Appendix B: Reading "Alice du Clós", and for the Birds[1]

> I believe in pure explication de texte. This may in fact be my principal form of piety.
>
> Wallace Stevens[2]

1. Preamble

"Alice du Clós" (**655**), like the first of Pound's *Cantos*, begins in the middle of its story. Yet, while Pound's last words are "So that," pointing to a narrative that goes on beyond the text, Coleridge concludes decisively with the death of the protagonist. The end arrives so suddenly that a reader must inevitably pause to catch up with the events that lead up to Alice's death, but the situation is unusual. The moment the fast-moving narrative concludes, the meanings it has gathered within itself and from other sources begin to unravel in slow-motion. Perhaps a better comparison than Canto I is Beckett's short story, "Dante and the Lobster," which ends:

> Well, thought Belacqua, it's a quick death, God help us all.
> It is not.[3]

Coleridge does not intervene directly like this. He brings us up short by an ending that might appear to contradict every feeling his narrative has elicited, every nuance a reader of his other poems might have picked up. And we may afterwards be troubled to learn that the sleight of hand involved is duplicitous, more characteristic of the villain here than the heroine.

In such ways "Alice du Clós" is unlike any other poem Coleridge wrote. Although it draws upon deep-rooted concerns that caused him anxiety and remained raw throughout his adult life, no other poem dispatches them with such brio. Why a finish that closes like a trap? Is the neatness of construction—the pared-down efficiency of the poem's working—a sign of impatience or even levity? How does a reader square the sympathies elicited by the narrative with the way they appear to be turned upside-down and written off by the plot? Was Coleridge contriving to affront or discomfort us? to provoke?

The sense of a conclusive ending that brings us up short in a narrative that could have gone on as the "Ancient Mariner" does after the shooting of the albatross—that is, simultaneously more and less of an ending than we have been led to expect—is closely connected to the way the plot turns on a pun. The stories of romance that kept Alice up all night entrap and destroy her when they are misreported; or, more accurately, when they are reported in such a literal manner that her situation is misunderstood. The use of the word "page" with two meanings—each separately innocent—becomes suddenly lethal when they are confused; and the shock we feel becomes a devouring irony when we reflect that the evil messenger who set the scene for Alice's destruction has done no more than the poet who, with his rhymes and half-rhymes, has used words in the same way to establish our sense of her innocence; an innocence that in retrospect contains fault-lines and slippages.[4] The pun opens a chasm under the rounded narrative by means identical with the way the entire poem works—modifying meanings by linking sounds, sometimes by rhymes that twist the sense—and the treachery of language underlines the blocked communication between Julian and Alice.

There is little evidence in the history of commentary that Coleridge's poem has been carefully or appreciatively read but it possesses an interest as a piece of writing remarkable for its skill, subtlety and directness.[5] Ballads held a special attraction for him as a form, yet beginning them proved easier than finishing them off. An eminent literary historian with a broad view of the subject singled out "Alice du Clós" as Coleridge's most successful piece of work of its kind, "an *Othello* in little":

> This poem shows what the ballad might be in the hands of a good poet who would take the pains to deal with it freely and sincerely. (Hustvedt 99)

At the same time, complete achievement and impressive though it is, it puts themes that occupied Coleridge from the beginning of his writing-life into a new perspective. The sparks that fly from "Alice du Clós"—the elements of surprise—are demonstrably of the same kind we meet in "The Eolian Harp" (**115**), "Frost at Midnight" (**171**) and "The Rime of the Ancient Mariner." At the same time, themes and aspects of style overlap poems written later, at the end of his writing-life, like "The Improvisatore" (**623**) and "The Garden of Boccaccio" (**652**). All round, we have a poem that performs a somersault, leaving Coleridge's central preoccupations intact, in their place but trembling.

It is important that an element of trickery is central. As in a Maupassant or O. Henry story, we are plunged into a situation that develops in real time with little opportunity to think outside it. The action advances through the uncertain period while dawn turns into day, as if within the mesmerised time we take to read. We are transported in space from a garden bower to a nearby woodland glade, and the second scene is superimposed on the first. The sense of elision is further increased by the small cast of characters—just four, who are in turn made up of two pairs—a lord and his attendant knight, a lady and her attendant squire. As I said, the working of the plot, the thoughts and feelings of the characters, come together with a speed and force that absorbs our whole attention. The pun that fashions the catastrophe comes out of the blue but, once seen, we understand it has lurked in the shadows and was always there. Or one could say the terminating pun echoes earlier sounds that have remained suspended within what we read. The process continues and remains the troubling subject of our thought; a thrust contained by and reverberating beyond the poem itself.

2. Narrative

A story-element is prominent in all ballads: usually one that can be told without much ado and quickly grasped. "Alice du Clós" conforms to tradition but turns on itself in the way I have described. Indeed, it is more like a modern short story in concentrating on the climactic moment, leaving the previous action to be understood by glimpses. The narrative breaks in on us like an urgent interruption and we are assailed by a request that is more like a command and told that we ignore it at our peril:

> "The Sun is not yet risen
> But the Dawn lies red on the dew:
> Lord Julian has stolen from the Hunters' away,
> Is seeking, Lady! for You.
>
> * * *
>
> O Lady! throw your Book aside!
> I would not that my Lord should chide."

Only afterwards do we discover that the speaker is the "Vassal Knight" Sir Hugh and the Lady is Alice, in some unconfirmed way his master's betrothed. He has been reported by an unnamed narrator who then, speaking in her own voice, at once digresses into a description of Alice's private world. It is a world of calm whose qualities are heightened as they contrast with the rough intrusion they follow, while retrospectively the sense of Hugh's effrontery is increased. The narrator's description of Alice extends in a way that continues to emphasise her innocence and vulnerability, making even clearer that Hugh has added insult to his task; and, when Alice comes to reply, we pick up with her threatened feelings. She dismisses him in forthright terms but trembles inwardly. He, for his part, crude and offensive as he is, carries away a disquieting sense of power and satisfaction in having achieved an unstated purpose:

> Like a huge billow from a Bark
> Toil'd in the deep Sea-trough
>
> That shouldering sideways in mid plunge
> Is travers'd by a Flash:
> And staggering onward leaves the Ear
> With dull and distant Crash.

When we turn back to the troubled Alice, there is a sudden change. Within the space of the following five-line stanza, with no explanation (unless she felt her "Scoff" had been too fierce), she recovers her spirits and follows the instructions she has been given. She dresses to join Lord Julian in "her Dress of Green,|Her Buskins and her Quiver," and we plunge into playtime. She is a child again, even younger than previously suggested, and, when she calls her youthful squire, Florian, she has a companion to share the fun (note his matching "quiver" in line 90). They stop for a moment to watch the sun rise on their setting out. It is an important transition, already poignant and fated to become more so. They are leaving behind a world of dreams to enter an adult masculine world of hunting.

Another small intrusion interrupts the narrative advance. The narrator explains that the place where Alice has been told to join Lord Julian has been altered to one that better suits a neighbour knight: not much further away but "A green and lightsome Glade" in the forest instead of a "Covert Lane." The narrator also takes the opportunity to describe how Julian experiences an odd difficulty in absorbing this change of plan. His failure to find good reason not to agree to the change has a decidedly unusual effect:

> He bit his lip, he wrung his Glove,
> He look'd around, he look'd above;
> But pretext none could find or frame!

Such prevarication and the mental disturbance it causes helps introduce his character and the scene that follows. An uncertain tyrant!

Sir Hugh arrives in the open glade and carefully postpones delivering the reply his Lord is waiting for. This of course only disturbs Julian's spirits the more:

> "God's Wrath! Speak out, Man!" Julian cried,
> O'ermaster'd by the sudden Smart:
> And feigning wrath, sharp, blunt and rude
> The Knight his subtle Shift pursued—

With false reluctance Hugh then reports Alice's response in a fashion that—while word for word accurate—is selective and utterly misrepresents her meaning. The repetition of Julian's word "Wrath" at first glance looks clumsy, but it foreshadows his reapplication of Alice's word "wanton" to her squire. The young pair break merrily onto the scene, their horses galloping out of control. Julian swallows the bait, believes Alice has spent the night in dalliance with Florian, hurls his hunting lance at Alice, end of story.

> The shaft was hurl'd!.a lifeless corse,
> Fair Alice from her vaulting horse,
> Lies bleeding on the glade.

3. Characters in Action

While Coleridge's poem can be compared to a modern short story, the parts can be said to move like contiguous scenes in a one-act play, achieving urgency by conforming to the Classical unities of time, place and action. In this respect, it justifies the comparison with the shortest, most perfectly wrought of Shakespeare's plays, *Othello*, cited above. The leading figures in the two texts indeed bear more than a passing resemblance; that is, Lord Julian, Sir Hugh and Alice when set against Othello, Iago and Desdemona. However, differences quickly arise when the comparison is pressed, as Coleridge probably intended. If one must suppose an allusion, it works in the same diminishing way as the pun.

Sir Hugh obviously resembles Iago in the way he deceives his master into destroying the woman he loves but his malignity is not, like Iago's, motiveless. Alice has already asked Julian not to employ him as a messenger. She is the target of Hugh's malign intentions; not the vehicle, as Desdemona is for Iago to assail Othello. Again, Hugh in his own way remains loyal to his master; if he is jealous of Julian, this only compounds his wounded pride in relation to Alice. He is sly but not so much in control of his feelings as to be called calculating. A poem by Coleridge first published at the time "Alice du Clós" was completed, "Not at Home" (**666**), is a commentary on how such feelings originate:

> That Jealousy may rule a mind
> Where Love could never be
> I know; but ne'er expect to find
> Love without Jealousy.
>
> She has a strange cast in her ee,
> A swart sour-visaged maid.
> But yet Love's own twin-sister she
> His house-mate and his shade. (*PW* 1:1118)

The play on names that serves Hugh's revenge—his loose use of the word "page" to substitute for what the narrator correctly calls "squire"—is a demotion of a kind Coleridge thought indicative of "resentment" and "suppressed passion, especially of hardly smothered dislike," "most common among the lower orders, & origin of Nick-names."[6] Compare his own well-known puns on the names Leibniz and Spinoza or even, in "Punic Greek," on his own name. They are all indicative of some kind of trivialising or low esteem one way or another.

Lord Julian shares the flavour of his servant's baseness, albeit in a differently stifled way. He is in some way engaged to be married to Alice, yet he issues an untimely command he expects her to follow and he has a deep compulsion to meet her in clandestine surroundings ("the Covert Lane") as if he shrank from acknowledging his love. As the narrator comments:

> It grieves me sore to think, to say,
> That Names so seldom meet with Love,
> Yet Love wants courage without a Name!

He can be roused to jealous action in a flash, like Othello, but otherwise his jealousy appears more like that of Leontes in *The Winter's Tale*. He is not by nature trusting; Alice obeys his instructions but with no hint of any bond but a legal one between them; there is nothing in him of the noble Moor. He is served as he deserves by his surly rough factotum. At the same time, Alice is no devoted Desdemona. She is compared at length to Venus, the morning star, that lingers on as if "To brave the' advancing Morn,"[7] but she betrays no positive feelings towards the man she is pledged to marry (lines 28–34). Only "flight and fear" enter the comparison. As Graham Davidson succinctly put the matter: "she has the innocence of the Christabel who has met Geraldine, an innocence of act but not of consciousness." And as Peter Cheyne added, it is important that Coleridge refers to the star under which Alice's fateful day begins as "he", not "she" (in line 33); that is, in its guise as Lucifer, not as Venus (as in AV Isaiah 14:12).

Hugh and Julian define themselves in the narrative against Alice's innocence, but one might indeed wonder if what she represents is wholly unqualified. The narrator lovingly portrays her as childishly innocent while "loosely wrapt in Maiden White," but she immerses herself in "Dan Ovid's mazy tale" which is the reverse of innocent, making "loosely" become a suspect word.[8] Again, Hugh's "taunting Vein… thrill'd like venom thro' her Brain" and Alice's tart retort is born of pride and anger. Perhaps she feels compromised by a dim awareness of shame, born of her reading and uncertain relationship with Julian. The narrator repeatedly emphasises her childishness by such formulations as the "lovely child of old Du Clos!" and always thinks of her as younger than we might assume she is. Alice's squire follows her as "a stripling" and is linked to her the more closely by his name, Florian, she being imaged as "the "earliest-open'd Flower." A stanza is given over to describing him as proud to be gallant in her service, blushing when he holds her train, and so not entirely innocent even if lacking in experience; and by such hints we are shown that the young pair who re-enter the poem to make its conclusion are already touched with the first signs of maturity. They dress up and set out on sedate palfreys like children; they arrive at their catastrophe, out of control, on galloping fillies. The narrator links Alice with "the flowring May-thorn Tree" in a description that culminates in a vision of joy. She forgets that may-thorn is also a promise of ill fortune, as she ignores other telling details she does not want to think about.[9]

The story in short is an accident waiting to happen, involving four characters who, the more fully they are considered, bring it on themselves. The unnamed fifth person—the narrator—is not involved in the action but she is no less present in a different way. Her interjections on Alice's behalf, following on Hugh's opening command, suggest she might be someone like an old family nurse. She supplies the long interruption that follows Hugh's opening command and situates us within Alice's point of view. Hers is the rising mood that accompanies Alice's recovering spirits as she prepares to join the hunt: as much to play with her young companion-squire as to obey a future husband's call. The same voice is heard as Alice moves off towards the hunt—"Alas! alas! and weladay!"—but it becomes more distant in the second half of the poem. The narrator shrinks back as the end comes in sight and we are left alone to move closer to the painful catastrophe. Of course, the nurse-as-narrator is a persona chosen by the author, and he is present too, manipulating rhymes and ironies and references outside her restricted purview. Who else to note that Alice has become like Diana, goddess of hunting, even though she is on the brink of being hunted to death in turn: an irony remarked by her "need" of Diana's diadem that was crowned by a crescent moon (lines 184–85).[10]

4. Enlarging Stanzas and Their Rhymes

The story is finely balanced and, if the ending is cruel, on whom does responsibility fall? The twinned villains obviously, but one has to allow the twinned victims could not say that guilt was a thing utterly impossible to them. Or does one suppose the fatal conjunction of all four together is the author's contrivance, and therefore his ultimate responsibility? Before addressing these questions, I must say more about the means Coleridge employed. The sudden shifts in point of view and focus I have described are part of his management.

Although the movement and structure of "Alice du Clós" conforms to the ballad tradition, its smaller elements do not. For a start, very few stanzas conform to the norm of alternating 4- and 3- stress lines rhyming abcb. The majority enlarge the pattern in ways that are not by themselves unusual, adding an additional rhyme here or extending a line there to drive home a point; but others again employ just two rhymes in stanzas of varying lengths in different combinations. Indeed, the two longest stanzas stretch to ten lines that some might prefer to call verse paragraphs, one of them employing three rhymes (lines 15–24) and the other five plus one line standing alone (lines 25–34), each in different ways. The odd line in the latter paragraph is part of an integrated ballad stanza that thereby prepares the way for a return to the four-line norm (in lines 35–38).

The ballad norm was established in Sir Hugh's opening instructions to Alice and immediately shifted into a more diffuse register when the narrator-nurse supplied her commentary in ten-line rhymed paragraphs. What is happening is that variations on the ballad stanza familiar from the "Ancient Mariner" are extended and combined with the rhyming schemes of "Christabel," and yet the ballad norm remains the context within which the variations are worked. Thus, after a stanza including two rhymes, the norm is picked up again when Alice begins her reply (lines 44–47) and, following another two-rhyme stanza, Hugh's departure continues in regular ballad stanzas that happen (uniquely in this poem: lines 52–59) to form a single grammatical unit. Moving on, when Alice is left alone and calls for Florian, we find a run of enlarged stanzas containing just two rhymes and also a larger than usual number of couplets in different positions. The patterning sets up protocols that govern the way we see and respond to characters in action.

We encounter nothing in the second half of the narrative like the nurse's extended meditative description of Alice. The waiting Lord Julian is introduced and described in a series of stanzas that mostly depart from the ballad norm; but significantly not all and none in quite the same way, and they thereby embody his conflicted and constricted state of mind. Sir Hugh then re-enters, unaccompanied by Alice, and delivers his initial, falsely considerate report on how he found Alice in her bower. His three wholly invariant ballad stanzas (lines 141–52) form the longest consecutive sequence in the poem, which is an irony given their blatant hypocrisy. As the climax builds, couplets re-enter all of the remaining stanzas and are used here to different effect than in the earlier scene with Alice and Florian. While they again serve to extend and delay the narrative movement, this has by now has gathered momentum to an extent that they open onto a pool of impending disaster. The manner in which rhyme is used to advance and retard our view of the action is a master class in manipulation.

The underlying continuo is provided by the structure of the basic ballad stanza: the pulsing forward rhythm of the first three lines is checked by the rhyme that ties the fourth line back to the second; and the rhythm is modified at every stage by anything between six and twelve syllables in any line and other factors. For example, the caesura, that usually finds a central place in 4-stress lines, necessarily leans one way or the other when the number of stresses is uneven. The concluding stanza (lines 187–93) is, as it should be, a definitive example: the a-rhyme is doubled, the c-rhyme is tripled (the only triplet in the whole poem), and each group of multiplied lines shifts the emphasis one way and the other to release their force onto the isolated b-rhymes that follow and tie the two sentences they conclude in a choking knot. At the same time, in this same stanza, sounds cross and intersect, keep echoes alive while others are renewed. The method for the most part works unconsciously. When it is noticed lending emphasis to different words and phrases, it can be relished.

A suitably different example is provided by the two crucially important paragraphs spoken by the nurse. The second paragraph, like the first, opens with a couplet but it contains a further couplet (lines 28–29) that repeats the initial rhymes of the previous, first paragraph (lines 15–17); and the syntax of this second paragraph runs across the line-endings in a completely different, more fluent way. Again, as one becomes familiar with the poem, one realises other details contribute to the complex interrelation. Words that contribute to the nurse's earlier, more optimistic point of view are overtaken by meanings that come from some more neutral space. For example Florian's "joy and pride" (82) becomes Julian's "shame and pride" (104); as I said before, Alice and Florian's horses, as they carry their riders to their unwitting destruction, change from staid palfreys (75) to "mad" fillies (180). Innocent words assume prescient meanings in retrospect, and the caring nurse's "advancing Morn" (line 34) ends in mourning sadness. Similarly, the words "buskins" and "quiver" that echo through the earlier part of the poem: the buskins of comedy are left behind and the airy, shimmering latticed light of Alice is overcast and violently stilled. And again the possibility remains, in the larger perspective and like a stain, that Alice (again like Desdemona) might somehow have collaborated in, even abetted her own destruction.

5. A Scheme of Echoes

These last examples show the author's hand, there is no gainsaying; and this is revealed to any who have read further in Coleridge in ways that leave no doubt where he stands. The title of this next stage of my argument is borrowed from an Irish poet, Trevor Joyce.[11] I use it here to describe not just the way Coleridge's poem sets up an interlocking scheme of sounds and values but contains clear traces of concerns touched on before at less or greater length in other poems. Thus, line 24, "A Snowdrop in a tuft of Snow!" repeats with slight variation the concluding line of Coleridge's "The Apotheosis; or, The Snow-drop" (**165**), a poem in answer to Mary Robinson's ode on the same theme (see *PW* 1:424–26). It thereby links Alice with a figure with whom Coleridge strongly identified as an abandoned victim of cruel love affairs. Again, original readers of "Alice du Clós" would have read, in line 91, the name Ellen and not Alice (see *PW* 1:1102 note, 2:1306); that is, they would have been reminded of the sisterly friend of the protagonist of Coleridge's continuation of Wordsworth's "The Three Graves," available for more than twenty years under his name as well as in the collection in which the poem Alice appeared. The context in Alice is very close to a passage in "The Three Graves" where "a perfect glory" is described (*PW* 1:348) as prelude to a disastrous turn in the narrative.[12] In short, the verbal slip betrays the promise of tragedy that for some reason must necessarily follow.

Connections of the same kind continue to be made through the poem. The narrator's sad reflection over Lord Julian's mixed feelings as he waits for Sir Hugh to return with Alice (lines 111–12) repeats lines Coleridge wrote in a notebook in December 1801 (*CN* 1:1066). In the context of the ballad, the narrator's statement that "Love wants courage without a Name" is gnomic and oddly out of character. But in the context of Coleridge's further development of the idea, in his published adaptation of Lessing's "Die Namen" (**236**; *PW* 1:588–89), the statement is a clarification of Julian's blocked impulses: his secrecy and shame and pride are aspects of a predicament that consumes him in jealous rage. As Graham Davidson comments: "Julian and Alice do not use personal names for each other," he "is still 'My Lord' to her, and she 'the daughter of old du Clós' to him," and it is questionable whether they have "reached any real intimacy despite being formally betrothed."

Another connection of the same kind is established between lines 175–78 and a poem Coleridge wrote into Sara Hutchinson's album, subsequently published in *Sibylline Leaves* and afterwards entitled "Time, Real and Imaginary" (**388**; *PW* 1:798–800). The situation in "Alice du Clós" reverses this other one in which a sister runs ahead of a blind brother, calling to him with "reverted face," the word *reverted* picking up with situations in Coleridge's poems as early as in "Absence: A Poem" (**60**; *PW* 1:99–103, line 80). In short, a reader of Coleridge's other poems is positioned to recognise his lifelong preoccupations working themselves out. They strengthen the impression that the vulnerable Alice is also, in some way, responsible for the situation she finds herself in; that her fear and Julian's rage are somehow interrelated, caused by some sort of blindness or inability to engage a central life-choice in a mature way. A biographer might even want to trace this back to Coleridge's inability to make such a choice in respect to Mary Evans: "a Passion which [he] felt neither the power or the courage to subdue" (*CL* 1:130) and admittedly lacked the "fortitude" to confront and engage with directly (*CL* 1:87–88).

The sense of the connectedness of this poem, which otherwise appears designed to make a firm, separate statement, grows with every reading. One of the few commentators to discuss the poem at any length suggests the star on the brow of the "moon-shiny Doe" imaged in lines 18–19 portends disaster, as in the "Ancient Mariner," which is plausible.[13] One might (I think more plausibly) suggest that such an emblematic doe brings into the poem Wordsworth's *White Doe of Rylstone* (1807), a poem long in the making and intimately connected with Coleridge's "Christabel." The character Christabel is directly recalled by the innocent but ambivalently culpable Alice, and in situations such as when Sir Hugh's words "thrill'd like venom thro' her Brain" (line 40). Indeed, single words in the poem like "glee" (line 68), "mazy" (line 37) and "giddy" (line 174) tremble with added significance when one remembers their prominent positions in poems like (respectively) "The Three Graves" (**155**) and "The Blossoming of the Solitary Date-tree" (**396**), "Religious Musings" (**101**) and "Kubla Khan" (**178**), "Oh! Mihi Præteritos" (**8**; sometimes known as "Quæ Nocent Docent"), and "The Garden of Boccaccio." They are an active presence, gathering and radiating a force beyond the use to which they are presently applied.

One last, minor connection will confirm the point and bring it to bear on the group of poems Coleridge had particularly in mind. The choice of Alice's surname, "du Clós," suggests a closeted existence, separate from the larger world like Coleridge's lime-tree bower perhaps, which is appropriate—just as the repeated conjunction of "du Clós" with "old" underlines her protected youthfulness. But the diacritical mark on Clós is another matter because it is in every respect superfluous: it makes no sense above the letter "o" in French usage. Coleridge took over such diacritics to mark the varying of accent from Percy's *Reliques*:

> And there came lords, and there came knights,
>   Fro manye a farre countryè,
> To break a spere for theyr ladyes love
>   Before that faire ladyè.[14]

I suggest he turned the diacritic the other way (to French acute instead of grave) not only to add to the irony that terminating clósure will overtake protected shelter but also to make visually strange and thereby connect his poem with others written thirty years earlier, where diacritics signalled affairs that were out of joint. It connects with the word "eye" spelled "ee" both in the "Ancient Mariner" and here (in line 89) with respect to Florian; and also with the wrenched mispronunciation, in "Christabel", of the name Geraldine so as to rhyme with Leoline (here "ee" becoming "eyne," reversing the direction of change in the Mariner).[15] I suggest that the earlier "Ballad of the Dark Ladiè" is at the centre of this destabilisation and stakes out the problem that "Alice du Clós" confronts.

6. Postponed Problems

"The Ballad of the Dark Ladiè" began as a companion piece to "Christabel," and Coleridge returned to work on it in late 1799 when he wrote the poem "Love" (**253**), the earliest version of which was published as the "Introduction" or "Preface" to the earlier ballad. Only the introductory stanzas of the ballad were committed to paper and published, and they describe two aspects of a single scene: an unnamed lady waiting anxiously for the arrival of a knight named Lord Falkland, to whom she appears to be betrothed; this followed by her distress at his obvious reluctance to celebrate their love in a public marriage. The knight is indecisive like Julian, but there are two important differences: his fiancée is passionately in love with him, has "given him all" and has thereby lost the respect of her friends; and he appears less confused than manipulative, ready with romantic promises that do not ring true.

The poem "Love," in its first short version introducing the ballad, promises a "woeful Tale of Love" concerning

> the cruel scorn
> That craz'd this bold and lonely Knight,
> And how he roam'd the mountain woods,
> Nor rested day or night. (*PW* 1:606)

In the second free-standing version, published soon afterwards in *Lyrical Ballads* 1800, the description of the now unnamed knight's state of mind is expanded. He is a victim of a proud lady's disinclination to recognise his suit, which he fruitlessly pursues for "ten long years." In his distracted state, he has a vision of "An angel beautiful and bright:|And . . . knew it was a Fiend," which one must suppose is based on her rejection; but this is followed by his rescuing her from the midst of a "murderous band" who threaten her with an "outrage worse than death" (*PW* 1:608). At this point, the "Lady of the Land" acknowledges his love, and tends and nurses him in an effort "to expiate|The scorn that crazed his brain." His "madness" goes away, and he dies having finally expressed feelings that have been reciprocated. Although the first short version of the poem, when it was an introduction to the ballad, promised a tale of "Of Man's perfid'ous cruelty" and a "cruel wrong" that "Befel the Dark Ladie," the lengthened version describes a disdainful Lady redeemed. Her suitor is as much her victim as her aggressor; and the burden of the story is reconciliation, not exploitation.

"The Ballad of the Dark Ladiè" and "Love" present both sides of the same coin. They share the same four-line ballad stanza, regularly rhyming abcb, the first three lines comprising eight syllables with six in the fourth line and only a few variations of syllabic count. We see Falkland in the "Ballad" through the eyes of his Lady as if his action was at best incomprehensible, at worst calculated abuse of her trust. Coleridge left no doubt in a manuscript note—he is indeed "a solemn Scoundrel" (*PW* 1:524 note)—and the woman clearly suffers. The position is reversed in the poem "Love": it is the unnamed knight who suffers because the woman he loves does not acknowledge him until it is too late; and, if she too suffers, she has brought it on herself by her unthinking, perhaps too-conventional behaviour.

Crucial to the difference—and present in both the preliminary and full versions of the poem "Love"—is Coleridge's decision to frame the story he is telling; that is, to incorporate it into a larger frame in which a lover tells it to his loved one. Here, the auditor, Genevieve, is hesitant rather than scornful and the narrator's purpose is simple persuasion. He turns around the beginning situation of the "Dark Ladiè" so as to represent the hero's state of mind as pathetic, set awry by nightmare and waiting to be saved by the heroine. He tells the story in such a way that neither he nor Genevieve have to declare their feelings openly: the manner of his telling draws them closer until they find themselves enacting the same resolution almost unselfconsciously. The element of awareness or even sly deceit is admitted—"'Twas partly Love, and partly Fear|And partly 'twas a bashful art"—but such means are held to justify the reconciliation of "All impulses of soul and sense":

> And hopes, and fears that kindle hope,
> An undistinguishable throng,
> And gentle wishes long subdued,
>   Subdued and cherish'd long! (*PW* 1:609)

What these two poems inherit from "Christabel" and earlier poems is clear. The plight of the Dark Ladiè/Lady of the Land is a shadowy mix of Christabel and Geraldine, and there are verbal echoes of "The Three Graves." The two poems together might be understood as an attempt to address problems explored in "Christabel" and left hanging. In particular, the supernatural dimension that "Christabel" shared with the "Ancient Mariner" is dropped and the focus narrows to the human emotions involved: the relation between fear and rage, the need to understand (articulate, name) contradictory and deep-buried emotions, the irony (indeed tragedy) of the fate of innocence. Each poem fixes on a moment of dawning realisation, Love attempting to work through its application to a world outside of a chivalric story; that is, by means of resources that work more closely with and by means of emotions (sound, pacing, shifts of point of view) so that a sense of change brings about actual change. The issues involved go back to Coleridge's very early days: the name Genevieve, for instance, carries forward from the sonnet he addressed at school to his nurse's daughter (**17**; *PW* 1:25). The Chinese-box structure of "Love" matches the theme of the self discovering itself in its own reflection that is endemic in his poems throughout the 1790s and almost parodied in his adaptation of an early Wordsworth poem in "Lewti" (**172**; *PW* 1:457–61):

> Nay, treacherous image! leave my mind.
> And yet, thou did'st not look unkind.[16]

This said, one must nevertheless reckon that "Love" just kicked many troubling issues down the road. It was a literary solution, certainly, but the real-life situation contained aspects that needed to be revisited and tested over again. To take just one example, "The Night-scene," the only published fragment of an unfinished play, *The Triumph of Loyalty* (**272**; *PW* 1:653–56 and see **271.X1**; 3:955–91) centres on the lasting impulse of two noble minds to deceive themselves, to give over totally to narcissistic feeling, the woman leading the man. It contains a striking reminiscence of the pantheistic moments in "The Eolian Harp," when "many idle flitting phantasies,|Traverse my indolent and passive brain" (*PW* 1:233), which points up the problem: the self finding itself in an other who is only a mirrored, solipsistic self-projection or delusion.

"Alice du Clós" was a fresh start on such topics. It begins in medias res, like the "Dark Ladiè." The baser instincts of Lord Julian, externalised in Sir Hugh, bring about destruction; but the doubling leaves space to hint at Julian's genuine confusion of mind. Subsequently, in the poem "Love," the hint of Genevieve's complicity is sophisticated by devolving active responsibility onto the teller of the tale. Twenty and more years later, the heroine Alice is tacitly and ambiguously complicit, although possessed of more child-like innocence, and the action is unmediated. Subtle extensions of the ballad stanza, every means of poematic manipulation, are brought to bear on the issues involved. Ted Hughes remarked (446–47) that the "Dark Ladiè" has "an amputated kind of completeness." The surgical skill employed on "Alice du Clós" is considerably more focused: the amputation is better prepared for and gives the impression of a body conceived to be born thus. Like "Love" it makes a completed thing of the experience it describes. Unlike "Love," it contains no trace of indulgence or hypocrisy.

7. A "Live" Solution

The first extant fragments incorporated into "Alice du Clós" date from December 1801 and the years following; the drive to fashion and complete the poem began perhaps in 1824, and intensified in 1828–29 (*PW* 1:1098–99, 2:1302–12). Coleridge might well have been encouraged to finish a poem that had long lived vaguely in his mind by thoughts of publication in one of the poetical albums that grew to be fashionable during the 1820s; indeed, he even came to an arrangement with Frederick Reynolds to publish it in *The Keepsake for 1829*. The albums and the culture surrounding them particularly involved women as authors and readers, and this has an obvious bearing on his poetry of the 1820s. However, the present poem is a timely reminder that his identification with female protagonists has deep personal roots and connects with an earlier, more radical phase of women's emancipation. "Alice du Clós" cannot be parcelled up with writers like Letitia Langdon and trends like Silver Fork fiction. As the allusions to Mary Robinson and masculine "pride" make clear, it exists within an older movement inaugurated by Charlotte Smith and Mary Wollstonecraft, writers in whom he had a much more serious interest.

While the poem must be read in terms of its deeper origins, it remains important that the later opportunity for publication was relinquished in 1828–29; and at this point "Christabel" re-enters the argument, a poem which had been published in a professedly unfinished state in 1816 and which continued to haunt its author afterwards, as the continuations of the narrative reported by James Gillman and Derwent Coleridge show (see *PW* 1:478–79). I strongly suspect Coleridge thought he was finished with what he could write when Part 1 was complete and he began "The Ballad of the Dark Ladiè"; and that Part 2 was added as a result of Wordsworth's urging, to fill out the new edition of *Lyrical Ballads* in 1800. The latter might even be a conscious demonstration that a narrative continuation in the same style—"witchery by daylight"—is not possible.[17] "Alice du Clós" probably began in the 1820s from the premise of a story that was truncated but complete. What indeed could happen next in narrative terms? Would Julian kill Hugh, and then be killed by a knight who rescues Alice? Or would Alice marry a somehow reformed Julian? Such suggestions are just as absurd as any of the attempted continuations of "Christabel": for instance, Martin Tupper's *Geraldine* (1838). Alice's complicity in her own destruction is more explicable than Christabel's, and we are shown by subtle hints how she creates her own fate: she is, in her surprising way, Julian's fitting counterpart. The narrative surely rested on this premise from the moment Coleridge began to address the task of composition seriously.

The poem communicates a sense of what Allen Grossman, in another context, happily terms "elate completeness."[18] Thirty years of trial and hard speculation over a wide variety of topics were resolved. It is worth recalling that Coleridge's experience in writing for the theatre played a crucial part: plays like *Diadestè* (**492.X2**; note the diacritic) and *Zapolya* (**517.X1**) carry traces of his thinking and assisted his sense of pacing and capacity to objectify. Meanwhile, sudden reversals in Coleridge's poetry were not new. The "mild reproof" that closes off the pantheistic speculations in "The Eolian Harp" (*PW* 1:234) is one striking example.[19] The Ancient Mariner's narrative progresses by sudden shifts and reversals of mood; and, as Julian's lance strikes Alice, we experience again the same wanton destruction of goodness:

> "Why look'st thou so?"—with my cross bow
> I shot the Albatross. (*PW* 1:378)

The difference of course is that "Alice du Clós" bundles beginning, middle and end into a compressed finale: a sequence into what is made to seem a moment. As always, this kind of writing, directed to such ends as moved Coleridge as he wrote, is more than a technical exercise. It involves a moral decision and is a realistic statement that "romantic" love cannot survive in a "real" world. Such love pursues its object blindly: the echo of "Time, Real and Imaginary" is crucial. The destructive pun is not cynical: it should be read against a poem like "Youth and Age" (**592**), where gains and losses are finely balanced. Again, to get its measure, it should be read against the work of young contemporaries like John Hamilton Reynolds and Thomas Hood where, fitted snugly within end-rhymes, the effect is trivialised:

> Ben Battle was a soldier bold,
> And used to war's alarms;
> But a cannon-ball took off his legs
> So he laid down his arms![20]

The shock Coleridge's pun delivers is a world away from this and all the more deeply disturbing. If it momentarily flattens the poem to the level of a string of words, the associations built by the use of overlapping sounds remain unaffected. The enigma of the poem rests on and continues to live within the duplicated word "wanton", with everything the word suggests for Coleridge. He uses it in the common sense of sexually abandoned and inviting in the "wanton glee" of "To an Unfortunate Woman" (**148**; *PW* 1:324 line 6:), in the "wanton dances" of "The Wills of the Wisp" (**281**; *PW* 1:670 line 2), and in "Love's accomplice" who "played the wanton" by half-disclosing her bosom in "The Picture" (**300**; *PW* 1:714 lines 59–67). But the additional dimension of teasing in the last instance here—of invitation withheld—shadows the "half-wanton, half-afraid" "wild Melody" of the "zephyr-travelld Harp" in the earliest manuscript version of "The Destiny of Nations" (**139**; *PW* 2:387 lines 14.1.1-4), with which one might compare the "coy maid half yielding to her lover" of "The Eolian Harp" (*PW* 1:232 line 15). These last two passages leave no doubt that the preoccupations that ignite Coleridge's pun are feelings and ideas that play across his entire life and writing: creative opposites that involve more than a rhetorical figure.

The final stanza appears for the first time in *Poetical Works* 1834, which raises a question: was the ending always intended or was it just impatiently slapped on for publication? The answer is both yes and no, and neither simply. The progress of the plot up to this point is an inevitable movement towards catastrophe. The shocking abruptness of the closing lines sends a judder backwards through the whole poem, but such an end connects with the violent beginning, tremors from which made themselves felt at crucial moments in the intervening lines. Wordsworth achieved the same troubling completeness when he deleted the last stanza of "Strange Fits of Passion," so as to end:

> "O mercy!" to myself I cried,
> "If Lucy should be dead!"[21]

Indeed, it is likely that Coleridge shrank from adding the bombshell ending to the holograph version he sent Reynolds because, at the moment he came to copy it into place, he realised his poem was unsuited to a Christmas gift-volume. He instead held it over and placed it first among the enlarged and newly titled group of "Miscellaneous Poems" in his last (1834) *Poetical Works*, where it occupies a prominent position following the "Ancient Mariner" and "Christabel."

8. Clarifying Comparisons

Mention of two further Coleridge poems written about the same time as "Alice du Clós" will help clarify his achievement. First, "The Improvisatore" (**623**; *PW* 1:1055-62, 2:1248-59): this was begun in summer 1826 and published the following year in Samuel Hall's album, *The Amulet for 1828*, so it is part of the literary culture of the time that lies behind the initial plans for "Alice". Indeed, "The Improvisatore" may be said to be more aware of its potential readership and less extensive in its personal retrospection.

It picks up with Coleridge's contemporaneous thinking about the situation of women: for instance, "The Man's desire is for the Woman, the Woman's desire is for the desire of the Man" (*TT* 1:91). It relates not only to Coleridge's identification with Alice but also to her implicit need to discover a real (not phantom) other. It relates to the lesson that Age teaches Youth, that the pursuit of Love by Hope might come in time to rest on different ground, that of Affection-Love:

> Yes, Lady! deem him not unblest:
> The certainty that struck HOPE dead,
> Hath left CONTENTMENT in her stead:
> And that is next to Best! (*PW* 1:1062)

"The Improvisatore" celebrates the resolution of a long-standing question with the recognition that it no longer applies, leaving its author the more secure. The resolution is congruent with the position mapped in "Alice du Clós," which shines a light on issues that once brought his writing to a standstill with unexpected clarity, even if Alice required a different reading-context.

The second comparison involves "The Garden of Boccaccio" (*PW* 1:1089–95, 2:1290–98). This was composed at the time Coleridge was considering the implications of what he had written in "Alice du Clós"; indeed, it substituted for "Alice" in Reynolds's *Keepsake* while he continued to ponder where "Alice" itself had taken him. The two poems share so much: from the basic situation of Coleridge musing on Stothard's illustration of Boccaccio that matches Alice reading Ovid down to shared phrases and significant words. The boar-hunting scene that Coleridge injects into Stothard interweaves with Lord Julian's hunt; again, "Boccaccio" incorporates the "Alice" situation as a story within a story in the manner of the poem "Love," the author's self in a Highgate garden replacing the unnamed narrator on the slopes of the Quantocks;[22] and with Anne Gillman actively handing him the illustration in place of the passive Genevieve, and thereby prompting his daydream. There is more than enough in "The Garden of Boccaccio" for us to muddle the person who dreams with the real-life Coleridge who is the subject of biographers, and it certainly helps to understand his relationship with the Friend whose "quiet hand" placed the illustration before him as one of "Affection-Love."

"Boccaccio" is not, however, a directly confessional poem, to be assimilated to the so-called Conversation Poems as they are conventionally understood.

It is not written in experimental blank verse, but in paragraphs of regular pentameters that develop from an opening string of rhyming couplets into elaborate patterns in which differently positioned couplets form a part. By such regulated means, the subject of Coleridge's ballad poems is translated back into a medium that has obvious—one might reckon misleadingly obvious—associations with poems like (say) "The Nightingale" (**180**), but there is a reason. "Boccaccio" shows Coleridge playing with materials and poetic means that once interested him, in order to play (with great skill) on slacker strings. The replay with modified means is fascinating, and the result served to meet a pressing commitment, but it is important that he appears to have lost interest in the poem even before it was gathered into *Poetical Works* 1829, where it was the last of a group under the subheading "Prose in Rhyme" (see *PW* 1:1091, 1272). One could argue that the delayed publication of "Alice" is proof he took the latter poem more seriously than "Boccaccio." The framing alibi is abandoned; the solutions that dreams bring are clearly not to be confused with reality; the prima facie objections to Affection-Love raised by some modern readers—is a degree of self-deception involved?—do not apply. The substitution of "Boccaccio" for "Alice" in *The Keepsake* suggests Coleridge exactly comprehended what he was about.

Coleridge reached conclusions in his prose-writing that he turned over in his verse to the end of his life.[23] He also wrote poems for comfort—or (better) consolation—"That woke the Tear yet stole away the Pang" (*PW* 1:1093), and others simply for fun. One can only conclude that "Alice du Clós" is a definitive statement of considered intent.

9. Beyond the Text

How does such an approach mesh with other, more current concerns? "Close reading" has come to have a bad name in some quarters as a limited and limiting exercise, but it is as it is and therein has its own integrity. It is a means of examining the anatomy of a poem, taking into account the nature of the beast, i.e. as a poem as opposed to any other form of writing. I chose to write about "Alice" because it is often passed over, or those who linger over it seem to miss the point. In particular, it may have been ignored because it does not fit a preconceived view of what its author is good for. Reading it with care is an opportunity to make a fresh start, perhaps more likely to succeed than starting with a poem already settled in place by fixed opinions.

A reading, in this sense, will take into account the poet's personality, character, circumstance, the conventions and contexts of his time, and his other writings: for instance, notebooks and letters. Conversely, a reader's primary interest might be in the poet himself and such a reader would be looking to the poem to reveal more about these matters. This is a valid quest, but it will only succeed if it is recognised that poems like "Alice du Clós" are primarily literary constructions and any other use of them must take that defining feature into account. One cannot pass it by, or catch up with it afterwards as an optional consideration, even if a different reason for reading remains the primary one. Any reading has to come through the text with an understanding of why it was projected as a poem for the words to stand as a reliable witness.

In the same way, cultural and political meanings can of course be elicited and I have touched on a couple: the historical filiations of Coleridge's instinct to identify with a woman's point of view and the dimension of cruel dispatch in rhyming puns following the long war with France. I should also mention another because it is of large, if not all-encompassing, importance. The narrative of "Alice du Clós" reflects a life-long hesitancy on Coleridge's part to commit to another self in whom he saw his own self reflected, hesitancy so extreme that left him in limbo, a condition of life-in-death:

> Such griefs with such men well agree,
> But wherefore, wherefore fall on me?
> To be beloved is all I need,
> And whom I love, I love indeed.
> (**335** "The Pains of Sleep"; *PW* 1:754–55)

Why should grief fall on him, the innocent, or is he not so innocent? And such hesitancy turns the question into one of cause: is it due to fear or pride? The dilemma—which Coleridge pursued at many levels and ultimately as a question of Will—underlay his difficulty as a writer in relating to a reading-public, the larger part of which he felt was unsympathetic. Although his feelings were unduly stretched, the predicament is representative; indeed one can see it as the central problem of government in a mass society. The resolution requires an amount of trust on both sides and Coleridge's own most elaborate attempt to bridge the gap—*Aids to Reflection*—could only remove objections and then appeal for a leap of faith. The gap since his time has grown wider.

I will bring this point to bear more closely and be done. The speed, intricacy and particular compression of "Alice" are part of the power it exerts. It wraps itself round us until it implodes on the pun. The method is hypnotic—it establishes control, places us in an enchanted place—and can be connected with facets of its author's personality.[24] It is certainly connected with his dominant habits as a conversationalist and speaker of verse—"Weave a circle round him thrice" (*PW* 1:514)—alongside the insecurity that wanted courage to speak its name. From here is a small step to his uncertain relation to a readership that evolved in a dramatic way during his lifetime. The same challenge has faced every reformer, and the conditions are speeded up and magnified today. The poem in question is a small gesture, perhaps, but to write such a thing is to take the measure of the world and to pass judgement on the condition of living. The way Coleridge does this is brave, elegant and sound. "Alice du Clós" happens to amount to something like a conclusive statement, in personal terms, but other poems exhibit the same qualities of mind and that is why they clamour to be read. Questions of whether he is a major poet, a failed thinker or a renegade politico are for the birds.

Notes

1. First published in *The Coleridge Bulletin* N.S. No.45 (Summer 2015): 1–21. Here with a few minor corrections and the references abbreviated. I must thank Peter Cheyne and Graham Davidson for their careful readings of an earlier version of my explication, both of whom improved it measurably.
2. To Bernard Heringman, 21 July 1953: *Letters* ed. Holly Stevens 793.
3. *More Pricks than Kicks* ed. Nelson 14. When Barry McGovern sent Beckett a copy of his taped reading of the story, Beckett suggested the last line should run "Like hell it is."
4. Discussed with further references by Fried "Rhyme Puns."
5. The poem found favour during the half-century between 1860 and 1910 (e.g. in the selections by A. C. Swinburne 1869, Joseph Skipsey 1884, Stopford Brooke 1895, Frederick Ellis 1896, Alice Meynell 1905 and Quiller-Couch 1907). It was omitted from the most widely-circulated selections during most of the twentieth century (e.g. by Stephen Potter 1935 and I. A. Richards 1950, Elisabeth Schneider 1951 and Kathleen Raine 1957, William Empson 1972 and John Beer 1996). The selections by H. J. Jackson (1985 and 1994) followed by Richard Holmes (1996 and 2003), in this respect at least, show a sign of recovery.

6. *CM* 4:842. For Leibniz, see *CL* 2:747; for Spinoza, *BL* 1:194; for his own name, *PW* 1:972 etc.
7. Coleridge's use of the apostrophe is peculiar in this poem: see also line 3. In the present instance it was possibly inserted to suggest an extra pause, and thus lengthen the line in reading.
8. See the references to "mazy" and "The Garden of Boccaccio" in my *Experimental Poetics* via the index.
9. Compare the may-thorn blossoms beneath boughs of dark green yew in the lines "Composed While Climbing the Left Ascent of Brockley Coomb" (**108**; *PW* 1:203–04) and also those that preside over the opening lines of Wordsworth's beginning-contribution to "The Three Graves" (*Early Poems and Fragments* ed. Landon 860).
10. Alice's mimicry of the language of hunting in lines 74–75 prefigures the identification; indeed, the age-old association between hunting and courting underlies the whole poem. A critical attitude towards hunting per se underlines poems otherwise as different as the "Ancient Mariner" and "The Story of the Mad Ox."
11. "Construction" in *Sole Glum Trek* 20. The phrase is used in exemplary fashion in Falci's essay, "Joinery: Trevor Joyce's Lattice Poems."
12. A similarity noted by Beer in *Coleridge's Play of Mind* 207.
13. Barbarese 688. The golden Morning Star of lines 29–34, as Coleridge presents it, is of course already not what it first seems. I might add to Barbarese's conjectures on naming that Julian shares the name of the Neoplatonic philosopher, emperor-apostate, in whose ideas and edicts Coleridge took a passing interest; and that Alice is a shortened form of Adelaide, who sings the song "Domestic Peace" (**66**; *PW* 1:114–15) in *The Fall of Robespierre* (**76.X1**; *PW* 3:22). Peter Cheyne adds the further suggestion that the name Julian recalls the Julian Laws (*lex Iula*) of the Emperor Augustus that encouraged the Roman higher classes to breed more, punished adultery and allowed men to kill straying wives.
14. "Sir Cauline" Part II, lines 53–56 in Percy (ed.) *Reliques* 1:53. See Percy's comment on this practice in his introductory Essay in *ibid* 1:liii. "Sir Cauline", which influenced Coleridge in particular in his enlargement of the ballad stanza, was largely rewritten by Percy.
15. I discuss this matter at greater length in an unpublished essay, "Contemplation in Coleridge's Poetry", and see also above Chap. 3, note 32.
16. The several wide-ranging issues in the preceding paragraph are discussed with reference to particular poems in my *Experimental Poetics* and further references therein.
17. See my *Experimental Poetics* 105–06 and endnotes.
18. In discussing Yeats's poem, "The Cap and Bells", in *Poetic Knowledge* 188.

19. A comment by Rzepka *The Self as Mind* 116 bears on the present context: "Sara's darting eye is particularly devastating because it destroys [the] mood of gentle, dreamy persuasion."
20. Hood "Faithless Nelly Gray: A Pathetic Ballad in Whims and Oddities" in his *Prose and Verse* (1826) 139–42 at 139.
21. He also rewrote in compressed form the stanzas that originally stood at the beginning: see *"Lyrical Ballads", and Other Poems* ed. Butler and Green 162 and compare 294.
22. See *PW* 1:604 for the manner in which "Love" conflates memories of Cothelstone Park in Somerset with a scene involving Sara Hutchinson at Sockburn in County Durham.
23. Ewan James Jones has written a valuable book based on exactly the opposite premise that I like to think does not contradict what I say here. See his *Coleridge and the Philosophy of Poetic Form* (2014)—which includes a chapter on punning with respect to "Limbo" (pp. 107–45)—and also his interview-response to "Five Questions" at www.bars.ac.uk/blog/?p.384 11 Aug 2014, accessed 10 Jan 2015.
24. As it has been, for example, by Rzepka *The Self as Mind* Chaps. 1 and 3 in particular, along with their extensive endnotes.

Bibliography[1]

Abrams, M. H., *The Mirror and The Lamp: Romantic Theory and the Critical Tradition*. New York: Oxford UP, 1953.
---------, ed. *Literature and Belief: English Institute Essays, 1957*. New York: Columbia UP, 1958.
---------, ed. *The Norton Anthology of English Literature*. 2 vols. New York: W. W. Norton, 1962.
---------. *Natural Supernaturalism: Tradition and Revolution in Romantic Literature*. New York: W. W. Norton, 1971.
---------. *The Correspondent Breeze: Essays on English Romanticism*. Ed. Jack Stillinger. New York: W. W. Norton, 1984.
---------. *Doing Things with Texts: Essays in Criticism and Critical Theory*. Ed. Michael Fischer. New York: W. W. Norton, 1989.
Allen, Donald M., ed. *The New American Poetry, 1945–1960*. New York: Grove Press, 1960.
[Allsop, Thomas.] *Letters, Conversations and Recollections of S. T. Coleridge*. 2 vols. London: Edward Moxon, 1836.
Altieri, Charles. *Reckoning with the Imagination: Wittgenstein and the Aesthetics of Literary Experience*. Ithaca, NY: Cornell UP, 2015.
Anderson, Peter. "'Thickening, deepening, blackening': Starlings and the Object of Poetry in Coleridge and Dante." *The Coleridge Bulletin* N.S. 32 (2008): 55–62.

---

[1] The bibliography does not include works by S. T. Coleridge, nor the different editions of *Lyrical Ballads*. These are listed under Abbreviations and References. It also does not include the many educational, pocket and illustrated editions of the "Ancient Mariner" referred to in passing. All references are to print sources unless otherwise noted.

Arac, Jonathan. *Critical Genealogies: Historical Situations for Postmodern Literary Studies.* New York: Columbia UP, 1987.
Arno, Christie. "New Roots: A Previously Unknown Version of 'The Barberry Tree'." *Times Literary Supplement* No.5759/60 (16–23 Aug 2013): 17–19.
Attridge, Derek. *The Rhythms of English Poetry.* London: Longman, 1982.
---------. *Poetic Rhythm: An Introduction.* Cambridge: Cambridge UP, 1995.
---------, and Daniel Ferrer, eds. *Post-structuralist Joyce: Essays from the French.* Cambridge: Cambridge UP, 1984
---------. See also Thomas Carper.
Ault, Donald. "Preface": see below Martin Wallen, ed. *Coleridge's Ancient Mariner.* vii–xv.
Averill, James H. *Wordsworth and the Poetry of Human Suffering.* Ithaca, NY: Cornell UP, 1980.
---------. "The Shape of *Lyrical Ballads.*" *Philological Quarterly* 60 (1981): 387–407.
Barbarese, J. T. "Dramas of Naming in Coleridge" *Studies in English Literature* 37 (1997): 673–98.
Barfield, Owen. "Coleridge Collected." *Encounter* 35.5 (Nov. 1970): 74–83.
Beare, Geoffrey, and Lorraine Janzen Kooistra. "Illustrated Editions of Coleridge's *The Rime of the Ancient Mariner.*" *IBIS Journal* 2 (2002): 53–98.
Beckett, Samuel. "Dante. . . Bruno. Vico. . Joyce" in *Our Exagmination Round his Factification for Incamination of Work in Progress.* Paris: Shakespeare and Company, 1929. 3–22.
---------. *Company, Ill Seen Ill Said, Worstward Ho, Stirrings Still.* Ed. Dirk Van Hulle. London: Faber and Faber, 2009.
---------. *Murphy.* Ed. J.C.C.Mays. London: Faber and Faber, 2009.
---------. *Watt.* Ed C. J. Ackerley. London: Faber and Faber, 2009.
---------. *More Pricks than Kicks.* Ed. Cassandra Nelson. London: Faber and Faber, 2010.
---------. *Waiting for Godot.* Ed. Mary Bryden. London: Faber and Faber, 2010.
Beer, John. *Coleridge the Visionary.* London: Chatto and Windus, 1959.
---------. "The Unity of *Lyrical Ballads*" in *1800: The New Lyrical Ballads.* Ed. Nicola Trott and Seamus Perry. Basingstoke, Hants.: Palgrave, 2001. 6–22.
---------. *Coleridge's Play of Mind.* Oxford: Oxford UP, 2010.
Beissner, Friedrich, et al., eds. *Friedrich Hölderlin: Sämtliche Werke. Grosse Stuttgarter Ausgabe.* 8 vols. Stuttgart: J. G. Cotta, 1943–85.
Belloc, Hilaire, with pictures by BTB. *Cautionary Tales for Children: Designed for the Admonition of Children between the Ages of Eight and Fourteen Years.* London: Eveleigh Nash, [1907].
Bennett, Betty T., ed. *British War Poetry in the Age of Romanticism, 1793–1815.* New York: Garland, 1976.

Beres, David. "A Dream, a Vision, and a Poem: A Psycho-Analytic Study of the Origins of *The Rime of the Ancient Mariner*." *The International Journal of Psycho-Analysis* 32 (1951): 97–116.
Blake, William. *The Complete Writings of William Blake* (1957). Ed. Geoffrey Keynes. London: Oxford UP, rev. ed. 1966.
Blunden, Edmund, ed. "An Introduction" to *The Rime of the Ancient Mariner, illustrated by H. Charles Tomlinson*. New York: Cheshire House, 1931. iii–xvi.
Bodkin, Maud. *Archetypal Patterns in Poetry: Psychological Studies of Imagination*. London: Oxford UP, 1934.
Bogdanov, Michael, adapt. *The Ancient Mariner: A Dramatisation*. London: Heinemann, 1984.
Borges, Jorge Luis. "Funes, the Memorious" in *Ficciones*. Trans Anthony Kerrigan. New York: Grove Press, 1962. 107–15
Bostetter, Edward E. "The Nightmare World of *The Ancient Mariner*." *Studies in Romanticism* 1 (1962): 241–54.
Boulger, James D. *Coleridge as Religious Thinker*. New Haven, CT: Yale UP, 1961.
---------. "Imagination and Speculation in Coleridge's Conversation Poems." *Journal of English and Germanic Philology* 64 (1965): 691–711.
---------. "Christian Skepticism in *The Rime of the Ancient Mariner*" in *From Sensibility to Romanticism: Essays Presented to Frederick A. Pottle*. Ed. Frederick W. Hilles and Harold Bloom. New Haven, CT: Yale UP, 1965. 439–52. Rev. as part of the "Introduction" to *Twentieth Century Interpretations of 'The Rime of the Ancient Mariner': A Collection of Critical Essays*. Ed. James D. Boulger. Englewood Cliffs, NJ: Prentice-Hall, 1969. 1–20.
---------. "Coleridge: The Marginalia, Myth-Making, and the Later Poetry." *Studies in Romanticism* 11 (1972): 304–19.
---------. "Coleridge on Imagination Revisited." *The Wordsworth Circle* 4 (1973): 13–24.
---------. "The Numinous in Poetry." *Thought* 54 (1979): 143–61.
---------. "Coleridge" in his *The Calvinist Temper in English Poetry*. The Hague: Mouton, 1980. 357–82.
Bradford, Richard. *Literary Rivals: Feuds and Antagonisms in the World of Books*. London: The Robson Press, 2014.
Brisman, Leslie. *Romantic Origins*. Ithaca, NY: Cornell UP, 1978.
Brown, Huntington. "The Gloss to the Ancient Mariner." *Modern Language Quarterly* 6 (1945): 319–24.
Burke, Kenneth. "On Musicality in Verse: As Illustrated by Some Lines of Coleridge." *Poetry* (Chicago) 57.1 (Oct 1940): 31–40. Rpt. as an Appendix to his *The Philosophy of Literary Form* (1941); 2nd ed. Baton Rouge: Louisiana State UP, 1967. 369–78.

Byron, Lord. *The Complete Poetical Works.* Ed. Jerome J. McGann. 7 vols. Oxford: Clarendon Press, 1980–93.
Caine, T. Hall. *Recollections of Dante Gabriel Rossetti.* London: Elliot Stock, 1882.
Campbell, Colin. *The Romantic Ethic and the Spirit of Modern Consumerism.* Oxford: Basil Blackwell, 1987.
Carlyon, Clement. *Early Years and Late Reflections.* 4 vols. London: Whittaker, 1836–58.
Carper, Thomas, and Derek Attridge. *Meter and Meaning: An Introduction to Rhythm in Poetry.* New York: Routledge, 2003.
Casement, Ann, and David Tracy, eds. *The Idea of the Numinous: Contemporary Jungian and Psychoanalytic Perspectives.* London: Routledge, 2006.
Cavell, Stanley. *In Quest of the Ordinary: Lines of Skepticism and Romanticism.* Chicago, IL: University of Chicago Press, 1988.
Chambers, E. K. *Samuel Taylor Coleridge: A Biographical Study.* Oxford: Clarendon Press, 1938.
Chandler, Alice. "Structure and Symbol in 'The Rime of the Ancient Mariner'." *Modern Language Quarterly* 26 (1965): 401–13.
Chandler James. "The Strange Design of a Lyrical Ballad" in his *An Archaeology of Sympathy: The Sentimental Mode in Literature and Cinema.* Chicago: University of Chicago Press, 2013. 287–91.
[Chatterton, Thomas.] *Poems Supposed to have been Written at Bristol by Thomas Rowley and Others.* Cambridge: B. Flower, 1794.
Cheyne, Peter, ed. *Coleridge and Contemplation.* Oxford: Oxford UP, forthcoming 2017.
Class, Monika. *Coleridge and Kantian Ideas in England, 1796–1817: Coleridge's Responses to German Philosophy.* London: Bloomsbury, 2012.
Coburn, Kathleen. "I.A.R. and S.T.C." in *I. A. Richards: Essays in his Honor.* Ed. Reuben Brower, Helen Vendler and John Hollander. New York: Oxford UP, 1973. 237–44.
———. *In Pursuit of Coleridge.* London: The Bodley Head, 1977.
———. *Experience into Thought: Perspectives in the Coleridge Notebooks.* Toronto: University of Toronto Press, 1979.
Coffin, Tristram. P. "Coleridge's Use of the Ballad Stanza in 'The Rime of the Ancient Mariner'." *Modern Language Quarterly* 12 (1951): 437–45.
Cohn, Jan, and Thomas H. Miles "The Sublime: In Alchemy, Aesthetics and Psychoanalysis." *Modern Philology* 74 (1977): 289–304.
Coleridge, Derwent. "Introductory Essay" to *Poems of Samuel Taylor Coleridge; With an Appendix.* Ed. Derwent and Sara Coleridge. New and enlarged ed. London: E. Moxon and Son, 1870.
Coleridge, Ernest Hartley, ed. *Letters of Samuel Taylor Coleridge.* 2 vols. London: William Heinemann, 1895.
———, ed. *The Complete Poetical Works of Samuel Taylor Coleridge.* 2 vols. Oxford: Clarendon Press, 1912.

[Coleridge, Samuel Taylor, and William Wordsworth.] *Lyrical Ballads with a Few Other Poems*. 2nd issue. London: printed for J. and A. Arch, 1798.
---------. See also under William Wordsworth.
Considering the Scholarly Edition in the Digital Age: A White Paper of the Modern Language Association's Committee on Scholarly Editions, 2 Sept 2015. https://scholarlyeditions.commons.mla.org/2015/09/02/cse-white-paper/ accessed 9 Sept 2015.
Cooper, Lane. *Late Harvest*. Ithaca, NY: Cornell UP, 1952.
Costelloe, Timothy M., ed. *The Sublime: From Antiquity to the Present*. Cambridge: Cambridge UP, 2012.
Crabb Robinson, Henry. *Henry Crabb Robinson on Books and their Writers*. Ed. Edith J. Morley. 3 vols. London: J. M. Dent and Sons, 1938.
Crawford, Walter and Edward S. Lauterbach, with the assistance of Ann M. Crawford. *Samuel Taylor Coleridge: An Annotated Bibliography of Criticism and Scholarship. Volume II: 1900–1939, with additional entries for 1795–1899*. Boston, MA: G. K. Hall, 1983. See also Richard D. Haven.
---------, with the research and editorial assistance of Ann M. Crawford. *Samuel Taylor Coleridge: An Annotated Bibliography of Criticism and Scholarship. Volume III: Part 1, 1793–1794 (Supplement to Vols. 1 and II, 1793–1939; Comprehensive Bibliography, 1940–1965; Selective Bibliography, 1966–1994). Part II, 1791–1993*. New York: G. K. Hall, 1996. See also Richard D. Haven.
Danby, John F. *The Simple Wordsworth: Studies in the Poems, 1797–1807*. London: Routledge and Kegan Paul, 1960.
Davie, Donald. "Dionysus in *Lyrical Ballads*" in *Wordsworth's Mind and Art*. Ed. A. W. Thomson. Edinburgh: Oliver and Boyd, 1969. 110–39.
Dearborn, Kerry. *Baptized Imagination: The Theology of George MacDonald*. Aldershot, Hants.: Ashgate, 2006.
De Quincey, Thomas. *The Collected Writings of Thomas De Quincey*. Ed. David Masson. 14 vols. Edinburgh: Adam and Charles Black, 1889–90.
De Vere, Aubrey. *Recollections of Aubrey De Vere*. London: Edwin Arnold, 1897.
Dickinson, Emily. *The Poems of Emily Dickinson: Reading Edition*. Ed. Ralph W. Franklin. Cambridge, MA: Harvard UP, 1999.
Dixon, Josie. "The Mind's Eye: Vision and Experience in Coleridge's Notebooks." *The Coleridge Bulletin* N.S. 31 (2008): 42–54.
Dorrien, Gary. *Kantian Reason and Hegelian Spirit: The Idealistic Logic of Modern Theology*. Chichester, West Sussex: Wiley Blackwell, 2012.
Drake, Nathan. *Literary Hours, or Sketches Critical and Narrative*. Sudbury, Suffolk: Printed by J. Birkitt, 1798.
---------. *Winter Nights; or Fire-side Lucubrations*. 2 vols. London: Longman, Hurst, Rees, Orme, and Brown, 1820.
Drew, John. *India and the Romantic Imagination*. Delhi: Oxford UP, 1987.

Duncan, Robert. "Towards an Open Universe" (1966) in *Collected Essays and Other Prose*. Ed. James Maynard. Berkeley, CA: University of California Press, 2014. 127–38.

---------. *Ground Work: Before the War*. New York: New Directions, 1984.

Dyce, Alexander. *The Reminiscences of Alexander Dyce*. Ed. Richard J. Schrader. Columbus, OH: Ohio State UP, 1972.

Dyck, Sarah. "Perspective in 'The Rime of the Ancient Mariner'." *Studies in English Literature* 13 (1973): 591–604.

Eaves, Morris. *The Counter-Arts Conspiracy: Art and Industry in the Age of Blake*. Ithaca, NY: Cornell UP, 1992.

Eilenberg, Susan. *Strange Power of Speech: Wordsworth, Coleridge, and Literary Possession*. New York: Oxford UP, 1992.

Empson, William. "*The Ancient Mariner*." *Critical Quarterly* 6 (1964): 298–319.

---------, and David Pirie, eds. *Coleridge's Verse: A Selection*. London: Faber and Faber, 1972.

Engell, James. *The Creative Imagination: Enlightenment to Romanticism*. Cambridge, MA: Harvard UP, 1981.

Erickson, Lee. *The Economy of Literary Form: English Literature and the Industrialization of Publishing, 1800–1850*. Baltimore, MD: The Johns Hopkins UP, 1996.

Espey, John. "The Inheritance of Τό Καλόν" in *New Approaches to Ezra Pound*. Ed. Eva Hesse. London: Faber and Faber, 1969. 319–30.

Falci, Eric. "Joinery: Trevor Joyce's Lattice Poems" in *Essays on the Poetry of Trevor Joyce*. Ed. Niamh O'Mahony. Bristol: Shearsman Books, 2014. 128–54.

Ferguson, Frances. "Coleridge and the Deluded Reader: 'The Rime of the Ancient Mariner'." *Georgia Review* 31 (1977): 617–35. Rpt. in *Post-Structuralist Readings of English Poetry*. Ed. Richard Machin and Christopher Norris. Cambridge: Cambridge UP, 1987. 248–63.

---------. *Wordsworth: Language as Counter-Spirit*. New Haven, CT: Yale UP, 1977.

François, Anne-Lise. *Open Secrets: The Literature of Uncounted Experience*. Stanford, CA: Stanford UP, 2008.

Freistat, Neil. "The 'Field' of *Lyrical Ballads*" in his *The Poem and the Book: Interpreting Collections of Romantic Poetry*. Chapel Hill, NC: The University of North Carolina Press, 1985. 47–94.

Fried, Debra. "Rhyme Puns" in *On Puns: The Foundation of Letters*. Ed. Jonathan Culler. Oxford: Basil Blackwell, 1988. 83–99.

Friedman, Albert B. "Comic, Romantic, and Gothic Ballad Imitations" in his *The Ballad Revival: Studies in the Influence of Popular on Sophisticated Poetry*. Chicago: The University of Chicago Press, 1961. 259–91.

Frost, Robert. *Collected Poems, Prose, and Plays*. [Ed. Richard Poirier and Mark Richardson.] New York: The Library of America, 1995.
Fruman, Norman. "Coleridge's Rejection of Nature and the Natural Man" in *Coleridge's Imagination: Essays in Memory of Pete Laver*. Ed. Richard Gravil, Lucy Newlyn and Nicholas Roe. Cambridge: Cambridge UP, 1985. 69–78.
Fry, Paul H., ed. *Samuel Taylor Coleridge: The Rime of the Ancient Mariner* [Case Studies in Contemporary Criticism]. Boston, MA: Bedford/St.Martin's, 1999.
Fulford, Tim. "Coleridge's Sequel to *Thalaba* and Robert Southey's Prequel to *Christabel*" in *Coleridge, Romanticism and the Orient: Cultural Negotiations*. Ed. David Vallins, Kaz Oishi and Seamus Perry. London: Bloomsbury, 2013. 55–70.
Fussell, Paul, Jr. *Poetic Meter and Poetic Form*. New York: Random House, 1965.
Gabler, Hans Walter, ed. *Ulysses: A Critical and Synoptic Edition*. 3 vols. New York: Garland, 1984.
Galperin, William. "Coleridge and Critical Intervention." *The Wordsworth Circle* 22 (1991): 56–64.
Gill, Stephen. *Wordsworth and the Victorians*. Oxford: Clarendon Press, 1998.
Glenn, Heather. *Vision and Disenchantment: Blake's "Songs" and Wordsworth's "Lyrical Ballads"*. Cambridge: Cambridge UP, 1983.
Griggs, Earl Leslie. "An Early Defense of *Christabel*" in *Wordsworth and Coleridge: Studies in Honor of George McLean Harper*. Ed. Earl Leslie Griggs. Princeton, NJ: Princeton UP, 1939. 172–91.
Groden, Michael, and Daniel Ferrer. "Post-Genetic Joyce." *Romanic Review* 86 (1995): 501–12.
Grossman, Allen. *Poetic Knowledge in the Early Yeats: A Study of "The Wind among the Reeds"*. Charlottesville, VA: The University Press of Virginia, 1969.
Halsey, Alan. "An Afterword." *The Coleridge Bulletin* Conference Issue [unnumbered] (July 1996): 21–24. See also Peter Larkin.
Harding, Anthony John. "Coleridge and Transcendentalism" in *The Coleridge Connection: Essays for Thomas McFarland*. Ed. Richard Gravil and Molly Lefebure. Basingstoke, Hants.: Macmillan, 1990. 233–53.
Harper, George McLean. "Coleridge's Conversation Poems" (1925) in his *Spirit of Delight*. New York: Henry Holt, 1928. 3–27.
Harris, Alexandra. *Romantic Moderns: English Writers, Artists and the Imagination from Virginia Woolf to John Piper*. London: Thames and Hudson, 2010.
Hartman, Geoffrey H. "False Themes and Gentle Minds" in his *The Unremarkable Wordsworth*. Minneapolis, MN: University of Minnesota Press, 1987. 47–57.
Haven, Richard, Josephine Haven, and Maurianne Adams. *Samuel Taylor Coleridge: An Annotated Bibliography of Criticism and Scholarship. Volume I: 1793–1899*. Boston, MA: G. K. Hall, 1976. See also Walter B. Crawford.
Hazlitt, William. *The Complete Works of William Hazlitt*. Ed. P. P. Howe. 21 vols, London: J. M. Dent and Sons, 1930–34.

Hodgson, Maurice. "The Literature of the Franklin Search" in *The Franklin Era in Canadian Arctic History, 1845–1859*. Ed. Patricia D. Sutherland. Ottawa: National Museums of Canada, 1985. 1–11.
Holmes, Richard. *Footsteps: Adventures of a Romantic Biographer*. London: Hodder and Stoughton, 1985.
---------. *Coleridge: Early Visions*. London: Hodder and Stoughton, 1989.
---------. *Coleridge: Darker Reflections*. London: HarperCollins, 1998.
Hood, Thomas. *Prose and Verse*. London: Lupton Relfe, 1826.
Hort, F. J. A. "Coleridge" in *Cambridge Essays, Contributed by Members of the University*. London: John W. Parker and Son, 1856. 292–351.
House, Humphry. *Coleridge: The Clark Lectures, 1951–52*. London: Rupert Hart-Davis, 1953.
Howe, Susan. *Pythagorean Silence*. New York: Montemora Supplement, 1982.
---------. *Tom Tit Tot*, with prints by R. H. Quaytman. New York: Library Council of the Museum of Modern Art, 2014.
---------. "Vagrancy in the Park." *The Nation* 15 Oct 2015; online at http://www.thenation.com/article/vagrancy-in-the-park/ accessed 16 Oct 2015.
---------, and David Grubbs. *Thiefth*. CD-ROM. Blue Chopsticks BC15CD, 2005.
---------. *Souls of the Labadie Tract*. CD-ROM. Blue Chopsticks BC17CD, 2007.
---------. *Frolic Architecture*. CD-ROM. Blue Chopsticks BC22CD, 2012.
---------. *Woodslippercounterclatter*. CD-ROM. Blue Chopsticks BC27CD, 2015.
Hughes, Ted. *Winter Pollen: Occasional Prose*. Ed. William Scammell. London: Faber and Faber, 1994.
Hunt, Leigh. *Foliage; or Poems Original and Translated*. London: C. and J. Ollier, 1818.
Hurlebusch, Klaus. "Conceptualisations for Procedures of Authorship." *Studies in Bibliography* 41 (1988): 100–35.
Hustvedt, Sigurd B. *Ballad Books and Ballad Men*. Cambridge, MA: Harvard UP, 1930.
Hutchinson, Thomas, ed. *Lyrical Ballads . . . 1798*. London: Duckworth, 1898.
Hyman, Stanley Edgar. *The Armed Vision: A Study in the Methods of Modern Literary Criticism*. New York: Alfred A. Knopf, 1948.
Jackson. J. R. de J., ed. *Coleridge: The Critical Heritage*. 2 vols. London: Routledge, 1970–91.
Jackson, Laura (Riding). *The Failure of Poetry, The Promise of Language*. Ed. John Nolan. Ann Arbor, MI: The University of Michigan Press, 2007.
---------. See also Laura Riding.
Jacobus, Mary. *Tradition and Experiment in Wordsworth's "Lyrical Ballads 1798"*. Oxford: Clarendon Press, 1976.
James, Ivor. *The Source of "The Ancient Mariner"*. Cardiff: Daniel Owen, 1890.

Janzen, J. Gerald. "Samuel Taylor Coleridge on Resonance in the Nature of Things" in his *When Prayer Takes Place: Forays into a Biblical World*. Ed. Brent A. Strawn and Patrick D. Miller. Eugene, OR: Cascade Books, 2012. 255–65.

---------. "A Tale of Two Samuels: Coleridge and his Father in the Conclusions to *BL* and *OM* 2." *The Coleridge Bulletin* N.S. 46 (2015): 37–50.

---------. "Notebook 55 as Contemplative Coda to Coleridge's Work and Life" in *Coleridge and Contemplation*. Ed. Peter Cheyne, forthcoming 2017?.

Jennings, Elizabeth. *Every Changing Shape*. London: Andre Deutsch, 1961.

Jones, Ewan James. *Coleridge and the Philosophy of Poetic Form*. Cambridge: Cambridge UP, 2014.

Jordan, John E. *Why the "Lyrical Ballads"?* Berkeley, CA: University of California Press, 1976.

Joyce, James: see Hans Walter Gabler.

Joyce, Trevor. *Sole Glum Trek*. Dublin: New Writers' Press, 1967.

Kant, Immanuel. *De Mundi Sensibilis atque Intelligibilis Forma et Principiis: Dissertatio etc*. [Königsberg]: privately printed, 1770.

---------. *Kant's Inaugural Dissertation and Early Writings on Space*. Trans. John Handyside. Chicago: Open Court, 1919.

Keane, Patrick J. *Coleridge's Submerged Politics: The Ancient Mariner and Robinson Crusoe*. Columbia, MO: University of Missouri Press, 1994.

Keats, John. *The Poems of John Keats*. Ed. Jack Stillinger. Cambridge, MA: Harvard UP, 1978.

Kilby, Clyde S. *Poetry and Life: An Introduction to Poetry*. New York: The Odyssey Press, 1953.

Kitson, Peter. "Coleridge, The French Revolution, and 'The Ancient Mariner': Collective Guilt and Individual Salvation." *Yearbook of English Studies* 19 (1989): 197–207.

---------. "'To Milton's Trump': Coleridge's Unitarian Sublime and the Miltonic Apocalypse" in *Romanticism and Millenarianism*. Ed. Tim Fulford. New York: Palgrave, 2002. 37–52.

Klesse, Antje. *Illustrationen zu S. T. Coleridges The Rime of the Ancient Mariner: Eine Studie zur Illustration von Gedichten*. Memmingen: Curt Visel, 2001.

Knox, Julian. "Coleridge and the Arts" in *The Oxford Handbook of Samuel Taylor Coleridge*. Ed. Frederick Burwick. Oxford: Oxford UP, 2009. 620–39.

Kroeber, Karl. "Mariner's Rime to Freud's Uncanny" in his *Romantic Fantasy and Science Fiction*. New Haven, CT: Yale UP, 1988. 72–94.

Lamb. Charles. *The Letters of Charles and Mary Lamb, 1796–1817*. Ed. Edwin W. Marrs. 3 vols. Ithaca, NY: Cornell UP, 1975–78.

Lang, Andrew, ed. *The Blue Poetry Book*, illus. W. J. Ford and Lancelot Speed. London: Longmans, Green, 1891.

---------. "Introduction" to *Selections from the Poets: Coleridge*. London: Longmans, Green, 1898. xi-xliii.

Larkin, Peter. "David Jones and The Ancient Mariner." *The Coleridge Bulletin* Conference Issue [unnumbered] (July 1996): 2–20. See also Alan Halsey.

Laws, G. Malcolm, Jr. *The British Literary Ballad: A Study in Poetic Imitation.* Carbondale and Edwardsville: Southern Illinois UP, 1972.

Levi, Albert William. *Literature, Philosophy and Imagination.* Bloomington, IN: Indiana UP, 1962.

Levinson, Levinson. "Insight and Oversight: Reading 'Tintern Abbey'" in her *Wordsworth's Great Period Poems*, Cambridge: Cambridge UP, 1986. 14–57.

Lipking, Lawrence. "The Marginal Gloss: Notes and Asides on Poe, Valéry, 'The Ancient Mariner,' The Ordeal of the Margin, *Storiella as She Is Syung*, Versions of Leonardo, and the Plight of Modern Criticism." *Critical Inquiry* 3 (1977): 609–55.

Lowes, John Livingston. *The Road to Xanadu: A Study in the Ways of the Imagination* (1927). Boston, MA: Houghton Mifflin, 2nd ed. 1930.

Macaulay, Thomas Babington. *The Journals of Thomas Babington Macaulay.* Ed. William Thomas. 5 vols. London: Pickering and Chatto, 2008.

MacDonald, George. *There and Back.* London: Kegan Paul, Trench, and Trübner, 2nd ed. 1891.

MacKinnon, D. M. "Coleridge and Kant" in *Coleridge's Variety: Bicentenary Studies.* Ed. John Beer. London: Macmillan, 1974. 183–203.

Magnuson, Paul. *Coleridge's Nightmare Poetry.* Charlottesville, VA: University of Virginia Press, 1974.

———. *Coleridge and Wordsworth: A Lyrical Dialogue.* Princeton, NJ: Princeton UP, 1988.

Mahon, Derek. Interviewed by Nicholas Wroe. "A Sense of Place." *The Guardian* 22 Jul 2006.

———. *Life on Earth.* Loughcrew, Co. Meath: Gallery Press, 2008.

Maxwell, Catherine. "Theodore Watts-Dunton's *Aylwin* and the Reduplications of Romanticism" in her *Second Sight: The Visionary Imagination in Late Victorian Literature.* Manchester: Manchester UP, 2009. 166–96.

Mayo, Robert. "The Contemporaneity of the *Lyrical Ballads.*" *Publications of the Modern Language Association* 69 (1954): 486–522.

Mays, J. C. C. "Coleridge's Borrowings from Jesus College Library, 1791–94." *Transactions of the Cambridge Bibliographical Society* 8 (1985): 557–81.

———. "New Light on Wordsworth's Coleridge" *The Wordsworth Circle* 29 (1998): 9–20.

———. "The Life in Death of Editorial Exchange: the Bollingen Collected Coleridge" in *The Culture of Collected Editions.* Ed. Andrew Nash. Basingstoke, Hants.: Palgrave Macmillan 2003. 183–200.

———. "The Wobbling Pivot" *TEXT: An Interdisciplinary Annual of Textual Studies* 16 (2006): 173–89.

———. *N11 A Musing.* Ballybeg, Co. Tipperary: Coracle, 2006.

———. "King Kubla's Folly" *Times Literary Supplement* No.5496 (1 Aug 2008): 13–15.
———. *Coleridge's Experimental Poetics*. New York: Palgrave Macmillan, 2013.
———. *Coleridge's Father: Absent Man, Guardian Spirit*. Bristol: Friends of Coleridge, 2014.
———. "Contemplation in Coleridge's Poetry" in *Coleridge and Contemplation*. Ed. Peter Cheyne, forthcoming 2017?
McElderry, Bruce R., Jr. "Coleridge's Revision of 'The Ancient Mariner'." *Studies in Philology* 29 (1932): 68–94.
McFarland, Thomas. "Poetry and the Poem: The Structure of Poetic Content" in *Literary Theory and Structure: Essays in Honor of William K. Wimsatt*. Ed. Frank Brady, John Palmer and Martin Price. New Haven, CT: Yale UP, 1973. 81–113.
———. *Originality and Imagination*. Baltimore, MD: The Johns Hopkins UP, 1985.
———. "Foreword: John Livingston Lowes and Coleridge's Poems" in *The Road to Xanadu: A Study in the Ways of the Imagination* by John Livingston Lowes (1930). Rpt. Princeton, NJ: Princeton UP, 1986. ix-xviii.
McGann, Jerome. "The Meaning of 'The Ancient Mariner'." *Critical Inquiry* 8 (1981): 35–67. Rpt. as "*The Rime of the Ancient Mariner*: The Meaning of the Meanings" in his *The Beauty of Inflexions: Literary Investigations in Historical Method and Theory*. Oxford: Clarendon Press, 1985. 135–72.
———. *The Romantic Ideology: A Critical Investigation*. Chicago: The University of Chicago Press, 1983.
———. *A New Republic of Letters: Memory and Scholarship in the Age of Digital Reproduction*. Cambridge, MA: Harvard UP, 2014.
McKendrick, Neil, John Brewer and J. H. Plumb, eds. *The Birth of a Consumer Society: The Commercialization of Eighteenth-Century England*. London: Europa Publications, 1982.
[Meynell, Alice.] "The Ancient Mariner." *The Pall Mall Gazette* (London) 65 No. 10,138 (22 Sept 22 1897): 3. Rpt. in *The Wares of Autolycus: Selected Literary Essays of Alice Meynell*. Ed. P. M. Fraser. London: Oxford UP, 1965. 67–70.
———, ed. "Introduction" to *Poems by Percy Bysshe Shelley*.London: Blackie and Son, 1903. v–viii.
———, ed. "Introduction" to *Poems of Samuel Taylor Coleridge*. London: Blackie and Son [1905]). iii–viii. Rpt. in *The Wares of Autolycus: Selected Literary Essays of Alice Meynell*. Ed. P. M. Fraser. London: Oxford UP, 1965. 154–57.
Miall, David S. "Guilt and Death: The Predicament of *The Ancient Mariner*." *Studies in English Literature, 1500–1900* 24 (1984): 633–53.
———. "The Campaign to Acquire Coleridge Cottage." *The Wordsworth Circle* 22 (1991): 82–88.

---------. "'I See It Feelingly': Coleridge's Debt to Hartley" in *Coleridge's Visionary Languages: Essays in Honour of J. B. Beer*. Ed. Tim Fulford and Morton D. Paley. Woodbridge, Suffolk: D. S. Brewer, 1993. 151–63.

---------. "Coleridge's Albatross: A Hypertext Essay on *The Rime of the Ancient Mariner*." https://www.alberta.ca/dmiall/MARINER/STCSTART.HTM last updated 9 September 1996, accessed 18 February 2015.

Mileur, Jean-Pierre. *Vision and Revision: Coleridge's Art of Immanence*. Berkeley, CA: University of California Press, 1982.

Miller, J. Hillis. *Poets of Reality: Six Twentieth-Century Writers*. Cambridge, MA: Harvard UP, 1965.

Milne, Ewart. *Forty North Fifty West*, illus. Cecil ffrench Salkeld. Dublin: The Gayfield Press, 1938.

Modiano, Raimonda. "Words and 'Languageless' Meanings: Limits of Expression in *The Rime of the Ancient Mariner*." *Modern Language Quarterly* 38 (1977): 40–61.

---------. *Coleridge and the Concept of Nature*. London: Macmillan, 1985.

---------. "Historicist Readings of *The Rime of the Ancient Mariner*" in *Samuel Taylor Coleridge and the Sciences of Life*. Ed. Nicholas Roe. Oxford: Oxford UP, 2001. 271–96.

Moir, D. M. *Sketches of the Poetical Literature of the Past Half-century*. Edinburgh: William Blackwood and Sons, 1851.

More, Henry. *Democritus Platonissans; or, An Essay upon the Infinity of Worlds out of Platonick Principles*. Cambridge; printed by Roger Daniel, 1646.

[Mozley, John Rickards.] Review of *The Poems of Samuel Taylor Coleridge*. Ed. Derwent Coleridge and Sara Coleridge (London, 1854). *Quarterly Review* 125 (1868): 78–106.

Muirhead, John H. *Coleridge as Philosopher*. London: George Allen and Unwin, 1930.

Newlyn, Lucy. *Coleridge, Wordsworth, and the Language of Allusion*. Oxford: Clarendon Press, 1986.

Nicholls, J. F. *Capt. Thomas James and George Thomas, the Philanthropist*, being Part 2 of his *Bristol Biographies*. 2nd ed. Bristol: for the Author, 1870.

Niebuhr, Richard R. *Streams of Grace: Studies of Jonathan Edwards, Samuel Taylor Coleridge, and William James* (1980. Rpt. Eugene, OR: Wipf and Stock, 2010.

Nodolny, Sten. *The Discovery of Slowness*. Trans. Ralph Freedman. New York: Viking Penguin, 1987.

O'Donnell, Brennan. *The Passion of Meter: A Study of Wordsworth's Metrical Art*. Kent, OH: The Kent State UP, 1995.

Oppen, George. *The Selected Letters of George Oppen*. Ed. Rachel Blau Du Plessis. Durham, NC: Duke UP, 1990.

---------. *New Collected Poems*. Ed. Michael Davidson. New York: New Directions, 2008.

Paley, Morton D. *Apocalypse and Millennium in English Romantic Poetry.* Oxford: Clarendon Press, 1999.
Palgrave, Francis Turner, ed. *The Golden Treasury of the Best Songs and Lyrical Pieces in the English Language.* Cambridge and London: Macmillan, 1861.
Parrish, Stephen Maxfield. *The Art of the "Lyrical Ballads".* Cambridge, MA: Harvard UP, 1973.
Pater, Walter. "Coleridge" (first pub. in parts in 1886 and 1880) in his *Appreciations, with an Essay on Style.* London: Macmillan, 1889. 64–106.
Pepys, Samuel. *The Diary of Samuel Pepys.* Ed. Robert Latham and William Matthews. 11 vols. London: G. Bell and Sons; Bell and Hyman, 1970–83.
[Percy, Thomas, ed.] *Reliques of Ancient English Poetry.* 3 vols. London: F. and C. Rivington, 4th ed 1794.
Pfau, Thomas. *Wordsworth's Profession: Form, Class, and the Logic of Early Romantic Cultural Production.* Stanford, CA: Stanford UP, 1997.
---------. *Minding the Modern: Human Agency, Intellectual Traditions, and Responsible Knowledge.* Notre Dame, IN: University of Notre Dame Press, 2013.
Piper, H. W. *The Active Universe: Pantheism and the Concept of Imagination in the English Romantic Poets.* London: The Athlone Press, 1962.
---------. *The Singing of Mount Abora: Coleridge's Use of Biblical Imagery and Natural Symbolism in Poetry and Philosophy.* Cranbury, NJ: Associated University Presses, 1987.
---------. "Coleridge and the Unitarian Consensus" in *The Coleridge Connection: Essays for Thomas McFarland.* Ed. Richard Gravil and Molly Lefebure. Basingstoke, Hants.: Macmillan, 1990. 273–90.
Poland, Lynn. "The Idea of the Holy and the History of the Sublime." *Journal of Religion* 72 (1992): 175–97.
Pound, Ezra. *The Cantos of Ezra Pound.* London: Faber and Faber, rev collected edn. 1975.
Pound, Louise, ed. *Coleridge's The Rime of the Ancient Mariner and Other Poems.* Philadelphia, PA: J. B. Lippincott, 1920.
Pradhan, S. V. "Philocrisy: Sources of Inspiration" in his *Philocrisy and its Implications: Essays on Coleridge.* Mumbai: Allied Publishers, 1999. 96–110.
Priestley, Joseph. *An History of the Corruptions of Christianity.* 2 vols. Birmingham: for J. Johnson, 1782.
Prynne, J. H. *Bands Around the Throat.* Cambridge; the Author, 1987.
---------. *Poems.* Hexham, Northd: Bloodaxe Books, 3rd ed. 2015.
Purves, Alan C. *The Verse Technique of Samuel Taylor Coleridge* (PhD dissertation (TS), Columbia University, NY, 1960). See *Dissertation Abstracts* 31 (1960): 190–91.
Raysor, Thomas Middleton, ed. *Coleridge's Shakespearean Criticism.* 2 vols. Cambridge, MA: Harvard UP, 1930.

---------, ed. *Coleridge's Miscellaneous Criticism.* Cambridge, MA: Harvard UP, 1936.

---------, ed. *The English Romantic Poets: A Review of Research.* New York: Modern Language Society of America, 1950; 2nd. ed. revised, 1956.

Reed, Arden. "The Rhyming Mariner and the Mariner Rimed" in his *Romantic Weather: The Climates of Coleridge and Baudelaire.* Hanover, NH: University Press of New England for Brown University Press, 1983. 147–81.

Reed, Mark L. *Wordsworth: The Chronology of the Early Years, 1770–1799.* Cambridge, MA: Harvard UP, 1967.

---------. *Wordsworth: The Chronology of the Middle Years, 1800–1815.* Cambridge, MA: Harvard UP, 1975.

---------. *A Bibliography of William Wordsworth, 1787–1930.* 2 vols. Cambridge: Cambridge UP, 2013.

Richards, I. A. *Principles of Literary Criticism.* London: Kegan Paul, Trench, Trubner, 1925.

---------. "The Lure of High Mountaineering" (1927) in his *Complimentarities: Uncollected Essays.* Ed. John Paul Russo. Manchester: Carcarnet New Press, 1976. 235–45.

---------. *Practical Criticism: A Study of Literary Judgment.* London: Kegan Paul, Trench, Trubner, 1929.

---------. *Coleridge on Imagination.* London: Kegan Paul, Trench, Trubner, 1934; 3rd ed., with Preface by Kathleen Coburn. Bloomington, IN: Indiana UP, 1960.

---------. *Coleridge's Minor Poems: A Lecture . . . Delivered in Honor of the Fortieth Anniversary of Professor Edmund L. Freeman at Montana State University on April 8, 1960.* Missoula, MT: Montana State University, 1960.

Riding, Laura, and Robert Graves. *A Survey of Modernist Poetry.* London: William Heinemann, 1927.

---------. See also Laura (Riding) Jackson.

Rowland, Christopher. Review of *Coleridge's Responses, Volume II: Coleridge on the Bible* (London: Continuum, 2008) in *The Coleridge Bulletin* N.S. 33 (2009): 119–27.

Ruoff, Gene W. "Romantic Lyric and the Problem of Belief" in *The Romantics and Us: Essays on Literature and Culture.* Ed. Gene W. Ruoff. New Brunswick, NJ: Rutgers UP, 1990. 288–302.

Rutherford, Mark: see William Hale White.

Rzepka, Charles J. *The Self as Mind: Vision and Identity in Wordsworth, Coleridge, and Keats.* Cambridge, MA: Harvard UP, 1986.

Sell, Roger D. "Dialogue *versus* Silencing: Coleridge's *The Rime of the Ancient Mariner*" in *Literary Community-Making: The Dialogicality of English Texts from the Seventeenth-Century to the Present.* Ed. Roger D. Sells. Amsterdam: John Benjamins, 2012. 91–130.

Seronsy, Cecil C. "Dual Patterning in 'The Rime of the Ancient Mariner'." *Notes and Queries* 201 (Nov 1956): 497–99.
Sewell, Elizabeth. *The Field of Nonsense.* London: Chatto and Windus, 1952.
---------. *The Orphic Voice: Poetry and Natural History.* New Haven, CT: Yale UP, 1960.
Shaffer, E. S. "Coleridge's Ekphrasis: Visionary Word-Painting" in *Coleridge's Visionary Languages: Essays in Honour of J. B. Beer.* Ed. Tim Fulford and Morton D. Paley. Woodbridge, Suffolk: D. S. Brewer, 1993. 111–21.
---------, and Edoardo Zuccato, eds. *The Reception of S. T. Coleridge in Europe.* London: Continuum, 2007.
[Shawcross, Hartley.] *Life Sentence: The Memoirs of Lord Shawcross.* London: Constable, 1995.
Sheats, Paul D. *The Making of Wordsworth's Poetry, 1785–1798.* Cambridge, MA: Harvard UP, 1973.
Shelley, Percy Bysshe. *The Poems of Shelley: Volume II, 1817–1819.* Ed. Kelvin Everest and Geoffrey Matthews. Harlow, Essex: Longman, 2000.
---------. *The Poems of Shelley: Volume III, 1819–1820.* Ed. Jack Donovan, Cian Duffy, Kelvin Everest and Michael Rossington. London: Routledge, 2011.
Shepherd, Justin. "'Where first I sprang to light': Coleridge's Autobiographical Reflections 1797–98." *The Coleridge Bulletin* N.S. No.35 (2010): 15–32.
---------. "The Integrity of the 1798 *Lyrical Ballads*: the Making of a Book." *The Coleridge Bulletin* N.S. No.41 (2013): 57–74.
Simpson, David. *Irony and Authority in Romantic Poetry.* London: Macmillan, 1979.
---------. "Public Virtues, Private Vices: Reading between the Lines of Wordsworth's 'Anecdote for Fathers'" in *Subject to History: Ideology, Class, Gender.* Ed. David Simpson. Ithaca, NY: Cornell UP, 1991. 163–90.
---------. "How Marxism Reads 'The Rime of the Ancient Mariner'" in *The Rime of the Ancient Mariner: Case Studies in Contemporary Criticism.* Ed. Paul H. Fry. Boston, MA: Bedford/St. Martin's, 1999. 148–67.
Sitterson, Joseph C., Jr. "'The Rime of the Ancient Mariner' and Freudian Dream Theory." *Papers on Language and Literature* 18 (1982): 17–35.
Skipsey, Joseph, ed. "Prefatory Notice" to *The Poems of Samuel Taylor Coleridge.* London: Walter Scott, 1884. 9–31.
Smith, James Elishama, ed. "Wildness and Extravagance." *The Family Herald: A Domestic Magazine of Useful Information and Amusement* 8 (1850): 332–33.
Snyder, Edward D. *Hypnotic Poetry: A Study of Trance-Inducing Techniques in Certain Poems and its Literary Significance.* Philadelphia, PA: University of Pennsylvania Press, 1930.
Soubigou, Gilles. "The Reception of *The Rime of the Ancient Mariner* through Gustave Doré's Illustrations" in *The Reception of S. T. Coleridge in Europe.* Ed. Elinor Shaffer and Edoardo Zuccato. London: Continuum, 2007. 61–87.

Stafford, Fiona, ed. *Lyrical Ballads, 1798 and 1802*. Oxford: Oxford UP, 2013.
States, Bert O. *Dreaming and Storytelling*. Ithaca, NY: Cornell UP, 1993.
St. Clair, William. *The Reading Nation in the Romantic Period*. Cambridge: Cambridge UP, 2004.
Stephen, Leslie. "S. T. Coleridge" (1888) in his *Hours in a Library*. 2nd ed. in 3 vols. London: Smith, Elder, 1892. 3.339–68.
Stevens, Wallace. *Letters of Wallace Stevens*. Ed. Holly Stevens. London: Faber and Faber, 1967.
---------. *Collected Poetry and Prose*. [Ed. Frank Kermode and Joan Richardson.] New York: The Library of America, 1997.
Stewart, George R., Jr. *Modern Metrical Technique, as Illustrated by Ballad Meter (1700–1920)*. New York: privately published, 1922.
---------. *The Technique of English Verse*. New York Holt, Rinehart and Winston, 1930.
Stillinger, Jack. *Coleridge and Textual Instability: The Multiple Versions of the Major Poems*. New York: Oxford UP, 1994.
Stork, Charles W. "The Influence of the Popular Ballad on Wordsworth and Coleridge." *Publications of the Modern Language Association* 29 (1914): 299–326.
Tate, Allen. "Literature as Knowledge" (1941) in his *The Man of Letters in the Modern World: Selected Essays, 1928–1955*. New York: Meridian Books; London: Thames and Hudson, 1955. 34–63.
Temple, Julien (dir.). *Pandaemonium*, screenplay by Frank Cottrell Boyce. London: Mariner Films, 2000; Optimum Releasing DVD no.VCD0243, 2002.
Thomas, Sophie. "Poetry and Illustration: 'Amicable strife'" in *A Companion to Romantic Poetry*. Ed. Charles Mahony. Malden, MA: 1-Blackwell, 2010. 354–73.
Thrupp, Frederick. *The Antient Mariner and the Modern Sportsman: An Essay*. London, 1881.
Tomko, Michael. *Beyond the Willing Suspension of Belief: Poetic Faith from Coleridge to Tolkien*. London: Bloomsbury, 2016.
Trickett, Rachel. *The Elders*. London: Constable, 1966.
Tsur, Reuven. *"Kubla Khan": Poetic Structure, Hypnotic Quality and Cognitive Style. A Study in Mental, Vocal and Critical Performance*. Amsterdam: John Benjamins, 2006.
Tuttle, Donald R. "*Christabel* Sources in Percy's *Reliques* and the Gothic Romance." *Publications of the Modern Language Association* 53 (1938): 445–74.
Twitchell, James B. "*The Rime of the Ancient Mariner* as a Vampire Poem." *College Literature* 4 (1977): 21–39.
---------. *The Living Dead: A Study of the Vampire in Romantic Literature*. Durham, NC: Duke UP, 1981.

Ulmer, William A. *The Christian Wordsworth, 1798–1805*. Albany, NY: State University of New York, 2001.
---------. "Necessary Evils: Unitarian Theodicy in 'The Rime of the Ancyent Marinere'." *Studies in Romanticism* 43 (2004): 327–56.
Voller, Jack G. *The Supernatural Sublime: The Metaphysics of Terror in Anglo-American Romanticism*. De Kalb, IL: Northern Illinois UP, 1994.
Wallen, Martin, ed. *Coleridge's 'Ancient Mariner': An Experimental Edition of Texts and Revisions, 1798–1828*. Barrytown, NY: Station Hill, 1993.
Warner, Richard. *A Walk Through Some of the Western Counties of England*. Bath: R. Cruttwell, 1800.
Warnock, Mary. *Imagination*. London: Faber and Faber, 1976.
Warren, R. P. "A Poem of Pure Imagination: Reconsiderations VI" *The Kenyon Review* 8 (1946): 391–427. Rpt. in *Samuel Taylor Coleridge: The Rime of the Ancient Mariner* illus. Alexander Calder. New York: Reynal and Hitchcock, 1946. 61–148; and *Selected Essays*. New York: Vintage, 1956. 198–305.
Watson, William. "Coleridge's Supernaturalism" in his *Excursions in Criticism; being Some Recreations of a Prose Rhymer*. London: Elkin Mathews and John Lane, 1893. 97–103.
Wellek, René. *Immanuel Kant in England, 1793–1838*. Princeton, NJ: Princeton UP, 1931.
West, Sally. *Coleridge and Shelley: Textual Engagement*. Aldershot, Hants: Ashgate, 2007.
Whalley, George. "The Bristol Library Borrowings of Southey and Coleridge, 1793–8." *The Library* 5th Series 4 (1949): 114–32.
---------. "'Late Autumn's Amaranth': Coleridge's Late Poems." *Transactions of the Royal Society of Canada* (Ottawa, ON) 2.4 (Jun 1964, section 2): 159–79.
---------. "England: Romantic-Romanticism" in *"Romantic" and Its Cognates: The European History of a Word*. Ed. Hans Eichner. Toronto: University of Toronto Press, 1972. 157–262.
---------. "Coleridge's Poetic Sensibility" in *Coleridge's Variety: Bicentenary Studies*. Ed. John Beer. London: Macmillan, 1974. 1–30.
[White, William Hale, under the pseudonym Mark Rutherford.] "Captain James's 'Strange and Dangerous Voyage'" (first printed in *The Nation*) in his *Last Pages from a Journal, edited by his Wife*. London: Oxford UP, 1915. 53–66.
Wilcox, Stewart C. "The Arguments and Motto of *The Ancient Mariner*." *Modern Language Quarterly* 22 (1961): 264–68.
Williams, Rowan. *The Edge of Words: God and the Habits of Language*. London: Bloomsbury, 2014.
Wilson, Katharine M. *Sound and Meaning in English Poetry*. London: Jonathan Cape, 1930.
Wolf, F. A. *Prolegomena to Homer*. Trans Anthony Grafton, Glen W. Most and James E. G. Zetzel. Princeton, NJ: Princeton University Press, 1985.

Woodring, Carl. "What Coleridge Thought of Pictures" in *Images of Romanticism: Verbal and Visual Affinities*. Ed. Karl Kroeber and William Walling. New Haven, CT: Yale UP, 1978. 91–106.

---------. "Wordsworth and the Victorians" in *The Age of William Wordsworth: Critical Essays on the Romantic Tradition*. Ed. Kenneth R. Johnston and Gene W. Ruoff. New Brunswick, NJ: Rutgers UP, 1987. 261–75.

Woof, Robert, ed. *William Wordsworth: The Critical Heritage. Volume I, 1793–1820*. London: Routledge, 2001.

Wordsworth, Dorothy. *The Grasmere and Alfoxden Journals*. Ed. Pamela Woof. Oxford: Oxford UP, 2002.

Wordsworth, William[, and Samuel Taylor Coleridge.] *Lyrical Ballads with Other Poems*. 2 vols. London: T. N. Longman and O. Rees, 1800.

---------. *Poems in Two Volumes*. 2 vols. London: Longman, Hurst, Rees, and Orme, 1807.

---------. *Poems*. 2 vols. London: Longman, Hurst, Rees, Orme, and Brown, 1815.

---------. *The Prose Works of William Wordsworth*. Ed. Alexander Grosart. 3 vols. London: Edward Moxon, Son, 1876.

---------. *Poetical Works: Volume II* (1944). Ed. E. de Selincourt. 2nd ed. Oxford: Clarendon Press, 1952.

Wordsworth, William and Dorothy. *The Letters of William and Dorothy Wordsworth: The Early Years, 1787–1805*. Ed. Ernest de Selincourt, rev. Chester L. Shaver. 2nd ed. Oxford: Clarendon Press, 1967.

---------. *The Letters of William and Dorothy Wordsworth: The Middle Years, 1806–1820*. Ed. Ernest de Selincourt, rev. Mary Moorman and Alan G. Hill. 2nd ed. 2 vols. Oxford: Clarendon Press, 1969–70.

---------. *Home at Grasmere: Part First, Book First, of "The Recluse"*. Ed. Beth Darlington. Ithaca, NY: Cornell UP, 1972.

---------. *The Prose Works of William Wordsworth*. Ed. W.J.B.Owen and Jane Worthington Smyser. 3 vols. Oxford: Clarendon Press, 1974.

---------. *The Letters of William and Dorothy Wordsworth: The Later Years, 1821–1853*. Ed. Ernest de Selincourt and Alan G. Hill. 2nd ed. 4 vols. Oxford: Clarendon Press, 1978–88.

---------. *The Prelude: 1799, 1805, 1850*. Ed. Jonathan Wordsworth, M. H. Abrams and Stephen Gill. New York: W. W. Norton, 1979.

---------. *"The Ruined Cottage" and "The Pedlar"*. Ed. James Butler. Ithaca, NY: Cornell UP, 1979.

---------. *Peter Bell*. Ed. John E. Jordan. Ithaca, NY: Cornell UP, 1985.

---------. *The White Doe of Rylstone; or The Fate of the Nortons*. Ed. Kristine Dugas. Ithaca, NY: Cornell University Press, 1988.

---------. *"Lyrical Ballads", and Other Poems, 1797–1800*. Ed. James Butler and Karen Green. Ithaca, NY: Cornell UP, 1992.

---------. *Early Poems and Fragments, 1785–1797*. Ed. Carol Landon and Jared Curtis. Ithaca, NY: Cornell UP, 1997.

Worthen, John. *The Gang: Coleridge, the Hutchinsons and the Wordsworths in 1802*. New Haven, CT: Yale UP, 2001.

Yeats, W. B. *The Oxford Book of Modern Verse, 1892–1935*. Oxford: Clarendon Press, 1936.

Yoshikawa, Saeko. *William Wordsworth and the Invention of Tourism, 1820–1900*. Farnham, Surrey: Ashgate, 2014.

Index[1]

A

Abrams, M. H., 154, 177, 184n15
Aikin, John, 58
Alfoxden (Somerset), 73, 83, 86, 93, 103, 114n35
Allen, Donald, 169
Allman, Thomas (publisher), 28, 114n38
Ampère, André-Marie, 176
Amulet, The, 225
Anderson, Peter, 38
Anti-Jacobin, 140, 163
Antin, David, 180
Arabian Nights, 28, 95
Arac, Jonathan, 139, 178
A rebours, 34
Armitage, Simon, 19, 23n19, 169
Arno, Christie, 113n5
Ashe, Thomas, 147–8
Attridge, Derek, 31, 137n14
Ault, Donald, 65, 75
Austen, Jane, 40
Averill, James H., 83, 91n4, 113n16

B

Barbauld, Anna Laetitia, 133
Barfield, Owen, 1–2, 157, 164
Barnes, William, 41, 168
Barnett, John Francis, 32
Barthes, Roland, 20
Bate, W. Jackson, 154
Baudelaire, Charles, 41, 147, 149
Beardsley, Aubrey, 173
Beare, Geoffrey, and Lorraine Janzen Kooistra, 45n20, 137n11
Beckett, Samuel, vii, 11, 13, 137n12, 137n15, 180, 184n23, 207, 229n3
Beddoes, Dr Thomas, 54
Beddoes, Thomas Lovell, 148
Beer, John, 38, 91n10, 91n11, 113n9, 151, 229n5, 230n12
Behmen, Jacob. *See* Boehme, Jakob
Beissner, Friedrich, 135
Bell, Vanessa, 149
Belloc, Hilaire, 28
Bennett, Betty T., 159n5

---

[1] Note: Page number with "n" denote notes.

254 INDEX

Berkeley, George, 53, 55, 66
Berlin, Sven, 39
Bernbaum, Ernest, 161n32
Bishop, Elizabeth, 169
Blake, William, 21, 25, 27, 38, 136, 162n38
Blavatsky, Madame Helena, 176
Bloom, Harold, 155
Blunden, Edmund, 79
Boas, Guy, 161n29
Boccaccio, Giovanni, 226
Bodkin, Maud, 46n30
Boehme, Jakob, 56, 68n6, 68n7, 78, 92n20, 92n21
Bogdanov, Michael, 32
Bonaparte, Napoleon, 164
Borges, Jorge Luis, 136
Boulger, James D., 22n7, 181, 184n21
Bowring, John, 160n21
Bradford, Richard, 96–7
Bristol, 6, 54, 69n20, 83, 84, 86, 88, 97, 113n10, 123, 155, 160n24, 173, 175
Brooke, Stopford, 160n21, 229n5
Browning, Robert, 148
Brun, Frederike, 61
Bruno, Giordano, 68n6
Bunting, Basil, 168
Bürger, Gottfried August, 74, 79, 101
Burke, Edmund, 175, 184n10
Burke, Kenneth, 34
Burnet, Gilbert, 128, 129
Byron, George Lord, ix, 23n19, 110, 112, 143

C
calculus, 55
Caleb Williams. See Godwin, William
Cambridge Union, 144
Campbell, Colin, 24n22

Campbell, James Dykes, 117, 130, 131, 148, 160n23, 160n24
Campbell, Thomas, 45n10
Carroll, Lewis (Charles Lutwidge Dodson), 78
Casement, Ann, and David Tracy, 46n30
Cavalcanti, Guido, 10
Cavell, Stanley, 56, 113n14
Cézanne, Paul, 149
Chambers, Edmund K., 4, 153
Chambers, William and Robert (publishers), 114n38, 142, 145, 159n7
Chandler, James, 113n16
Chatterton, Thomas, 79
Cheddar Gorge (Somerset), 175
Cheshire, Paul, 23n17
Cheyne, Peter, x, 56, 213, 229n1, 230n13
Chidley, John (publisher), 142
Christ's Hospital (London), 50, 77, 92n20
Clarke, Austin, 41
Clarke, Harry, 173
Clarke, H. G. (publisher), 142
Coburn, Kathleen, 68n7, 151, 152, 157, 158, 162n38
Cohn, Jan, and Thomas H. Miles, 184n9
Coleridge, Ann (mother), 65, 75–6, 120–1, 128
Coleridge, Berkeley (son), 53
Coleridge, Derwent (son), 78, 131, 141, 160n15, 223
Coleridge, Ernest Hartley (grandson), 91n5, 91n8, 117, 130, 131, 135, 146, 148
Coleridge, Hartley (son), 60, 89, 90
Coleridge, Henry Nelson (nephew/son-in-law), 141, 146, 152
Coleridge, Jack (brother), 65, 70n30

Coleridge, John (father), 49, 55, 57, 65, 69n18, 70n30, 76, 91n10, 128, 175
Coleridge, Samuel Taylor

(A) CONTEXTS:
audience for his poetry
  copyright considerations, 121, 131, 141–2, 145, 159n6, 160n23
  early consolidation of, 140–4
  notably diverse nature of, 7, 11–12, 149
  his reserved position regarding, ix, 10, 17–22, 94, 166, 168
  Wordsworth's part in creating, 110–12, 139, 148
Bollingen edition
  Coburn's pivotal role, 152, 157–8
  earlier volumes meet an interest in politics, 164
  later volumes enlarge overall understanding, 8, 18, 157–8
  other editions of "Mariner" (*see esp.* E. H. Coleridge, Stillinger, Wallen *in main index*)
  PW Reading and Variorum Texts, their dialogic relation, 134–6
distractions and obstructions
  biographical paradigm of apostasy and failure, viii–ix, 4, 9–10, 111, 155
  contexts that mislead, 19, 135, 148–9
  his literary criticism separated from his verse, ix, 149–50, 152–3, 154
  measured by Wordsworth's achievement as man and poet, 9, 111, 139–40, 148–9
  multiplicity of textual versions, 11–12, 117–21, 134–6
  secular inhibition, 9, 14–15, 17, 42–4, 48, 51–2, 175–9, 182
  source hunting along *The Road to Xanadu*, 1–2, 5–6, 150–1, 157 (*see also* Wordsworth, William, the hunt motif and the Albatross)
literary concepts
  Biographia Literaria
    changing reputation of, 152–3
    muddled construction of, 13–14, 48
    as response to Wordsworth, 8, 49–50, 105–6
  emotion and feelings, place of, 40, 51–2, 90, 93–4, 166–7, 178, 218
  Imagination
    developing concept of, 7–8, 48–50, 132
    and Fancy, 8, 14, 48–9, 151
    narrowed as a simply literary term, 14–15, 51–2, 60–1, 174
    "spirituality of the senses", 25–7, 44, 59
  poem vs. poetry, 3–4, 13–14, 174
  the sublime and sublimation, 14–15, 175–7
philosophical concepts (*see also* Berkeley, Hartley, Kant, Spinoza, etc. *in main index*)
  Association of Ideas, 50, 53–4, 57–8, 74, 82, 224
  Coincidence of Opposites (polarity), 56–7, 171, 173, 225

256 INDEX

(A) CONTEXTS: (*cont.*)
  Neoplatonism, 8, 14–15, 47, 51, 55–6, 58–9, 60–1, 68n1, 151, 152, 178–9, 230n13 (*see also* Plato/Platonic *in main index*)
  Order of the Mental Powers, 14, 51, 62, 174
  Pantheism, 15–16, 53–4, 57–8, 134, 175, 222
  Reason, 8, 14, 23n12, 42, 51, 59, 62, 106–7, 132, 154, 173–4, 176, 178–9
  Transcendental Idealism, 43, 53–7, 59, 118, 130, 154, 174, 178
  Understanding, 8, 39–40, 42, 51, 53, 57, 62, 64, 132, 174, 179
  Will (human and divine), 12, 58, 62, 78, 80, 108, 120, 124, 134, 176, 228
 position of "Ancient Mariner" in his overall career
  new beginning, 7, 15, 53, 68, 179
  unique place, 13, 35–6, 43–4, 63–7, 179–80
  with him to the end, 12–13, 127–30
 status as poet
  comparisons with modern poets, ix, 17, 19–20 (*see also* Duncan, Howe, Prynne, *etc. in main index*)
  as experimental, 4–5, 17–22, 87–8, 180
  as failure, viii, 9–10, 21–2, 111, 140
  as non-professional ("other" or "ingenuous"), ix, 19–22, 95, 135, 165–8

  theological concepts (*see also* literary concepts | Imagination *and* philosophical concepts | Reason *above*)
  Enthusiasm, 15, 184n15
  Gnosticism, 10, 77–8, 81, 92n21
  Trinity, 8, 12, 51, 95, 175
  Unitarianism, 8, 57–8, 69n17, 175, 182
 the times surrounding
  apocalyptic, 57–8, 77, 175
  changing politics, 140, 163–4, 165
  consumerism, 20–1
  periodical criticism, 95, 107, 122, 140–1, 168
  slavery, 56–7, 134, 155, 173
  war, 6, 141, 159n5, 228
Coleridge, Samuel Taylor

(B) "ANCIENT MARINER":
 allusions in
  contradictory, 6, 34–5, 40, 44n2, 57, 130, 136, 178
  Gothick, 2, 65, 74, 79, 84, 98, 122–3, 127–8, 137n4
  Kant's Two Worlds, 56
  personal
   mother and father, 65, 75–6, 120–1, 128
   Wordsworthian Hermit, 29, 33, 77, 114n36, 122
 connections with
  fin de siècle authors, 117, 146–7, 173
  French *symbolistes*, 38, 41, 51, 147, 149 (*see also* Beckett, Duncan, Howe, Prynne, Stevens, Yeats *in main index*)

epigraph, 9, 128–9, 132
footnotes, 80, 129–30
genres and applications
  ballad, 6, 12–13, 16, 29–32, 34, 63–6, 70n31, 75, 78–9, 141, 167, 180, 208, 215–16
  children's book, 28, 145–6, 163
  gift book, 28, 38, 142, 146, 155
  illustrated book, 38–9, 131–2, 144–7
  joke/parody, 2, 11, 43, 53, 58, 65, 78, 87–8, 98, 122, 127–8, 133
  nonsense, 26, 78–9, 91n14, 95
  "a poem of pure imagination", 67, 133
  school text, 28, 32, 131, 144–6, 148–50, 153
gloss
  complications introduced by, 9, 52, 65, 117, 128, 131–2
  difficulty of reading, 9, 130–1
  options for placement, 121, 131, 137n9
  poetry or pastiche?, 133–4
illustrated editions
  attraction for illustrators, 17, 38–40, 144–6
  distraction for readers, 17, 39–40
  "supplement," another form of, 131–2
imagery
  "of high latitudes", 56–7, 81
  pictorial, 31–2, 39–40, 93–4
  sight into sound, 38–40, 62
  Sun and Moon, 29, 34–5, 36, 40, 62, 72–3, 81, 83, 109, 114n35, 127, 133–4, 178 (*see also* symbolism *below*)

language
  antique spelling/archaisms, 79, 98, 122, 123
  meanings at the edge, 26, 41–3, 51, 53, 58–9, 82–3, 181–3
  simplicity, 34–5 (*see also* joke/parody *above and* words *below*)
LB 1798
  as context for poem, 83–7, 96–7
  first version of "Ancient Mariner," 11–12, 79, 81–2, 117–18, 119–20
  reviving interest in volume, 47, 91n4, 148, 152
  the way this version was read, 140–1, 143–4, 147, 163–4
moral
  appropriateness of the trite admonition, 28, 30, 41, 132–3
  differently understood by Wordsworth, 9, 73, 96–7, 98–9, 122, 125, 132–3
  reinforced or undercut by revisions, 87–8, 118–19, 123–4, 128, 180
  Wordsworth's alternative formulations, 73–4, 95, 100–4, 105–6, 109–10, 123–5
narrative method, aspects of
  change of plan, 3, 35–8
  division into parts, 29, 33, 34, 35
  doubled over, 36–8, 81
  epiphanic moments, 42, 59–60, 62, 178
  incomplete and inconsequential, 2, 25–6
  mounting and reversing pace, 2–3, 57, 224

(B) "ANCIENT MARINER":
  (*cont.*)
  multiple frames and levels,
    128–30, 130–1
  rounded story, 3, 28–9, 81
  readership (*see* audience *and* times
    surrounding *under (A)
    CONTEXTS*)
  reputation of
    early popularity, 140–4, 147
    influence of educationists,
      145–6
    influence of illustrators, 144–5
    late nineteenth century
      re-launch, 146, 173
    in twentieth-century criticism,
      147–56, 174
  revision (*see* versions *below*)
  simplicity of poem
    described, 28–9
    difficulty of confronting, 1–2,
      178–9
    impossibility of understanding
      3–4, 51, 62, 176
    transparency, 28, 30, 42, 179
      (*see also* distractions *and*
      obstructions *under (A)
      CONTEXTS*)
  sound matters
    consonants and vowels, 16,
      30, 34
    echo, 15, 32–5, 38, 41, 65, 66,
      73, 75, 101, 104–5, 173,
      174, 217–19
    figures
      chiasmus, 34, 101
      zeugma, 16
    how absorbed by readers, 31–3
    metrical experiment, 30–1, 34,
      44n5, 81
    musical settings, 17, 32
    pitch, 30, 33, 172
    rhyme, 32, 34, 35, 37, 41, 64
    rhythm, 16, 30–1, 33, 50, 134
    stanza construction, 12–13, 16,
      30–4, 64, 75
    trisyllabic substitution, 75
  story, elements of
    dream, 31, 39, 53, 56–7,
      80, 124
    fear and dread, 35–8, 41, 42, 94
    Hand of Glory, 122
    Hermit, 28, 29, 33, 37, 77,
      114n36, 122
    homecoming, 36–7, 81–2, 134
    magic, 52–3, 77, 82, 111,
      148–9, 153
    reverie, 98, 123–4, 125
    Spectre Ship, 12, 35, 65, 120,
      122, 123, 127
    Two Voices, 32, 33, 35, 38, 41,
      42, 57, 77, 122–3
    voyage, 3, 6, 38, 57, 81, 120,
      124–5, 141, 147, 178,
      183n6
  symbolism
    albatross as narrative marker, 29,
      35, 36, 59, 208, 224
    ambivalence of redemptive
      theme, viii, 58, 77, 82–3,
      124, 133–4
    inadvertent consequence of
      Wordsworth's
      contribution, 41, 46n27,
      80–1, 124–5, 132–3
    nineteenth-century
      misunderstanding, 132,
      143, 144, 147
    twentieth-century
      misunderstanding, 4–5,
      10, 26, 134–6, 152–3,
      154–5
  versions and revisions
    1797-98

composed orally?, 31, 121
doubled in length, 37–8, 81–2
too easily set aside, 11–12, 133
1800-1805
   Coleridge's revisions, 121, 122–5
   Wordsworth's treatment of Coleridge in, 98–100, 123–5
1817 and afterwards
   anticipations of the further revision, 125, 126
   changes in text and added footnotes, 127–8, 129
   epigraph, 128–9
   gloss. (*see* gloss *separately above*)
   late tinkering, 129–30
digital presentation of variants, 135–6
words
   creativity of, 15–17
   different words, effect of, 35, 37, 38
   proper names, lacking, 28
   repetition of, 29, 35, 80 (*see also* story, elements of | fear and dread)
   simplicity of, viii, 2, 16, 28–9, 34–5
   spellings
      difficulty exaggerated, 133
      "ee", 32, 70n32, 75, 219, 230n17 (*see also* language *above*)
   "rime", 89, 124
Coleridge, Samuel Taylor

(C) SELECTED OTHER TITLES:

"Alice du Clós" (**655**)
   ballad stanza, variations of, 215–16

brevity, effect of, 207–08, 223–5
Calvinist dimension, 22n8, 119
comparison with "The Garden of Boccaccio", 226–7
echoes, system of, 217–19
final statement on issues raised by "Mariner", 12–13, 67, 165, 222–4
human inadequacy, 228
hunt narrative and "Ancient Mariner", ix, 125, 144, 210–11, 214, 226, 230n10
malignity, 208, 212–14
narrative structure, 209–11, 212
"The Ballad of the Dark Ladiè" (**182**)
   connections with "Alice du Clós", 219, 222
   connections with "Mariner", 12, 63, 65–6, 120–1
   relation to poem "Love", 66–7, 219–21
"Christabel" (**176**)
   connections with "The Ballad of the Dark Ladiè", 63, 66, 120–1, 223
   following on from "Ancient Mariner", 63, 65–6
   metrical evolution of, 64, 215
   omission from *LB* 1800, 98–100
   Part I supernatural same kind as "Ancient Mariner", 63, 66, 70n27, 99, 223
   Part II compared to "Ancient Mariner" gloss, 133, 158
   Preface compared to "Ancient Mariner" epigraph, 128–9
"Continuation of 'The Three Graves'" (**155**)
   ballad stanza, handling of, 75

(C) SELECTED OTHER TITLES: (*cont.*)
  curse, 74, 75, 82, 86
  local imagery, 82, 94
  mother figure, 75, 76
  sun through leaves, 62, 217
"The Eolian Harp" (**115**)
  epiphanic structure, 59
  music of versification, 17, 30
  pantheism in, 17, 222, 224–5
  revision parallels that of the "Mariner", 118
  sensory detail of, 93–4
"Frost at Midnight" (**171**)
  ending curtailed, 60, 89
  excluded from *LB 1798*, 73, 89, 90
  frost and rime, 89, 124
  Wordsworthian springboard 59–60, 90
"Kubla Khan" (**178**)
  connections with "Ancient Mariner", viii, 4, 8, 68
  different resonances, 35, 151
  effect of preface compared to "Mariner's" parerga, 128–9
  excluded? from *LB 1800*, 101
  and Lord King's summer-house, 5, 22n3
  reputation compared to "Mariner's", 143, 147, 149, 156, 160n17
  and Wordsworth's "Hart-leap Well", 100, 102, 125
"Love" (**253**)
  connections with "The Ballad of the Dark Ladiè" and "Christabel", 12, 66–7, 84, 219–22
  nineteenth-century reputation, 141, 143, 146, 147, 160n17
  psychological dimension more prominent than supernatural, 118, 221–2
"The Wanderings of Cain" (**160**)
  divided brothers and redemptive child, 76–7
  failed collaboration entirely, 75–6
  Gnostic-Hermetic dimension, 77–8, 82
  purgatory and apocalypse, 77
Coleridge, Sara (daughter), 141, 152, 157
Coleridge, Sara (wife), 87, 231n19
Coleridge, Stephen, 125
Collins, Billy, 169
Collins (publisher), 45n17, 145
Conrad, Joseph, 147
Cooke, George, 5
Cooper, Lane, 80, 96, 114n36
Costelloe, Timothy M., 184n9
Cothelstone Park (Somerset), 231n22
Cottle, Joseph (publisher), 81, 83, 84, 86, 88, 97, 99, 111, 113n11, 119, 123
Courtois, Bernard, 176
Cox, Thomas (publisher), 142
Crantz, David, 68n3
Crashaw, Richard, 184n15
Critical Review, 79, 137n3, 141
Cruikshank, John, 80
Cudworth, Ralph, 129
Culbone (Somerset), 5, 149

D
Daly, Charles (publisher) 137n9, 142
Dante degli Alighieri, 62, 69n16
Davidson, Graham, x, 213, 217, 229n1
Davies, John, 174–6
Davy, Humphry, 36, 176

INDEX 261

Dearborn, Kerry, 184n7
De Quincey, Thomas, 1, 100, 111, 143
Derrida, Jacques, 9, 131
De Vere, Aubrey, 115n41
Dibdin, Thomas Frognall, 20
Dickinson, Emily, 139
Dixon, Josie, 40
Donne, John, 156
Donoghue, Denis, 181
Doré, Gustave, 17, 144–5
Dowden, Edward, 148
Drake, Nathan, 143
Drew, John, 91n10
Dugas, Kristine, 108
Duncan, Edward, 144
Duncan, Robert, ix, 11, 170, 180
Dyce, Alexander, 80, 81, 143
Dyck, Sarah, 137n7

E
Earnshaw, C., 159n6
Edgar, Pelham, 157, 162n38
Edinburgh Review, 95, 107, 111, 140
Einstein, Albert, 154
Eliot, Thomas Stearns, 2, 42
Emerson, Hunt, 79, 132
Emerson, Thomas, 178
Empson, William, 155, 161n26, 229n5
Engell, James, 68n2, 154
Etonian, The, 141, 146
Evans, John, 159n6
Evans, Mary, 103, 218
Evans, William, 69n18
Exmoor, 5, 78

F
Falci, Eric, 230n11
Fenton, James, 22n7
Ferguson, Frances, 65, 103–04
Ferrer, Daniel, 135
Finlay, Ian Hamilton, 182
Firbank, Ronald, 149
Fitzgerald, Edward, 38, 45n18
Foster, Myles Birket, 144, 145
Fox, George, 179
François, Anne-Lise, 10, 104, 114n24
Franklin, John, 136, 144
Freistat, Neil, 91n4
Frend, William, 57, 69n18
Freud, Sigmund, 154, 175
Fricker, Martha, 119
Fried, Debra, 229n4
Frost, Robert, 19, 174, 177
Fruman, Norman, 93, 155
Frye, Northrop, 162n38
Fry, Roger, 149
Fulford, Tim, 102
Fussell, Paul, 114n34

G
Gabler, Hans Walter, 135
Galignani, A. and W. (publishers), 142
Gall and Inglis (publishers), 45n10, 114n38
Garnett, Richard, 147
George, Andrew, 131, 150, 152, 160n23
Gessner, Salomon, 76
Gilbert, William, 103
Gillman, Anne, 226
Gillman, James, 223
Gillray, James, 163
Godwin, William, 49, 90–1n2, 92n24
Golden Treasury of English Verse. *See* Palgrave, Francis
Göttingen (Germany), 54
Grant, Duncan, 7, 17, 40, 132, 149
Grasmere (Cumbria), 99, 101, 113n6
Greta Hall. *See* Keswick, Cumbria

262 INDEX

Griggs, Earl Leslie, 153, 162n36, 184n8
Grigson, Geoffrey, 149
Groden, Michael, 135, 137n14
Grossman, Allen, 223
Grubbs, David, 17, 182
Guinizelli, Guido, 15, 172

H

Hall, Samuel, 225
Halsey, Alan, 137n11
Hamilton, William Rowan, 111
Haney, John L., 148
Hanson, Lawrence, 153
Harding, Anthony, 178
Harper, George McLean, 160n21
Harris, Alexandra, 160n20
Hart, Clive, 137n16
Hartley, David, 50, 53, 54, 57, 58, 90, 151
Hartman, Geoffrey, 113n16
Hayes, Nick, 132
Hazlitt, William, ix, 4, 23n9, 57, 83, 86–8, 100, 109, 140, 155, 164, 165, 183n3
Heaney, Seamus, 19, 156, 169
Heber, Richard, 20–1
Henry, O. (William Sidney Porter), 209
Herder, Johann Gottfried, 175, 184n10
Higginbottom, Nehemiah, 78
Highgate, London, 19, 105, 158, 226
Hölderlin, Friedrich, 63, 135
Holford Glen (Somerset), 103
Holmes, Richard, 4, 6, 229n5
Hood, Thomas, 224
Hooker, Herman (publisher), 137n9, 142
Hopkins, Gerard Manley, 41, 148
Hort, Fenton J. A., 30, 143

House, Humphry, 1, 45n12
Howe, Susan, ix, 17, 19, 40, 46n25, 180–3
Hughes, Ted, 222
Hume, David, 48
Hunt, Leigh, ix, 141, 143, 165, 183n3
Huntington, Tuley Francis, 150
Hurlebusch, Klaus, 20, 22
Hustvedt, Sigurd, 32, 208
Hutchinson, Sara, 15, 42, 49, 62, 97, 155, 217, 231n22
Hutchinson, Thomas, 91n8, 148
Huysmans, J.-K., 34
Hyman, Stanley Edgar, 154

I

Ilfracombe (Devon), ix–x, 5–6, 156
Irving, Edward, 125, 126, 128

J

Jackson, Laura (Riding), 166. *See also* Riding, Laura
Jacobi, Friedrich Heinrich, 54
Jacobus, Mary, 91n6
Jacquet, Claude, 135
James, Ivor, 160n24
James, Thomas, 57, 160–1n24
Janzen, J. Gerald, x, 14, 62, 69n13, 137n10, 154
Jeffrey, Francis, 95, 107
Jennings, Elizabeth, 184n15
John Lane/Bodley Head (publishers), 146
Jones, David, 17, 40, 132, 137n11, 150
Jones, Ewan James, 231n23
Jones, Stephen?, 159n6
Jordan, John E., 92n27, 114n35, 114n37

INDEX 263

Joyce, James, 42, 135
Joyce, Trevor, 217
"Juan de Fuca route," 57

K
Kant, Immanuel, 27, 48, 51, 53–6, 58–9, 62, 69n10, 106, 118, 175, 179
Keats, John, 19, 21, 44, 112, 142, 143
Keepsake, The, 222, 226, 227
Kermode, Frank, 181
Keswick, Cumbria, 97, 99
Kierkegaard, Søren, 52
Kilby, Clyde, 23n11
Kilve (Somerset), 80
Kitson, Peter, 69n19
Klesse, Antje, 45n17
Knight, David, 184n12
Knight, William, 148
Knox, Julian, 45n22
Kroeber, Karl, 133, 162n35

L
Lake School (of poetry), 113n5, 140, 168
Lamb, Charles, 78, 95, 97, 123–4, 133, 137n3, 140, 159n2
Lamley (publishers), 149
Lang, Andrew, 42, 43, 146, 147, 173
Langdon, Letitia Elizabeth, 223
Larkin, Peter, 137n11
Larkin, Philip, 174
Laurel (Stan) and Hardy (Oliver), 140
Lear, Edward, 78
Leibniz, Gottfried Wilhelm, 55, 69n10, 212
Lessing, Gottfried Ephraim, 113n20, 217
Levi, Albert William, 48

Lewis, Matthew ("Monk"), 79, 123, 137n4
Lewis, Percy Wyndham, 149
Littledale, H., 148
Longinus, 175, 184n10
Longman (publisher), 28, 97, 99, 107, 126, 145, 146, 160n16
Lowell, James Russell, 45n10, 79, 146
Lowell, Robert, 19
Lowes, John Livingston, 13, 38, 48, 68n3, 75, 150–1, 155, 156, 160–1n24, 161n25
Lynton (Devon), 6, 22n3, 76, 78, 81

M
Macaulay, Thomas Babington, 7, 32, 78, 147
MacDonald, George, 117, 118, 134, 173
MacGreevy, Thomas, 181
MacKinnon, Donald M., 69n9
Mahon, Derek, 156
Malta, 107, 125, 126
Manet, Édouard, 149
Mark Rutherford. *See* White, W. Hale
Maupassant, Guy de, 209
Maurice, Frederick Denison, 111
Mayo, Robert, 92n27
McCartney, Paul and Linda, 170
McFarland, Thomas, 1–2, 14, 23n10, 26, 68n2, 107, 151, 161n25
McGann, Jerome J., 136, 137n16
McGovern, Barry, 229n3
Meadows, Kenny, 145
Meynell, Alice, 25–7, 29, 42, 44, 45n24, 59, 147, 151, 229n5
Miall, David, 45n14, 45n16, 160n18
Miller, J. Hillis, 181
Milne, Ewart, 17, 23n18

Milton, John, 17, 69n16, 144, 168, 172
Mirandola, Pico della, 69n12, 77, 92n20
Modern Language Association of America, 135
Modiano, Raimonda, 91n11, 184n11
Moir, D. M. ("Delta"), 140
Monthly Magazine, 54, 58, 74, 78, 79, 141
Monthly Review, 5, 141
More, Hannah, 147, 160n15
More, Henry, 47, 60, 68n1, 129
Morgan, John, 184n8
Moxon publishers, 38, 45n17, 131, 137n8
Mozley, John Rickards, 161n28
Muirhead, John H., 150

N
Nadolny, Sten, 136
"Nehemiah Higginbottom", 78
Nether Stowey (Somerset), 5, 78, 80, 148, 175
New Directions (publishers), 181
New School (of poetry), 74, 78, 95, 113n5, 165
Nicholls, J. F., 160n24
Niebuhr, Richard, 23n16
Nietzsche, Friedrich, 175
Northwest Passage. *See* allusions | contradictory *under (B)* *"ANCIENT MARINER"*
Norton, Mrs Charles Eliot, 91n14

O
O'Donnell, Brennan, 92n25, 92n26
Odyssey, 29
Olson, Charles, ix, 169, 172, 181

Omega Workshops (London), 149
Oppen, George, 41, 163
Osgood, James R. (publisher), 145
Ottery St. Mary (Devon), 50, 57, 89, 128, 157
Otto, Rudolf, 176
Ovid (Publius Ovidius Naso), 213, 226
Owen, Wilfred, 160n19

P
Paley, Morton, 69n19
Palgrave, Francis, ix, 160n17
Palmer, Samuel, 149
Pamphleteer, 141, 159n4
Parrish, Stephen M., 74, 158
Pater, Walter, 146, 147
Patmore, Coventry, 145
Paton, Joseph Noel, 144, 145
Payne, Joseph, 145
Peake, Mervyn, 7, 17, 40, 131–2
Pepys, Samuel, vii
Percy, Thomas, 31, 64–6, 75, 79, 108, 219, 230n14
Pfau, Thomas, 23n21
Picasso, Pablo, 154
Pickering, William (publisher), 131
Piper, Herbert W., 69n17
Pirie, David, 155
Plato/Platonic, 23n13, 54–6, 60, 62, 68n1, 68n6. *See also* philosophical contexts | Neoplatonism *under (A)* *CONTEXTS*
Poe, Edgar Allan, 149
Pogany, Willy, 150
Poole, Thomas, 55–6, 69n13, 97, 110, 121
Porlock (Somerset), 6
Porlock Weir (Somerset), 5
Potter, Stephen, 131, 229n5

Pound, Ezra, 10, 11, 21, 149, 161n31, 207
Pound, Louise, 44–5n9
Pradhan, S. V., 69n9
Prideaux, W. F., 148
Priestley, Joseph, 57–8, 92n20
Prynne, Jeremy H., ix, 11, 19, 168–73, 180, 181, 183
Purchas, Samuel, 57, 102
Purves, Alan, 44n5

Q
Quantock Hills (Somerset), 149, 226
Quarterly Review, 141, 159n7, 161n28
Quaytman, R. H., 182

R
Racedown (Dorset), 74
Ransom, John Crowe, 174
Raysor, Thomas M. 153, 161n32
Read, Herbert, 157
Reed, Arden, 92n30
Reed, Mark L., 113n10
Reynolds, Frederick, 222, 225, 226
Reynolds, John Hamilton, 109, 224
Rhys, Ernest, 147
Richard of St. Victor, 177
Richards, Ivor Armstrong, 48, 151–2, 157, 161n26, 174, 229n5
Riding, Laura, and Robert Graves, 161n26. *See also* Jackson, Laura (Riding)
Rimbaud, Arthur, 38, 147
Robinson, Henry Crabb, 140
Robinson, Mary, 217, 223
Rogers, Bruce, 40
Rogers, Samuel, 149
Rooke, Barbara, 1, 157
Rossetti, Christina, 91n14
Rossetti, Dante Gabriel, 110, 146
Rossetti, William Michael, 38, 131
Rousseau, Jean-Jacques, 92n24
Rubaiyat of Omar Khayyam. See Fitzgerald, Edward
Ruoff, Gene, 184n15
Rutherford, Mark. *See* White, W. Hale
Ryle, Gilbert, 48
Rzepka, Charles J., 231n19, 231n24

S
Sampson, George, 148, 161n29
Sampson, Low (publishers), 144, 145
Sartre, Jean-Paul, 48
Schelling, Friedrich Wilhelm Joseph, 8, 50–2, 62
Schiller, Friedrich, 97, 142
Scott, David, 39, 144
Scott, Walter, 21–2, 79, 101, 149
Scrutiny, 152
Seccombe, Thomas, 38
Sennert, Daniel, 129
Seronsy, Cecil C., 34
Sewell, Elizabeth, 46n30, 91n14
Shakespeare, William, 1, 3, 7, 26, 38, 54, 62, 65, 68n7, 152, 153, 168, 172, 208, 212–13, 216
Sharp, Richard, 183n2
Shawcross, John, 152, 161n30
Shelley, Percy Bysshe, 16, 23n19, 40, 53–4, 60–1, 142, 143
Shelvocke, George, 80
Shepherd, Justin, 69n11, 91n4
Shepherd, Richard Herne, 147, 148
Sherwood, Gilbert and Piper (publishers), 142
Shorter, Thomas, 28, 145
Sidney, Philip, 172
Siegle Hill (publishers), 149
Simpson, David, 92n24, 183n6

Skipsey, Joseph, 43–4, 229n5
Smith, Charlotte, 223
Smith, James Elishama, 159n10
Snyder, Alice D., 150
Snyder, Edward D., 44n8
Sockburn (Durham), 97, 231n22
Sotheby, William, 49
Southey, Robert, 32, 48–9, 87, 97, 109, 122, 137n3, 140, 149, 163, 173
Spenser, Edmund, 64, 120, 130
Spicer, Jack, 170
Spinoza, Baruch, 16, 54, 58, 212
St. Clair, William, 23n21, 45n17
Stange, G. Robert, 155
Stephen, Leslie, 48
Sterling, John, 111
Sterne, Laurence, 106
Stevens, E. T., and D. Morris, 145
Stevens, Wallace, 26, 46n25, 61, 62, 176–7, 181, 207
Stevenson, Robert Louis, 36, 45n13
Stillinger, Jack, 119–21, 125–7, 135
Stothard, Thomas, 226
Strand, Mark, 169
Strauss, Richard, 170
Swinburne, Algernon Charles, 43, 146, 148, 152, 229n5
Symons, Arthur, 147

T
Talfourd, Thomas Noon, 141
tantalum/ Tantalus, 170–2
Tate, Alan, 23n11, 174
Taylor, William, 74, 79, 88
Temple, Julien, 101, 113n14
Tennemann, Wilhelm Gottlieb, 51
Tennyson, Alfred Lord, 143, 144, 146
Teresa of Avila, St., 179, 184n15
Thatcher, Margaret, 171
Thelwall, John, 52, 140, 164
Thomas, Dylan, 41
Thomas, Edward, 149, 160n19

Thomas, Sophie, 45n19
Thorneycroft, Hamo, 160n17
Thrupp, Frederick, 125
Tilt, Charles (publisher), 137n9, 142
Tom Hickathrift, 39
Tomlinson, Charles, 169
Town End. *See* Grasmere (Cumbria)
Treasure Island. *See* Stevenson, Robert Louis
Trickett, Rachel, 21–2, 24n24, 166
Tristram Shandy. *See* Sterne, Laurence
Tsur, Reuven, 44n8
Tupper, Martin, 223
Turner, J. M. W., 5

U
Ulmer, William A., 114n33

V
Vallon, Annette, 72
Vaughan, Henry, 41–2
Voysey, Charles, 149

W
Wallen, Martin, 65, 119–20, 123, 127, 137n8
Wallenstein translations. *See* Schiller, Friedrich
Walters, John, x, 6
Wandering Jew, 29
Warner, Richard, 5–6, 22n3
Warnock, Mary, 48
Warren, Robert Penn, 48
Watchet (Somerset), 5–6, 81, 156
Watts-Dunton, Theodore, 146
Wedgwood, Thomas and Josiah, 19, 57, 69n17, 165
Wehnert, Edward, 144
Wellek, René, 150
Westminster Review, 146 160n21
Whaley, Arthur, 149

Whalley, George, 2, 69n20, 93, 157, 161n28, 161n33
White, W. Hale, 160n23, 160n24
Whiter, William, 54, 68n7
Williams, Rowan, 41
Wilson, John, 92n29
Wilson, Katharine, 34, 45n15, 46n27
Wilson, Patten, 146
Wolf, F. A., 136
Wollstonecraft, Mary, 223
Woodring, Carl R., 2, 45n22
Woolf, Virginia and Leonard, 149
Wordsworth, Dorothy, 39, 74, 81, 83, 90, 93, 97, 99, 101, 103, 111, 114n35
Wordsworth, Jonathan, 95
Wordsworth, William
  apropos "Ancient Mariner" (**161**)
    background in "The Three Graves" (**155**), 71–2, 74–5, 82, 86, 94, 217
    background in "The Wanderings of Cain" (**160**), 71–2, 75–8, 82
    dislike of 1798-version spellings, 97–8
    his resistance to its deeper meanings, 89–90, 100–1, 105–6
    his specific contributions to its beginning, 79–81, 129
    the hunt motif and the Albatross, 41, 81, 101, 109, 124, 132–3
    prompts breakthrough-moment in Wordsworth's writing, 73–4, 83–90
  apropos Coleridge in general
    anxiety concerning *LB 1798*, 96–7
    Coleridge's forgiving admiration of his genius, 18–19, 94, 96, 100, 105, 110–11
    created the taste by which Coleridge was understood, 9–10, 18, 90, 95, 139
    first, most extensive and serious critic of poem, viii, 6–7, 90
    his *LB* contributions more challenging than experimental, 73–4, 87–8
    material success and later reputation, 18, 21–2, 154, 166
    resistance to what he found "painful", 75, 83, 94, 108, 112, 214
  differences with Coleridge over
    diction, 50, 87, 96–7, 106, 168
    guilt and the supernatural, 9, 72, 81–4, 87, 107, 109–10, 122, 128
    metrics and stanza forms, 75, 85–7, 109, 112
    the sense of place and homecoming, 36–7, 81–2, 89–90, 93–4, 134
    the sublime, 95, 173, 178
  personal
    ambition as poet, 18, 50, 90, 95, 166
    anxiety to "answer" Coleridge's poem, 9, 73–4
    in *LB 1798*, 83–90, 96–7
    in *LB 1800*, 97–105
    in *Peter Bell*, 88–9, 96, 105, 107, 109–10, 114n36, 161n29
    in *The White Doe of Rylestone*, 105, 107–9, 218

Y
Yeats, William Butler, 11, 147, 160n19, 173, 174, 183, 230–1n18

MAY 20 2019

CPSIA information can be obtained
at www.ICGtesting.com
Printed in the USA
LVHW021545210419
614969LV00015B/698/P